Who Should Read This Book?

"**R**ead" may be the wrong word. "Engage" would be better, because this is not so much a book as it is a classic text, and Jewish classics are not read so much as they are engaged. Included here are a classic text of Jewish prayer, spanning 2,000 years of Jewish experience with the world and with God; and ten thoughtful commentaries on that text, each one reaching back in a different way, again through 2,000 years of time. The question ought to be "Who should engage this book in personal dialogue?"

If you like to pray, or find prayer services baffling: Whether you are Orthodox, Conservative, Reconstructionist, or Reform, you will find that *My People's Prayer Book* tells you what you need to know to pray.

- The Hebrew text here is the most authentic one we have, and the variations among the Jewish movements are described and explained. They are all treated as equally authentic.
- The translation is honest, altogether unique, and outfitted with notes comparing it to others' translations.
- Of special interest is a full description of the Halakhah (the "how to") of prayer and the philosophy behind it.

If you are a spiritual seeker or Jewishly curious: If you have wondered what Judaism is all about, the prayer book is the place to begin. It is the one and only book that Jews read each and every day. The commentaries explain how the prayers were born, and synopsize insights of founding Rabbis, medieval authorities, Chasidic masters, and modern theologians. The layout replicates the look of Jewish classics: a text surrounded by many marginal commentaries allowing you to skip back and forth across centuries of insight.

If you are a teacher or a student: This is a perfect book for adult studies, or for youth groups, teenagers, and camps. Any single page provides comparative insight from the length and breadth of Jewish tradition, about the texts that have mattered most in the daily life of the Jewish people.

If you are a scholar: Though written in friendly prose, this book is composed by scholars: professors of Bible, Rabbinics, Medieval Studies, Liturgy, Theology, Linguistics, Jewish Law, Mysticism, and Modern Jewish Thought. No other work summarizes current wisdom on Jewish prayer, drawn from so many disciplines.

If you are not Jewish: You need not be Jewish to understand this book. It provides access for everyone to the Jewish wisdom tradition. It chronicles the ongoing Jewish-Christian dialogue, and the roots of Christian prayer in Christianity's Jewish origins.

The My People's Prayer Book: Traditional Prayers, Modern Commentaries series

My People's Passover Haggadah: Traditional Texts, Modern Commentaries

The Prayers of Awe Series

My People's Prayer Book

TRADITIONAL PRAYERS, MODERN COMMENTARIES

Vol. 3 —*P'sukei D'zimrah* (Morning Psalms)

EDITED BY RABBI LAWRENCE A. HOFFMAN

CONTRIBUTORS

MARC BRETTLER

DAVID ELLENSON

JUDITH HAUPTMAN

LAWRENCE A. HOFFMAN

LAWRENCE KUSHNER

NEHEMIA POLEN

ELLIOT N. DORFF

ELLEN FRANKEL

JOEL M. HOFFMAN

REUVEN KIMELMAN

DANIEL LANDES

Jewish Lights Publishing

My People's Prayer Book: Traditional Prayers, Modern Commentaries
Vol. 3 —*P'sukei D'zimrah* (Morning Psalms)

2016 Hardcover Edition

Library of Congress Cataloging-in-Publication Data
My people's prayer book : traditional prayers, modern commentaries /
edited and with introductions by Lawrence A. Hoffman.
p.   cm.
Includes the traditional text of the siddur, English translation, and
commentaries.
Contents: vol. 3. *P'sukei D'zimrah* (Morning Psalms).
ISBN: 978-1-879045-81-1 (hc)
ISBN: 978-1-68336-210-4 (pbk.)
1. Siddur. 2. Siddurim — Texts. 3. Judaism — Liturgy — Texts.
I. Hoffman, Lawrence A., 1942–   . II. Siddur. English & Hebrew.
BM674.39.M96   1997

296.4'5 — dc21   97-26836
                                  CIP

First edition

ISBN 978-1-58023-756-7 (eBook)

Manufactured in the United States of America
Jacket design: Glenn Suokko
Text design: Reuben Kantor
Text composition: Douglas S. Porter

Published by Jewish Lights Publishing
 www.jewishlights.com

Contents

CONTENTS

CONTRIBUTORS

MARC BRETTLER	*Our Biblical Heritage*
ELLIOT N. DORFF	*Theological Reflections*
DAVID ELLENSON	*How the Modern Prayer Book Evolved*
ELLEN FRANKEL	*A Woman's Voice*
JUDITH HAUPTMAN	*Our Talmudic Heritage*
JOEL M. HOFFMAN	*What the Prayers Really Say*
LAWRENCE A. HOFFMAN	*History of the Liturgy*
REUVEN KIMELMAN	*Rhetorical Structure*
LAWRENCE KUSHNER AND NEHEMIA POLEN	*Chasidic and Mystical Perspectives*
DANIEL LANDES	*The Halakhah of Prayer*

About My People's Prayer Book

My People's Prayer Book is designed to look like a traditional Jewish book. Ever since the dawn of modern printing, Jews have arranged their books so that instead of reading in a linear fashion from the first line of the first page to the last line of the last one, readers were encouraged to linger on a single page and to consult commentaries across the gamut of Jewish thought, all at one and the same time. Every page thus contained a cross-cut of the totality of Jewish tradition.

That intellectual leap across many minds and through the centuries was accomplished by printing a text in the middle of the page and surrounding it with commentaries. Readers could scan the first line or two of the various commentaries and then choose to continue the ones that interested them most, by turning the page — more or less the way newspaper readers get a sense of everything happening on a single day by glancing at all the headlines on page one and then following select stories as they are continued on separate pages further on.

Each new rubric (or liturgical section) is, therefore, introduced in traditional style: the Hebrew prayer with translation in the middle of the page, and the beginning lines of all the commentaries in the margins. Commentaries are continued on the next page or a few pages later (the page number is provided). Readers may dwell for a while on all the comments, deciding which ones to pursue at any given sitting. They may want to compare comments, reading first one and then another. Or having decided, after a while, that a particular commentator is of special interest, they may instinctively search out the opening lines of that commentator's work, as they appear in each introductory page, and then read them through to arrive at a summary understanding of what that particular person has to say.

Introduction to the Liturgy

Why the *P'sukei D'zimrah?*

Lawrence A. Hoffman

Liturgy can seem confusing, more like a shapeless mass of verbiage than a carefully constructed whole; a jumble of noise, not a symphony; a blotch of random colors, hardly a masterpiece of art. But prayer *is* an art form, and like the other arts, the first step toward appreciation is to recognize the pattern at work within it.

There are three daily services: morning *(Shacharit),* afternoon *(Minchah),* and evening *(Ma'ariv* or *Arvit).* For the sake of convenience, the latter two are usually recited in tandem, one just before dark, and the other immediately after the sun sets. All three follow the same basic structure, but the morning service is the most complete. It is composed of seven consecutive units that build upon each other to create a definitive pattern. Though the words of each unit have been fluid for centuries, the structural integrity of the service has remained sacrosanct since the beginning.

Services are made of prayers, but not all prayers are alike. Some are biblical quotations, ranging in size from a single line to entire chapters, usually psalms. There are rabbinic citations also, chunks of Mishnah or Talmud that serve as a sort of Torah study within the service. Medieval poetry occurs here too, familiar things like *Adon Olam* or older staples (called *piyyutim* — sing., *piyyut*) marked less by rhyme and rhythm than by clever word plays and alphabetic acrostics. And there are long passages of prose, the work again of medieval spiritual masters, but couched in standard rabbinic style without regard for poetic rules.

Most of all, however, the Siddur is filled with blessings, a uniquely rabbinic vehicle for addressing God, and the primary liturgical expression of Jewish spirituality.

Blessings (known also as benedictions, or, in Hebrew, *b'rakhot* — sing., *b'rakhah*) are so familiar that Jewish worshipers take them for granted. We are mostly aware of "short blessings," the one-line formulas that are customarily recited before eating, for instance, or before performing a commandment. But there are "long blessings" too, generally whole paragraphs or even sets of paragraphs on a given theme. These are best thought of as small theological essays on topics like deliverance, the sanctity of time, and the rebuilding of Jerusalem. They sometimes start with the words *Barukh atah Adonai*... ("Blessed are You, Adonai..."), and then they are easily spotted. But more frequently, they begin with no particular verbal formula and are hard to identify until their last line, which invariably does say, *Barukh atah Adonai*... ("Blessed are You, Adonai...") followed by a short synopsis of the blessing's theme ("...who sanctifies the Sabbath," "...who hears prayer," "...who redeems Israel," and so forth). This final summarizing sentence is called a *chatimah,* meaning a "seal," like the seal made from a signet ring that seals an envelope.

The bulk of the service as it was laid down in antiquity consists of strings of blessings, one after the other, or of biblical quotations bracketed by blessings that introduce and conclude them. By the tenth century, the creation of blessings largely ceased, and eventually, Jewish law actually opposed the coining of new ones, on the grounds that post-talmudic Judaism was too spiritually unworthy to try to emulate the literary work of the giants of the Jewish past. Not all Jews agree with that assessment today, but the traditional liturgy that forms our text here contains no blessings later than the tenth century.

The word we use to refer to all the literary units in the prayer book, without regard to whether they are blessings, psalms, poems, or something else, is *rubric.* A rubric is any discrete building block of the service, sometimes a single prayer (this blessing rather than that, or this quotation but not that poem), and sometimes a whole set of prayers that stands out in contradistinction to other sets: The *P'sukei D'zimrah,* for instance (our topic here in Volume 3 of this series) is a large rubric, composed mostly of Psalms and other biblical citations, and bracketed by an introductory and a concluding benediction. Relative to the *P'sukei D'zimrah* as a whole, however, each of these two blessings (for instance) is a subrubric, but sometimes, when considered relative to each other, they may be called rubrics as well. The term is flexible. It is just a convenient way to refer to a particular body of material without having to stipulate what kind of thing — a psalm? a blessing? a *piyyut?* — it is.

The *P'sukei D'zimrah*		
Opening Blessing	Psalms & Biblical Citations	Closing Blessing

At the liturgy's core are three large rubrics: the *Sh'ma* and Its Blessings (the topic of Volume 1 of this series); the *Amidah,* known also as the *T'fillah* or *Sh'moneh Esreh* (Volume 2); and the public reading of Torah. The *Sh'ma* and Its Blessings and the *Amidah* were recited every day; Torah is read on Monday and Thursday (market days in antiquity, when crowds were likely to gather in the cities), and on Shabbat and holidays, of course. The *Sh'ma* and Its Blessings is essentially the Jewish creed, a statement of what Jews have traditionally affirmed about God, the cosmos, and our relationship to God and to history. The *Amidah* is largely petitionary. It is convenient to think of the *Sh'ma* as a Jewish conversation *about* God and the *Amidah* as a Jewish conversation *with* God. The Torah reading is a recapitulation of Sinai, an attempt to discover the will of God through sacred scripture. Since the *Sh'ma* and Its Blessings begins the official service, it features a communal call to prayer at the beginning: our familiar *Bar'khu*. We should picture these units building upon each other in a crescendo-like manner, as follows:

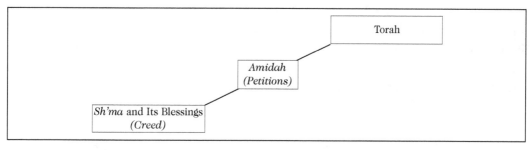

It is, however, hard for individuals who are normally distracted by everyday concerns to constitute a community given over wholeheartedly to prayer. Already in the second century, therefore, we hear of some Rabbis who assembled prior to the actual Call to Prayer in order to sing psalms of praise known as a *Hallel*; and even before that — at home, not the synagogue — it was customary to begin the day immediately upon awakening by reciting a series of daily blessings along with some study texts. By the ninth century, if not earlier, these two units also had become mandatory, and the home ritual for awakening had moved to the synagogue, where it remains today. The warm-up section of psalms (our topic here) is called *P'sukei D'zimrah*— meaning "Verses of Song" — and the prior recital of daily blessings and study texts (the topic of a future volume in this series) is called *Birkhot Hashachar*— "Morning Blessings." Since both of these rubrics now precede the main body of the service, gradually building up to it, the larger diagram can be charted like this:

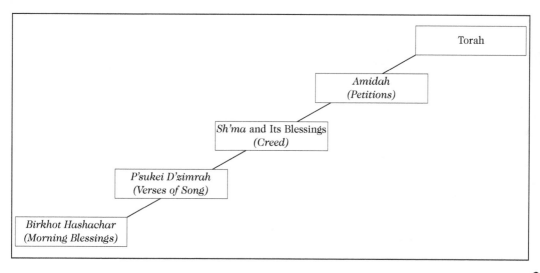

Two other expansions of this basic structure probably occurred in the first two centuries C.E., although our evidence for their being that early is less certain.

First, a Conclusion was added. It featured a final prayer called the *Kaddish*, which as yet had nothing to do with mourning, but merely followed the Torah reading, and therefore closed the service, by looking ahead to the coming of God's ultimate reign of justice. Eventually, other prayers were added to the Conclusion, including the *Alenu*, which had originally been composed as an introduction to the blowing of the shofar on Rosh Hashanah, but was moved here in the Middle Ages.

Second, the Rabbis, who were keenly aware of the limits to human mortality, advised all Jews to come to terms daily with their frailty and ethical imperfection. To do so, they provided an opportunity for a silent confession following the *Amidah*, but before the Torah reading. In time, this evolved into silent prayer in general, an opportunity for individuals to assemble their most private thoughts before God; and later still, some time in the Middle Ages, it expanded on average weekdays into an entire set of supplicatory prayers called the *Tachanun*.

The daily service was thus passed down to us with shape and design. Beginning with daily blessings that celebrate the new day and emphasize the study of sacred texts *(Birkhot Hashachar)*, it then continues with songs and psalms *(P'sukei D'zimrah)* that create a sense of spiritual readiness. There then follows the core of the liturgy: an official call to prayer (our *Bar'khu*), the recital of Jewish belief (the *Sh'ma* and Its Blessings), and communal petitions (the *Amidah*). Individuals then pause to speak privately to God in silent prayer (later expanded into the *Tachanun*), and then, on select days, they read from Torah. The whole concludes with a final *Kaddish*, to which other prayers, most notably the *Alenu*, were added later.

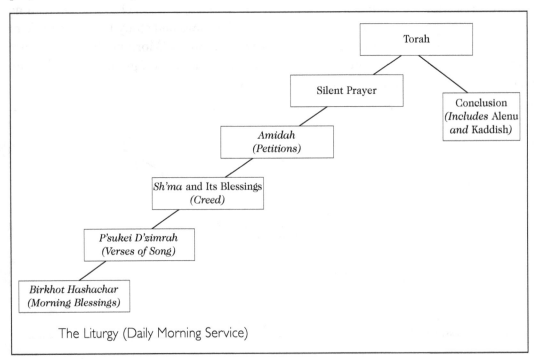

The Liturgy (Daily Morning Service)

On Shabbat and holidays, this basic structure expands to admit special material relevant to the day in question, and contracts to omit prayers that are inappropriate for the occasion. On Shabbat, for instance, the petitions of the *Amidah* are excluded, as Shabbat is felt to be so perfect in itself as to make petitioning unnecessary. But an entire service is added, a service called *Musaf* (literally, "Addition"), to correspond to the extra sacrifice that once characterized Shabbat worship in the Temple. Similarly, a prophetic reading called the *Haftarah* joins the Torah reading, and extra psalms and readings for the Sabbath are inserted here and there. The same is true for holidays when, in addition, numerous *piyyutim* are said, especially for the High Holy Days when the sheer size of the liturgy seems to get out of hand. But even there, the basic structure remains intact, so that those who know its intrinsic shape can get beyond what looks like random verbiage to find the genius behind the liturgy's design.

THE *P'SUKEI D'ZIMRAH* ("VERSES OF SONG"): A WARM-UP OF PSALM AND SONG

Our earliest law code, the Mishnah (c. 200) relates that "the pious ones of old used to tarry an hour and then pray, so as to focus themselves on God" (Ber. 5:1). I suspect that originally, these "pious ones" whom the Mishnah remembers would meditate before saying their prayers. In time, however, the meditation, which probably took place in silence, dropped out and was replaced by a preparatory rubric of words. It is as if before the Rabbis prayed, they prayed that they might pray. The *P'sukei D'zimrah* is best regarded as "the prayer before the prayer." It functions as the warm-up for the morning service, a recognition that prayerfulness cannot be summoned on demand. The two morning staples, the *Sh'ma* and Its Blessings and the *Amidah* (see Volumes 1 and 2 of this series), are therefore introduced by the *P'sukei D'zimrah* as a transition from the daily secular routine to the sacred act of communal prayer.

Tannaitic works (rabbinic works prior to the year 200 C.E., such as the Mishnah) do not discuss anything called *P'sukei D'zimrah*. As late as the third century, then, it was still coming into being. In fact, the service as a whole was still much shorter than what we are used to today. Except for those who retained the practice of preparatory meditation, it was common and still proper for people to arrive at the synagogue only for the Call to Prayer that formally inaugurates the *Sh'ma* and Its Blessings and then to leave immediately after the *Amidah* was completed — a total of perhaps twenty-six Hebrew pages in today's Siddur. On the days when the Torah was read, the service would be expanded, but only with a Torah reading, not with the extended liturgy that we use nowadays to take the Torah from the ark and then to replace it there when the reading is completed. All of that liturgy came later, as did most of the other material that now composes the 156-page morning service as we have it.

To be sure, the lengthy rubric called the Morning Blessings *(Birkhot Hashachar)* would have been said privately at home upon awakening, and there may have been a daily *Kaddish* attached to the Torah reading (the *Kaddish* was not a mourner's prayer yet, but only a petition that accompanied study and requested the arrival of the ultimate reign of God upon the earth). But even so, the service was relatively tiny.

All of that would change, however, largely because of the process by which *kavvanah* was slowly transformed into *keva*. *Kavvanah* and *keva* are the two Hebrew words used to describe the opposite ends of the psychological continuum between heartfelt spontaneity *(kavvanah)* and rigid requirement *(keva)*. Every religion struggles to balance these two essentials. For that matter, every culture — and even every way of life — does the same thing. We get dressed in the morning with the bare necessities to keep us warm and cover our nakedness *(keva)*, but we do so with the latest fashions and matching colors *(kavvanah)*. We eat to provide nourishment *(keva)*, but we serve food nicely prepared and beautifully presented *(kavvanah)*. When public prayer first began, it required a fixed set of topics, one after the other *(keva)*, but the prayer leader improvised the poetry or prose in which the topics were conveyed that day *(kavvanah)*.

As the practice of prayer expanded beyond the rabbinic class to become common among the Jewish population as a whole, however, improvisation became more difficult. It became less likely that prayer leaders in the new synagogues being constructed both within the Land of Israel and outside of it would be able to fashion ever-new creative versions of the required liturgy, because they were not necessarily as educated as the Rabbis who had initiated the practice of communal prayer in the first place. They were unfamiliar with the Bible, for example, and the Bible was the primary source on which the Rabbis drew for their improvisations. Also, as the system of rabbinic Judaism grew, and more and more legal minds worked at spinning out consequences of rabbinic law, the rules increased regarding every aspect of life, including prayer. Leading a congregation in prayer was no longer as simple as it had been. *Keva* soon came to mean not just the necessary topical order, but the standard wording that emerged as the normal way to say a benediction. Different places developed their own favorite verbiage, but whatever they developed, the words recited by a prayer leader one day tended to be repeated the next, rather than to be improvised anew. With the expansion of *keva* to include not just topical but also verbal fixity, the meaning of *kavvanah* changed also. No longer was *kavvanah* the free-flowing spontaneous invention of novel words. Instead, it came to mean the little extra things that a prayer leader, or an individual worshiper, might do to provide sincerity in what could otherwise deteriorate into a humdrum routine. Part of *kavvanah* was adding extra prayers that came from the heart, beyond what was demanded, strictly speaking. But a large part of *kavvanah* was simply putting one's heart into the liturgical staples that were required, making them a "heartfelt" prayer, rather than rote recitation. Worshipers were expected to do more than rattle by rote through the fixed and memorized text. They were told to "direct their heart" — *l'kaven et libo* to God. The verb "to direct" *(l'kaven)* is the root of *kavvanah*. *Kavvanah* came to mean the act of directing one's heart to God during the course of fixed prayer.

Kavvanah meant even more than "heartfelt" prayer, however. It has a profound intellectual component. Much as we identify the heart with human feeling, the Rabbis saw the heart as the seat of the intellect. To "direct one's heart" meant not just sincerity but contemplation of the meaning of each and every word spoken. Prayer had become outfitted with a fixed text, but worshipers were to concentrate on every word of the text as they spoke it. Fastening their attention on the meaning of the words, they would be able to mean what they said, perhaps reading new meaning into old words the way prayer leaders had once injected new words into old themes. Prayer was thus an obligation (a *mitzvah*) defined by a growing set of rules and regulations. Yet it remained what it always had been: an opportunity to open one's heart and mind to God. Ironically, the most important rule was precisely not to let the rules stand in the way of true *kavvanah*.

THE DAILY *HALLEL*: THE CORE OF THE *P'SUKEI D'ZIMRAH*

The growing need to pay attention to *kavvanah* is what led, ultimately, to the rubric called *P'sukei D'zimrah*. We hear about it first with regard to the practice of Yose bar Chalafta, a second-century Rabbi, who is reported as saying, "May my lot be among those who complete a *Hallel* every day." Nowadays, we usually use the word *Hallel* to designate a particular set of psalms, Psalms 113–118. They are recited after the *Amidah* on festivals, for instance, and they are part of the Passover Seder. But originally, *Hallel* meant *any* set of psalms of praise, not just Psalms 113–118. Psalms 113–118 are a particular *Hallel*, "The Egyptian *Hallel*" (to be precise), a name derived from the first verse of Psalm 114, "When Israel left Egypt...." That is why it forms part of the *Haggadah*. Another *Hallel* was called "The Great *Hallel*," which the Talmud identifies as Psalm 136. It too is said at the Seder and also as an extra psalm in the *P'sukei D'zimrah* for Shabbat. Yet a third *Hallel* is "The Daily *Hallel*," and that is the *Hallel* that Rabbi Yose bar Chalafta meant when he said that he wanted to complete a *Hallel* every day. Nowadays, the Daily *Hallel* is made up of the last six psalms in the Book of Psalms, Psalms 145–150.

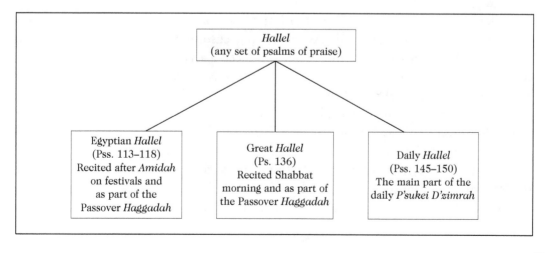

It is not certain that Yose bar Chalafta meant just those psalms, however. The name "Egyptian *Hallel*" was derived from the content of Psalm 114, so it could not refer to just any psalms in the Bible (although it too fluctuated somewhat, probably being just Psalms 113–114 at first and then growing to include Psalms 115–118). The other *Hallels*, however, might well have meant several things. When the Talmud says that the Great *Hallel* is Psalm 136, it probably reflects only one tradition out of many. The Talmud explains its choice by citing Rabbi Yochanan, a third-century Palestinian authority, who says, "In Psalm 136, God is pictured as standing at the height of the universe distributing food to every creature" — an act that Rashi later calls "a great thing indeed." But other psalms too may have been called "Great" for other reasons.

Certainly the choice of psalms for the Daily *Hallel* varied widely at the beginning. We know that for sure because of the Genizah fragments, the manuscripts that show us how our ancestors in the Land of Israel prayed during the several centuries that preceded the Crusades. Many fragments leave out the psalms altogether, as if the prayer leader was expected to choose different psalms every day. One manuscript has Psalms 120–150 — thirty-one psalms in all! The most interesting fragments have no complete psalms at all, but just snatches of verses from various psalms joined together into a long litany of praise. That is probably how the title for this rubric came into being: *P'sukei D'zimrah*, "*Verses* of Song" — not whole chapters, but just verses selected from here and there in the Psalter into a glorious song to God.

We do not know when or why Psalms 145–150 came to be chosen eventually. The choice had to have been made by the ninth century because our first comprehensive prayer book, *Seder Rav Amram* (about 860 C.E.), has them. But an eighth-century work called *Massekhet Sofrim* has them also. Presumably, these six psalms were a common option, but not the only one, until Rav Amram codified them as the proper choice in his epic work that became the basis for Jewish liturgies all over the world thereafter.

We can only guess at the thinking behind the decision to incorporate these six psalms, but I think the choice followed from a literal reading of Rabbi Yose's remark, on one hand, and a special affection for Psalm 145, on the other. Rabbi Yose had said, "May my lot be among those who complete a *Hallel* every day." Taking the word "complete" literally, people sought to finish the Book of Psalms. The only question was what psalm they should start with. As we saw, one custom was to start all the way back at Psalm 120, but that practice must have produced a service that was far too long for most people. A far more convenient starting point was just a few psalms short of Psalm 150, and here the special regard that people had for Psalm 145 came into play.

Nowadays, and probably from the eighth century on, Psalm 145, known simply but profoundly as "David's Psalm" *(T'hillah l'david)*, has been said as a staple of Jewish prayer three times daily. It is found here, in the *P'sukei D'zimrah*, then again later in the morning service *(Shacharit)*, and a third time as the introduction to the afternoon service *(Minchah)*. Indeed, our printed version of the Talmud advises, "Those who say Psalm 145 three times daily can rest assured that they will receive a share of the world-to-come" (Ber. 4b). The words "three times" are actually a medieval addition to the talmudic text, reflecting the practice of the time. But even without those two words, the original text expresses the high regard for Psalm 150, which was to be said every day because it guaranteed the worshiper a share in the world-to-come. What better time for it than within that rubric of the morning service dedicated to giving praise to God? In devising the ideal set of morning psalms, then, it seemed advisable to say at least Psalm 150 (in order to "finish" a *Hallel*) and to count back at least as far as Psalm 145 (in order to include the all-important "David's Psalm") but not necessarily any farther.

OPENING AND CLOSING BLESSINGS: BRACKETING BOOKENDS FOR THE *P'SUKEI D'ZIMRAH*

We saw above that the Rabbis' favorite form of prayer was the blessing. Lengthy biblical readings that found their way into the liturgy were therefore usually bracketed by blessings pertinent to the readings that they introduced and concluded. That is why the *Sh'ma* (which is biblical) is organized as "the *Sh'ma* and Its Blessings." Here too, then, we do not just read psalms to warm up before the Call to Prayer. We read them as a larger liturgical unit — bracketed, like the *Sh'ma*, by an introductory and a concluding benediction. The blessing that introduces them is called *Barukh she'amar* ("Blessed is the One who spoke..."), a title derived from the first words in the blessing. Similarly, the concluding blessing is sometimes called by its first Hebrew word, *Yishtabach* ("Praised be [your name forever]"). But the final blessing is also known as *Birkat Hashir,* "The Blessing of Song."

Introductory Blessing	Daily *Hallel*	Concluding Blessing
Barukh she'amar....	Psalms 145–150	*Yishtabach....* also called *Birkat Hashir* ("Blessing of Song")

Structure of P'sukei D'zimrah

All three forms of *Hallel* conclude with one version or other of a Blessing of Song, an appropriate indication of the function that a *Hallel* serves. As praise of God, these psalms were intended all along to be sung, not just read. Though we have no way of knowing what melodies accompanied them early on, we have every reason to believe that such melodies existed. Psalms 146–150 all begin with "Halleluyah," a shout of joy to God. Their mood and subject matter almost demand music for a full appreciation of what they are about. The last line (the *chatimah*) of the concluding Blessing of Song is explicit: Blessed is God "who chooses songs."

BIBLICAL INTERLUDES: MORE PRAISE YET IN THE *P'SUKEI D'ZIMRAH*

Indeed, the theme of praising God, especially through song, was so powerful that over the course of time, other biblical material illustrative of praising God with song was added to the *P'sukei D'zimrah*, either between the opening blessing and the Daily *Hallel* or after the *Hallel* but before the final benediction, so that the final shape of the rubric as a whole looks like this:

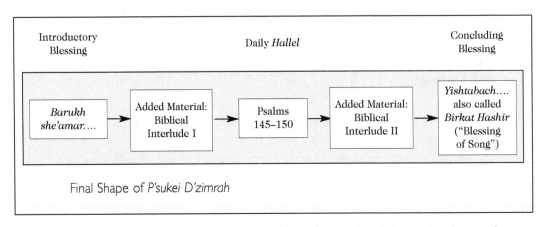

My commentary on the liturgy identifies each of the units that makes up the *P'sukei D'zimrah* and gives further detail on how they came into being. It should be clear from what has been said so far, however, that this rubric has been planned with enormous regard for its structural integrity. Its centerpiece, the Daily *Hallel*, is now bracketed by later additions to illustrate how biblical men and women sang God's praises, and the whole thing is further introduced and followed by blessings that affirm the mutual joy that both we and God have as we awake each morning to praise our creator.

THE CENTRALITY OF PSALMS IN JEWISH WORSHIP

One final word is in order about the role of psalms in Jewish worship. The Temple of old had very little prayer in it, if by prayer we mean a spoken liturgy. Instead, it was almost wholly animal sacrifice. But some words were recited as part of the cult, and to the extent that we can call those words an actual liturgy of words, we can say that the Temple's spoken liturgy was almost wholly composed of psalms. There are some notable exceptions: the Priestly Blessing from Num. 6:24–26 ("May Adonai bless you and keep you…"), for instance (see Volume 2, *The Amidah*, p. 176). But mostly, we hear about psalms that the Levites sang.

The sacrificial system was a noisy and not altogether pleasant business. Live animals were tethered on one side of the altar area, then taken, slaughtered, cut into pieces, and offered up in what must have resembled an enormous barbecue pit. Incense cut down on the smell that must have permeated the open air arena where it all occurred. The noise of the animals alone must have been considerable. The whole thing was typical of Greco-Roman religion, where all the deities in the pagan system had temples devoted to them. People came for reasons of piety, but also for entertainment. Watching the sacrifice was usually accompanied by feasting and even drunkenness, a condition of which even the Jewish priests at the Temple are regularly suspected by the Rabbis, who go so far as to ban the Priestly Blessing at the time of the afternoon sacrifice because the priests may already be too drunk to get it right. How can God's blessings be invoked if the invokers are inebriated?

Part of the sacred "show" was the music. Pagan temples featured virtual orchestras along with vocal music, and so too did the Jewish Temple in Jerusalem. Above the noise of the animals and the slaughter there rose the sound of a variety of instruments and a levitical choir. The psalms formed the repertoire for the choir.

We no longer know the entirety of what was sung when, but the Mishnah provides some recollections and so too (whether accurately or not) do other later rabbinic works. There was a separate psalm for each day, for instance. Other psalms were associated with specific sacrifices. Some are obvious references to Shabbat or to the festivals. Sacrifices without psalms would have fulfilled the bare skeleton of the Torah's commandments to offer sacrifices to God. But it would hardly have been the memorable ritual that moved an eyewitness, a gentleman-farmer known to us as Ben Sirah, to recall the high priest Simon ben Onias in all his glory:

> How glorious he was, surrounded by the people,
> As he came out of the sanctuary!
> …He was like a young cedar in Lebanon,
> And they surrounded him like the trunks of palm trees,
> All the descendants of Aaron in their splendor,
> With the Lord's offering in their hands,
> Before the whole assembly of Israel;
> And when he finished the service at the altars,
> To adorn the offering of the Most High, the Almighty,
> He stretched out his hand to the cup,
> And poured out some of the blood of the grape;
> He poured it at the foot of the altar,
> A fragrant odor unto the Most High, the King of all.
> Then the descendants of Aaron shouted;
> They sounded the trumpets of beaten work;
> They made a great sound heard
> For a reminder, before the Most High.
> The singers too praised Him with their voices;
> They made sweet music in the fullest volume,
> And the people entreated the Lord Most High
> With prayer before Him who is merciful,
> Until the worship of the Lord should be finished,
> And they completed the service.*

*Translation from Edgar J. Goodspeed, *The Apocrypha: An American Translation* (New York: Vintage, 1959).

When the synagogue service developed in place of the cult, psalms played a major role there too. As much as possible, psalms for special occasions were just moved from one locale to the other. Our morning service still ends with a psalm for the day, for instance, and the Egyptian *Hallel* was transferred from Temple to synagogue use as holiday liturgy. Other psalms had never been used in the Temple the way they came to be said in the synagogue. Psalms 92 and 93, for instance, are known as the psalm for Friday and Shabbat, respectively, but they were apparently said every evening in the old Palestinian synagogues. The Daily *Hallel*, too, is such a synagogue innovation.

In the early synagogue, however, the psalms were not accompanied by instruments because the Rabbis banned instrumental music as part of the prayer service. They were probably reacting to the continued use of instrumentation in pagan temples, hoping to mark off the synagogue as a different kind of sacred venture. It would be without the entertainment aspect that had been central even to the Temple in Jerusalem. Elsewhere too, they fought against the tendency of merging religion with overt festivities that would lead to drunkenness — as, for instance, in the Seder, where they limited the amount of wine a person might drink after dinner. Eventually, other reasons for dispensing with instruments were offered. Instrumental music was inappropriate in an era of mourning for the Temple, it was said. Also, fixing broken instruments on Shabbat constituted a breach of Shabbat work regulations. It was feared that if a musician's instrument broke while it was being used, the temptation to fix it would be too overwhelming to refuse.

So psalms were introduced everywhere in our liturgy, and others were added later during the Middle Ages. But they were now just read or sung. And as the total verbiage grew, people tended to hurry through the *P'sukei D'zimrah*, rather than to appreciate it as a profoundly moving spiritual experience in its own right. Nowadays, the problems are compounded by the appearance (or even the substitution) of English. People complain that they wonder why God needs all this praise or even that they have trouble believing in a God who needs praise so much.

APPROACHING THE *P'SUKEI D'ZIMRAH* AS MODERN MEN AND WOMEN

For several reasons, biblical psalms are no longer as appreciated as they once were. In part, that is because they were composed in such difficult Hebrew that they are hard to get through even by rote, let alone with an understanding of what they mean. In part, too, their poetic style is no longer familiar to us. They look like poetry — indeed, they are poetry — but it is hard to convey their poetry in translation, and even the Hebrew form is not readily recognizable to most modern readers. A third reason for our lost appreciation of psalms is that they were composed to be sung and we no longer have tunes for most of them. And finally, the themes of the psalms come from an ancient world where their metaphors were never questioned because no one doubted the reality of a God who sat enthroned on high like a "king of kings" awaiting thanks and praise from his subjects. Psalm 92 proclaims, "It is good to give grateful acknowledgment to Adonai, to sing hymns to your name, O Most High." Modern worshipers may feel thankful but may have trouble with ancient words that identify the only God to whom thanks are due as a God who is "most high."

Still, the *P'sukei D'zimrah* is nothing if not giving "grateful acknowledgment" and "singing hymns" to our God, however we may choose to identify God, in our day. We should not feel constrained by the metaphors of the Bible, for they are just that: metaphors to suggest the nature of a divine reality that regularly escapes being captured in mere words. The essence of the *P'sukei D'zimrah* is the affirmation within ourselves of the feeling of gratitude and praise for the tenuous mystery of life, and the parallel recognition that beyond the mystery of life there lies yet a deeper mystery whom we call God. Reciting the age-old passages from psalms connects us with another mystery we call history, and not just history as an academic discipline, but history of our own roots and beginnings: the origins of the Jewish project that still continues, some four thousand years later. Modern prayer books often provide newly composed poetry and songs to supplement the psalms, but worshipers are advised to turn to the psalms each morning to connect their own fragile life span with the larger Jewish past and to speak or sing the words of poetry now two thousand years old. For good reason, Halakhah (Jewish law) does not prohibit modern additions to our service of praise. For good reason also, it does not release us into free-fall from history, where everyone's private sentiments are expressed in equally privatized ways, cut off from the sources of our past. To make sense of the sometimes outdated imagery that the psalms express, worshipers should feel free to do what Jews have always done so well: we interpret what we read in ways we find acceptable, recognizing that what we are reading is poetry, and the very essence of poetry is its ability to succeed and fail at the same time. It succeeds because it says the unsayable; and it fails because insofar as its topic is unsayable, everything that it says, when taken literally, is false.

For us, a truly deep engagement with the *P'sukei D'zimrah* involves its utilization as poetry and as song to connect our deepest human aspirations to the grandest conception of reality that we can muster, to recognize how deeply we yearn to connect our feelings of gratitude and joy to a source beyond ourselves, and to identify the reality of that source as the God whom we hope to meet, somehow, in the sacred act of prayer. As introduction to the larger service, the *P'sukei D'zimrah* sets the tone and prepares the way for our further conversation *about* God (the *Sh'ma* and Its Blessings) and then our conversation *with* God (the *Amidah*). It provides a transition from the daily grind of secular life to the meditative and sacred frame of mind that we want for our liturgy. Only when we finish the *P'sukei D'zimrah* are we ready for the *Bar'khu,* the official call to public prayer.

This "warm-up" section of the service is also a beautifully crafted set of poetic prayer in its own right. All too often we hurry through it so we can get to the "real liturgy." But it deserves better, and so do we. The *P'sukei D'zimrah* is waiting to be reclaimed as the thing of beauty that our ancestors knew it to be.

Prayer in the Bible and the Use of the Bible in Later Jewish Prayer

Marc Brettler

Even the terms used for the Hebrew Bible reflect its central role within Judaism and western culture. In classic rabbinic texts, the Hebrew Bible is often called *mikra,* meaning "that which is read," while the English term "Bible" ultimately derives from the Greek, *biblia,* "the books." Whether we are talking about what one normally reads or what must be seen as *the* book, the Bible fits the bill.

Given the central importance of the Bible within Judaism, it is not surprising that it should exert a disproportionate influence on the liturgy. In some cases, entire biblical texts like Exod. 15:1–19, the Song of the Sea *(Shirat Hayam),* or Deut. 6:4–9, the *Sh'ma* itself, are cited in full as part of the liturgy. The same is true of psalms. Entire psalms are regularly cited verbatim in this or that liturgical context.

In other cases, biblical texts are woven together to create a new but still biblically styled prayer. Even when the biblical text is not quoted, however, the form of the later liturgical composition often reflects a continuation of forms found first in the Bible.

For these reasons, it is impossible to appreciate rabbinic liturgy without a clear understanding of its biblical predecessors, the earliest recorded examples of Jewish prayer.

Certainly, biblical prayers were in many ways quite different from what we have in mind when we think of Jewish liturgy. For example, they were not synagogue-based, and they predate the various attempts to formalize the structures and wording of the statutory prayers like the *Amidah* or the rabbinic blessings over food that regularly (nowadays) begin formulaically with *Barukh atah Adonai.* Yet, it is altogether proper to begin a historical consideration of the Siddur with an exploration of "Prayer in the Bible" (below), which highlights the continuities and discontinuities between biblical and post-biblical Jewish prayer. Explicit utilization of biblical prayers in the post-biblical Siddur can then be examined separately in "The Use of the Bible in Later Jewish Prayer."

PRAYER IN THE BIBLE

"Adonai is near to all who call upon Him; to all who call upon Him in truth" (Ps. 145:18). This verse from Psalms, now part of the liturgy also, expresses the premise of biblical prayer: one prays to a God who can hear and who is fundamentally responsive, at least to those who call "in truth" *(b'emet)*. Other psalms indicate that this response is not always automatic; sometimes God needs to be reminded to listen or to be more attentive, as when the psalmist asks God: "Awake! Don't sleep, O Lord! Wake up! Do not forget forever! Why are You hiding your face, forgetting our oppression and affliction?" (Ps. 44:24–25; cf. 35:22–23). Yet, the psalmist assumes that this outcry or reminder can be effective. God, who has been inactive, can be roused to action by something as simple as a spoken prayer: "They cry out, and Adonai hears, saving them from all of their troubles" (Ps. 34:18).

This notion that prayer works to get God to act on behalf of the individual or community is very common throughout biblical literature and is especially prevalent in the Book of Psalms. It is not, however, the only biblical notion of prayer. The main section of the psalm associated with the Sabbath opens: "It is good *[tov]* to give thanks to Adonai and to sing hymns to your name, Most High" (Ps. 92:2). Hymns that extol God's nature and activities are in themselves good. Prayer is not just a medium for requests and thanksgiving. Individuals may encounter the religious moment simply by reciting statements like, "How great are your actions, Adonai; your designs are so very deep" (v. 6).

These two urges, to petition and to praise, seem to stand in a certain amount of tension. Yet that tension is apparent only, since many petitions contain a significant element of praise, and many psalms that are pure praise might have been used as a part of a broader liturgy, followed, perhaps, by elements of request. Nevertheless, in both biblical and post-biblical (rabbinic) prayer, these two elements, petition and praise, must be distinguished from each other and seen as representing the fundamental human urges for having a relationship with God. On the one hand, the individual hopes for personal benefit (petitionary prayer); on the other, the relationship with God that naturally evokes praise (hymns) is valuable in and of itself.

The Bible knows many kinds of prayer, not just poetry, but prose as well. In fact, there are approximately one hundred prose prayers in the Bible. But the psalms, which epitomize the poetry of the Bible, play a particularly important role in both Jewish and Christian liturgy, to the point where biblical prayer is associated predominantly, if not solely, with the psalms. Certainly the psalms represent a particularly fine example of biblical poetry, which is characterized by a combination of the following features:

- Heightened or unusual vocabulary or imagery
- Significant figuration (especially metaphors and similes)
- Parallelism

The parallelism is especially noteworthy. A verse is commonly divided into two sections of near-equal length, and the second section typically mirrors the first. For example, Ps. 6:2 reads, "Adonai, do not punish me in your anger, do not chastise me in your fury." The verse has two parts: (a) "Adonai, do not punish me in your anger"; (b) "do not chastise me in your fury." The second part is a restatement of the first. Later, the psalmist, expressing his great grief, says, "With my tears I melt my bed" (v. 7), an instance of the tendency toward heightened imagery. It is obviously a poetic exaggeration, where the word used for "bed" is not the usual *mitah* but the much more rare and poetic word *eres*. This preference for difficult vocabulary, extreme figuration, and especially the poetic parallelism, which is quite foreign to the English ear, makes biblical poetry especially difficult to translate.

The poetic aspect of the psalms raises a significant issue that is often overlooked: Why do poetic prayers exist at all? Given the difficulty of the poetry, isn't it likely that worshipers didn't even understand the psalms they were saying? This question becomes even more significant in the post-biblical poetic period, which (by the fifth or sixth century) featured ever-more complex liturgical poetry known as *piyyutim*. Certainly the average synagogue Jew would never have understood the excessively difficult Hebrew of these poems, which allude obliquely to biblical texts and early rabbinic writings, and which depend on these allusions to make their point. Why would people pray in a style or register that they do not understand?

This question is best answered by seeing the contexts in which prose and poetic prayer might have coexisted. Already in the biblical period, there was a tension between official, formal prayer and personal, spontaneous prayer, which existed side by side. This tension is seen most clearly in the first two chapters of Samuel, which deal with Hannah's childlessness and her subsequent conception and birth of the prophet Samuel. In 1 Sam. 1:11, Hannah offers a prose prayer in the form of a vow: "O Lord of Hosts, if You attentively see the affliction of your maidservant and remember me, and if You do not forget your maidservant and give your maidservant a boy, I will dedicate him to Adonai all of the days of his life, and no razor shall ever touch his head." The vocabulary of Hannah's vow is typical: unlike poetic prayers in the Bible, it contains no similes or metaphors and it is not balanced into parallel parts. It is easy to imagine such a prayer as the spontaneous utterance of the pained Hannah.

In contrast, after Samuel is born, a poetic prayer is put in Hannah's mouth. Though not technically part of the Book of Psalms, it is nonetheless readily recognizable as a biblical psalm. She proclaims, for example (1 Sam. 2:8a), "He [God] raises the poor from the dust, lifts the needy from the dunghill." This verse has the three characteristics of psalms mentioned above: heightened or unusual vocabulary or imagery, significant figuration (especially metaphors and similes), and parallelism. It uses the rare word "dunghill" *(ashpot)*; it refers metaphorically to God's saving grace in general; and the second half of the verse repeats and reflects the first half, in different language.

But why does the biblical author attribute this psalm to Hannah? The question becomes even sharper when we realize that most of the psalm is concerned with the military victory of the Israelite king over his enemies — a context that is totally inappropriate to the natural outcry of a mother who has just given birth to a long-awaited child. Granted, Samuel is the prophet who will eventually anoint the first king, Saul, but that will occur only much later in the narrative. Why would anyone imagine that a psalm of military victory would be said by a mother who finally bears the child for whom she has dreamed and prayed for years?

The key is found in the second half of 2:5, "until the barren women gives birth to seven, and the one with many children languishes," a single line that is indeed thematically relevant to Hannah and additionally describes well her relationship to her co-wife Peninah, who had children, while Hannah did not. This psalm was probably in existence before the Book of Samuel was composed. The biblical author used it for Hannah because its allusions in verse 5 could be read in the context of the rivalry between the co-wives Hannah and Peninah.

The assignment of the psalm to Hannah is therefore secondary, but it reflects something crucial about the nature of the recitation of psalms in ancient Israel: a psalm could be recited even if it was not fully appropriate, as long as some small section of it dealt with the issue at hand. We might imagine that a woman like Hannah would want some "official" way, using elaborate language, to thank God for her great triumph. She would then go to a particular type of functionary, perhaps a Levite, and ask for the relevant psalm. It is unlikely that the Levite would compose such a psalm; instead, he would find the one that was most appropriate, even if the fit was somewhat tenuous.

It is not really so surprising that the psalm put in Hannah's mouth is not fully appropriate — how often might any one of us today recite a standard, statutory prayer that is only marginally relevant to our concerns? We all concentrate on certain prayers or sections of prayers that are particularly pertinent to the concerns or problems of the moment. Antiquity was no different — a woman like Hannah could have recited what is basically a royal military psalm, while ignoring its primary meaning, and allegorizing a particularly timely line, "until the barren women gives birth to seven, and the one with many children languishes." A woman would have chosen such a psalm, rather than compose her own, because she felt that nothing she could have written would express her gratitude as well as a ready-made composition that had been used by others before her.

The existence in the Bible of both prose and poetic prayer thus anticipates an issue that would later be explicitly articulated regarding rabbinic prayer: what is the relation between standard, already formulated prayer *(keva)* — like the psalm in 1 Samuel 2 — and spontaneous, newly created prayer *(kavvanah)* — like Hannah's vow in chapter 1? The same tension that exists in the Bible between prose and poetic prayer, innovation and conservatism, is endemic to worship. In Judaism, it begins in the Bible, then continues in rabbinic liturgy, and is found in our own prayer life today.

Whether in prose or in poetry, biblical prayers follow set patterns. Through natural development and outside influence, these patterns change somewhat over time, but overall, they remain remarkably stable. The basic existence of these patterns is hardly surprising, given people's desire to systematize and organize all aspects of human endeavor. What is somewhat surprising, however, is the extent to which biblical prayer relies heavily on the world of human relationships and interaction, what has been called "social analogy."

For example, the structure and some of the vocabulary used when a person supplicates an individual in power are mirrored in prayers in which a person supplicates God. We can, for instance, easily imagine a poor individual addressing a rich landlord in ancient Israel: "Mr. Boaz [address], I know that I am not even worthy enough to speak to you [self-deprecation]; nevertheless, will you please allow me to glean in your field [request]? I know that God will surely reward you if you do [motivation]." The following prayer, recited by Jacob as he is anticipating a confrontation with his brother Esau, is fundamentally similar (Gen. 32:10–13): "O God of my father Abraham, and God of my father Isaac, Adonai, who said to me, 'Return to your native land and I will deal bountifully with you' [address], I am unworthy of all the kindness that You have so steadfastly shown your servant... [self-deprecation]. Deliver me, I pray, from the hand of my brother, from the hand of Esau [request]; else, I fear that he may come and strike me down, mothers and children alike. Yet You have said, 'I will deal bountifully with you, and make your offspring as the sands of the sea, which are too numerous to count [motivation].'"

These parallels in structure are not limited to prose prayers. Psalm 6, which we looked at before, is considered a lament of an individual who is suffering from various troubles. The main part of the psalm opens with an invocation or address, "Adonai," which is followed by a series of requests, such as "Do not punish me in your anger, do not chastise me in your fury. Have mercy on me...heal me.... Turn, Adonai...." This is followed by a motivation: "For there is no remembrance of You in the land of death; in Sheol, who will praise You?"

The most striking example of the power of the social analogy is in the use of the "blessed" or *barukh* formula in biblical and later liturgical writings. As was pointed out in relation to the official call to prayer, "Bless Adonai who is to be blessed" *(Bar'khu et Adonai ham'vorakh)* — see Volume 1, *The Sh'ma and Its Blessings*, p. 29 — it seems odd to bless God, who is, from the biblical perspective, the source, not the recipient of all blessings. It makes perfect sense to say to a powerful patron who has done you a great favor, "May you be blessed by Adonai, by the creator of heaven and earth" (Ps. 115:15). But who can bless God? Yet, the use of social analogy is so widespread that the language by which people invoke blessing on those who show them kindness is transferred also to God.

THE USE OF THE BIBLE IN LATER JEWISH PRAYER

Post-biblical prayer emulates many of the features of its biblical predecessors, including the continued tension between poetic, formulaic prayer and spontaneous, prose prayer, as well as the continued use of genres such as petition and hymns. Beyond these broad influences, biblical formulas for prayer as well as entire sections, even whole chapters, from the Bible entered the liturgy verbatim. These include various psalms, such as the concluding chapters of the Book of Psalms (145–150) that are recited in *P'sukei D'zimrah* (see "The Daily *Hallel*," p. 107) and the psalms that focus on God's kingship that are part of *Kabbalat Shabbat* (Psalms 95–99). The most familiar material from other biblical books may be the Priestly Blessing, Num. 6:24–26 (see Volume 2, *The Amidah*, p. 176). The *P'sukei D'zimrah*, however, is especially rich in biblical citations. Aside from Psalms 145–150, we also find a prayer from 1 Chron. 16:8–36 (see pp. 78–90) immediately following the opening blessing, *Barukh she'amar* ("Blessed is the One by whose speech the world came to be"), and a string of three prayers, from 1 Chron. 29:10–13, Neh. 9:6–11, and Exod. 14:30–15:18, which are used toward the conclusion of the rubric (see pp. 156–175), just prior to the final benediction, *Yishtabach* ("Let your name be forever praised"). In addition to the complete citations, the liturgy contains prayers that are basically nothing more than pastiches of biblical verses, organized together thematically. The best example in the *P'sukei D'zimrah* is *V'hu rachum...* ("And He is merciful..." [see pp. 92–97]). In other cases still, prayers allude to a biblical verse or tradition, even though it is not quoted, for instance, *Birkat David* ("Blessing for David") in the weekday *Amidah* (see Volume 2, *The Amidah*, p. 142), which contains phrases from various biblical texts concerning David. The three paragraphs of the *Sh'ma* represent a special category, since in the Bible they are not prayers at all, but they have been moved to the liturgy and recontextualized to become central to the prayer book.

The influence of the Bible on the liturgy goes even farther still. The blessing formula *Barukh atah Adonai eloheinu melekh ha'olam* ("Blessed are You, Adonai our God, ruler of the world") is central to rabbinic liturgy. We see early signs of it in the late biblical books, such as David's prayer in 1 Chron. 29:10, which opens, "Blessed are You, Adonai, the God of Israel our father, from the beginning of time to the ends of time." Similarly, Ps. 119:12 says, "Blessed are You, Adonai. Teach me your statutes." But this is already a second stage of development. An earlier biblical formula, "Blessed is Adonai" *(Barukh Adonai)* can be found in Gen. 9:26 and Ps. 41:14. Although the longer formula *Barukh atah Adonai* is rare in the Bible, it becomes more common in the Dead Sea Scroll literature, which may here, as is often the case, be seen as an important transitional link between biblical literature and the later rabbinic liturgical traditions.

Various biblical forms continue to influence classical liturgical compositions. For example, Psalm 18 (with its parallel, 2 Samuel 22) opens with various descriptions of God, which function as praise, and then moves directly to requests of

God — a direct parallel to the structure of the daily *Amidah,* where three opening blessings of praise lead to thirteen blessings of petitions. These latter blessings, a series of petitions, have no direct correlation in earlier biblical literature, however, since the petitions of the *Amidah* are for general benefits that anyone can say and that can form the basis of a regularized daily liturgy irrespective of the particular circumstances of whoever the worshiper happens to be. In the Bible, however, there is no regularized daily prayer service that generation after generation of people say. Biblical requests are explicitly specific; they focus on a particular problem or affliction of the petitioner. Psalm 6 is something of an exception, in that the supplicant is suffering from both physical illness (v. 3) and from a threat by enemies (v. 8). It therefore moves in the direction of becoming an all-purpose prayer, listing anything likely to be wrong and requiring help. But it does not become a daily staple that worshiper after worshiper recites as part of a regular fixed worship service such as we have today. That kind of service is the invention of the post-biblical period, when, in fact, Psalm 6 is eventually taken over as a daily prayer that people say whether they are actually suffering or not. It is part of the rubric called the *Tachanun,* the subject of a later volume in this series.

Additionally, the biblical urge simply to praise God is not lost in post-biblical liturgy, not only from the rabbinic era, but even in later medieval compositions, such as *Adon Olam* and *Yigdal,* two popular hymns that now belong to the early morning rubric called "Morning Blessings" *(Birkhot Hashachar).* Finally, acrostic poems, that is, poems that follow the order of the Hebrew alphabet, are common in the Bible too. Usually, each verse gets a different letter of the alphabet, as, for instance, Psalm 145, which is part of the *P'sukei D'zimrah* (see p. 112). This same pattern is frequently found in later liturgical compositions, for example, *El Adon,* a Sabbath expansion of the blessing that precedes the morning *Sh'ma.* In post-biblical liturgy, however, the principle of using acrostics is expanded to include prayers in which every single word gets a different letter of the alphabet — for instance, E*l* b*arukh* g*'dol* d*e'ah* ("*A*lmighty *b*lessed *g*reat *d*iviner…"), a section of the same blessing in the daily prayers (see Volume 1, *The Sh'ma and Its Blessings,* p. 55).

There are several indications that classical biblical prayer might have been associated either with sacrificial offerings or perhaps with the offering of the incense. Psalm 141:2, for instance, says, "Let my prayer be counted as incense before You, and the lifting up of my hands as an evening sacrifice." This obviously was not the case with synagogue prayer as it developed. However, some ritualistic acts that accompanied biblical prayer continued into the classical liturgy of the synagogue. Bowing, a sign of obeisance, is often recorded in biblical texts in the context of prayer. We hear, for instance, that when King Solomon completed his prayer to God, "he rose from where he had been kneeling" (1 Kings 8:54). The act of at least symbolically bending the knees is incorporated later in places like *Bar'khu* and the opening and closing blessings of the *Amidah* (see Volume 1, *The Sh'ma and Its Blessings,* p. 29, and Volume 2, *The Amidah,* pp. 60, 70, 165, and 174). 1 Kings 8:48 and Dan. 6:11 (two late passages reflecting the realities of living outside the Land of Israel) note the practices of facing Jerusalem while praying, and Daniel is pictured as praying three times daily as well, two conventions that became central by the time of the Rabbis of the Mishnah and that continue to this day. Yet not all of the physical rituals associated with prayer in the biblical period continued into later times. For example, as we saw above in Ps. 141:2 ("Let my prayer be counted as incense before You, and the lifting up of my hands as an evening sacrifice"), the central position of prayer in the biblical period was to approach God with upraised hands. Solomon too prays not just kneeling, but "with his hands spread out toward heaven" (1 Kings 8:54). Though this position is still maintained by the *kohanim* (the priests) during the Priestly Blessing, it is no longer the predominant position of prayer.

The use of the Bible in the liturgy parallels the use of the Bible throughout post-biblical Jewish culture in general. It is quoted extensively, and its themes and structures are extremely influential. Yet, as Judaism continued to evolve, new themes (such as the resurrection of the dead) and new structures (such as rhythmic, rhyming poetry) were absorbed from outside cultures and incorporated into the liturgy. The result is the Siddur as we have it, much of which the biblical authors would have recognized and felt comfortable with, even though the vast majority of its material is of post-biblical origin.

The Twofold Halakhic Status of P'sukei D'zimrah

Daniel Landes

The halakhic status of *P'sukei D'zimrah* is ambiguous. On the one hand, it is an independent entity with its own integrity. On the other, it is merely preparatory to the really central rubrics of our liturgy: the *Sh'ma* and Its Blessings, and the *Amidah*. Both aspects of the *P'sukei D'zimrah* are supportable by talmudic discussion.

The first such talmudic source, Shabbat 118a, is part of a longer discussion regarding certain halakhic practices, whether ritual or ethical, that various Rabbis express themselves as anxious to undertake. Each begins with the phrase "Let my portion be among...." In that context, we learn, "Rabbi Yose stated: 'Let my portion be among those who complete [i.e., recite] *Hallel* [literally, "praise"].'"

The Talmud immediately questions this practice, however: "Can this be correct? Didn't the master state, 'Anyone who reads *Hallel* every day insults and blasphemes!'"

So Rabbi Yose's view is clarified: "We are referring to *P'sukei D'zimrah*."

At issue is the meaning of word *Hallel*. It can mean praise of God in general, but it also denotes Psalms 113–118, praise of God in particular for having delivered Israel from Egypt. Rabbi Yose was referring to the former usage. He wanted to speak God's praise daily. The Talmud's objection derived from the mistaken view that he wanted to recite Psalms 113–118 every day, a practice that is regarded as a form of blasphemy, since these psalms are reserved for specific holiday recitation alone. Rashi [Solomon ben Isaac, Troyes, France, 1040–1105] explains, "The early prophets legislated [*tiknu*] these psalms as praise and thanksgiving, at specific times.... One who recites them continuously, rather than at their specific time, is like one who makes them into a secular song, thereby mocking their original intent."

Three points emerge regarding *P'sukei D'zimrah*. First, if it was confused with the Egyptian *Hallel*, it may be that it postdates that *Hallel*, which was already around in Yose's day and, therefore, easily mistaken for what Yose wanted to do. Second, it was not originally established as a required prayer service. Otherwise, Yose could hardly have said of it only the wish, "Let my portion be among those" who do it. Third, though it is not the same as the Egyptian *Hallel*, it is nonetheless a legitimate form of *Hallel* in its own right. The implication of this last point is that it has its own integrity as a prayer rubric and that it functions as a discrete unit of prayer with its own distinctive structure and rules. That is why *P'sukei D'zimrah* was provided with an opening and closing blessing ("Blessed is the One by whose speech..." [*Barukh she'amar*] and "Let your name be forever praised" [*Yishtabach*]). The Egyptian *Hallel* had such blessings, so it was fitting to supply them for the *P'sukei D'zimrah* as well.

The major distinction between these two forms of *Hallel* is that the *Hallel* of Egyptian deliverance has greater halakhic standing, in that it is either an early enactment of the later prophets, as Rashi surmised and as Maimonides (Egypt, 1135–1204) too believed (Laws of Chanukah 3:6), or, according to other authorities (e.g., *Halakhot G'dolot* by Shimon Kayara, Iraq, ninth century), even a Torah commandment.

In sum, what emerges from this first talmudic discussion is that *P'sukei D'zimrah* is a form of *Hallel*. It began as a *minhag* (a custom) but then, following the model of the earlier *Hallel* of Egyptian deliverance (known as the Egyptian *Hallel*), it was given a parallel identity and structure, complete with beginning and ending blessings. It became a *Hallel* for every day.

Indeed, it is not only *permitted* to be said every day; it is *required*. At the heart of *P'sukei D'zimrah* is Psalm 145, known by its first two words, *T'hillah l'david* ("David's Psalm"). The Talmud grants special significance to this psalm, which asserts God's beneficent presence standing behind the entire natural order. We learn that "whoever recites this psalm three times daily will merit the world-to-come" (Ber. 4b). No wonder *P'sukei D'zimrah* has such special significance! It is a regularized extolling of God. Every day, we are to say to God what is halakhically considered the core verse of this core psalm: "You open your hand, and satisfy every living being."

There is, however, a second and countervailing talmudic source, Berakhot 32a, which presents a different attitude toward the liturgical status of *P'sukei D'zimrah*:

> Rabbi Simlai expounded: A person should always praise the holy One blessed be He and afterwards pray. From where do we know this? From Moses, as it is written, "I pleaded with Adonai at that time..." (Deut. 3:23), and it is written immediately thereafter (Deut. 3:24), "O Lord God, You...whose powerful deeds no god in heaven or on earth can equal!" Only after all of that it is written, "Let me, I pray, cross over and see the good land..." (Deut. 3:25).

The Talmud identifies Moses' first statement, "O Lord God, You...whose powerful deeds no god in heaven or on earth can equal," as praise, and his second statement, "Let me, I pray, cross over and see the good land...," as petition, thus proving that praise of God should precede the standard rubrics that constitute the core of our daily liturgy.

To be sure, this source does not explicitly mention *P'sukei D'zimrah*, and because Moses' prayer is a petition, many commentators think that it refers not to the *P'sukei D'zimrah* at all but to the first three blessings of the *Amidah*, which indeed are blessings of praise and which introduce the middle thirteen benedictions that express our petitions (see *Kesef Mishneh* by Joseph Caro, Turkey, Greece, and Safed, Israel, 1488–1575; and Maimonides, Laws of Prayer 1:2). It is, however, directly associated with *P'sukei D'zimrah* by the *Tur* (*Orach Chayim* [O. Ch.] 51), the formative law code by Jacob ben Asher (called also Ba'al Haturim, Spain, 1270–1340). After quoting it, he adds, "Therefore, they legislated [*tiknu*] them [the psalms] before prayer and fixed one blessing before them and another after them."

For the *Tur*, then, *P'sukei D'zimrah* is not an independent prayer. Unlike the Egyptian *Hallel*, it cannot stand alone. It is intended as an intensive rendering of praise in anticipation of the *Sh'ma* and the *Amidah*, the prayers that follow. The *Sh'ma* and *Amidah* are "the real thing," as it were, while the *P'sukei D'zimrah* (which introduces them) is merely *preparatory*. Indeed, Joel Sirkes (Poland, 1561–1640, known usually as the Bach, an acronym formed from the initials of his work, *Bayit Chadash*) goes so far as to say that by itself, *P'sukei D'zimrah* as described in the Talmud would not be required but only recommended for "receiving a great reward in the world-to-come." He thinks that the sources are insufficient to have us conclude that the *P'sukei D'zimrah* is obligatory. "And since it is not obligatory, there is no reason to establish a blessing [before and after]." Nonetheless, Sirkes would mandate *P'sukei D'zimrah* because of Rabbi Simlai's dictum demanding praise to God before petitions. In other words, the obligation (*chiyuv*) to recite *P'sukei D'zimrah* has nothing to do with its discrete status as a *Hallel* akin to the Egyptian *Hallel*—indeed, it is not akin to it at all and does not even require opening and closing blessings. It does, however, provide the necessary praise that anticipates our daily petitions to God in the *Amidah*.

The *P'sukei D'zimrah* can thus be seen as falling into either category: an independent prayer like the Egyptian *Hallel*, or a preparation for the "real" prayer of the *Amidah*. In practice, both models are reflected in the Halakhah, as we can readily see from two separate halakhot (laws).

The first halakhah of importance in this regard is that *P'sukei D'zimrah* is said as part of group prayer, unlike the large rubric that comes before it, the *Birkhot Hashachar* ("Morning Blessings"), which may be said by individuals at home, before arriving for congregational worship. *Birkhot Hashachar* consists of morning blessings and study sections that are customarily said privately and personally, upon arising. With *P'sukei D'zimrah*, however, not only do we require a group, but we are even encouraged to meet in a synagogue to say it together. David ben Abu Zimra (the Radbaz, Egypt, 1479–1573) considers it altogether unfitting to sing God's praise in any way that is not communal. He even says, "If the *Sh'khinah* [the "divine presence"] comes to synagogue and sees people reciting the psalms with some behind and others ahead, She immediately departs" (*Responsa* 1:887).

The *P'sukei D'zimrah* is recited communally with a prayer leader. But it is not of the same communal status as the *Sh'ma* and the *Amidah* that follow it — as we see from the following legal stipulation. The final benediction in the *P'sukei D'zimrah* is normally concluded by a *Kaddish,* for which a quorum of ten worshipers (a *minyan*) is required. If the congregation has reached that benediction, but no quorum is yet present, the leader will commonly wait for up to half an hour hoping that more people will arrive (Moses Isserles [the R'ma] to *Shulchan Arukh,* O. Ch. 53:3, Poland, 1530-1572; and Abraham Gombiner [*Magen Avraham*], Poland, 1637–1683). Yet individuals are not to stop their own individual worship at that time. Instead, they are supposed to continue on their own and finish the rubric privately, and only then to wait for the prayer leader to catch up (Israel Meir HaCohen Kagan, Poland, 1838–1933, *Mishnah B'rurah* to O. Ch. 53:3, No. 9).

The upshot is that *P'sukei D'zimrah* should be recited in a formal prayer structure with a *minyan* and a prayer leader, but unlike the *Sh'ma* and the *Amidah,* it is not required to be done that way. The *Sh'ma* and the *Amidah,* however, are communal in their essence: they *must* be recited as public prayer within a community of worshipers. Only if no opportunity for such a communal gathering exists may a worshiper say these prayers privately.

The second halakhah that illustrates the twofold nature of the *P'sukei D'zimrah* arises with regard to the technical matter of interrupting a prayer in progress. Technically it is forbidden to interrupt the recitation of *P'sukei D'zimrah* once one has begun its opening benediction (*Shulchan Arukh,* O. Ch. 51:4). One may not, for instance, extend a greeting to someone who arrives late, even if, at the time, one is naturally pausing between the various chapters of psalms that make it up (*Mishnah B'rurah* to O. Ch. 41:12). When Maimonides was asked whether someone could stop to put on *tallit* and *t'fillin* in the middle of the rubric, he answered, "There is no *issur* [nothing expressly forbidden] about making a blessing on *tsitsit* [the *tallit*] and *t'fillin* during the songs of praise. Such an interruption during *P'sukei D'zimrah* is not forbidden, for it is not like the *Amidah* or the *Sh'ma,* where interruptions such as these are forbidden" (Maimonides, *Responsa* 183, Blau ed., p. 335; see also the Re'ma 54:3 and *Mishnah B'rurah* 53:5–6, which permit reciting the blessings between the psalm chapters when there is no other opportunity to put on the *tallit* and *t'fillin*). In fact, necessary announcements to the worshipers (e.g., page numbers) can even be given, a practice that would most definitely not be allowed during the *Sh'ma* and the *Amidah* (*Iggrot Moshe* of Rabbi Moshe Feinstein of blessed memory, Russia, and New York, 1895–1986). The point again is that to some extent, *P'sukei D'zimrah* has its own integrity. It is a discrete rubric in its own right, but not on the level of the *Sh'ma* or the *Amidah.*

The third example of both models acting dialectically concerns the vexing issue of skipping part of the *P'sukei D'zimrah.* Halakhic authorities like *Mishnah B'rurah* (O. Ch. 52) urge worshipers to recite the *P'sukei D'zimrah* without leaving any of it out. Worshipers are urged to come early to synagogue in order to make sure they will have the time necessary to say it completely or, if that is impossible, to wait for a later *minyan* and say it then without omitting anything (*Kaf Hachayim* 52:1, Yaakov Chayim Sofer, Baghdad and Jerusalem, early twentieth century).

Nonetheless, the authorities realize that in practice, it constantly happens that people come late to synagogue and have to skip part of *P'sukei D'zimrah* in order to catch up with the recital of the *Sh'ma* and the *Amidah*. They therefore rank the prayers of the *P'sukei D'zimrah* hierarchically according to importance: the minimal amount that must be said is the opening and closing blessings and Psalm 145, known as *Ashre*.

We might think of *P'sukei D'zimrah* as a prayer that was born as a mere custom but that quickly became accepted by Jews as a formalized service with all its specific trappings. The record of its origin as "custom" is provided by Maimonides (Laws of Prayer 7:12):

> The sages praised the person who recites songs from the Book of Psalms every day, meaning thereby from *T'hillah l'david* (Psalm 145) to the end of the book, and the people customarily read verses before and after. The sages also legislated [*tiknu*] a blessing before the songs *(Barukh she'amar)* and a blessing afterward *(Yishtabach)*. Afterward one says the blessing of the *Sh'ma* and reads the *Sh'ma*.

Begun as a custom, the *P'sukei D'zimrah* eventually became concretized as a prayer in its own right with all the integrity of the Egyptian *Hallel*, and on the same theme: praise of God. Sometimes it is best viewed in that independent way. And sometimes it is conceived still as customary preparation for the *Amidah*, the petitions *par excellence*, which require prior prayers of praise. In the latter capacity, it leads individuals who are just gathering together in a group to a deepened feeling of subservience to a God capable of creating our wondrous world (*Arukh HaShulchan* 51; Yechiel Mikhel Halevi Epstein, Russia, 1829–1908). Praise of God the creator leads halakhically to the acceptance of God's Oneness, in the *Sh'ma*, then to our ability and desire to address Him in petitionary prayer of the *Amidah*.

P'sukei D'zimrah and the Problem of Length in Modern Prayer Books

David Ellenson

Two principles have guided liberal Jews in their approach to the construction of the modern prayer book: a principle of content and a principle of length. The principle of content meant that as they reformulated the classical Jewish service, they refashioned the manifest content of the Siddur to comport to the actual beliefs of modern worshipers. They simply changed the wording wherever the content of the traditional prayers was deemed problematic. The previous two volumes in this series described and analyzed how a variety of non-Orthodox prayer books accomplished this task by rewording the *Sh'ma* and Its Blessings and the *Amidah*.

But the principle of content was supplemented by the principle of length, in that non-Orthodox prayer books also addressed what their authors viewed as the undue length of the traditional service. From the very first liberal prayer book that came out of Hamburg in 1819 all the way down to our own day, Reform Jewish liturgists have felt that the traditional service is so long that it precludes proper devotion in prayer. They have therefore abbreviated the liturgy by omitting parts of the service that seemed superfluous or needlessly repetitious, not because they had ideological objections to what those prayers said, but just to shorten the service. They were convinced that by excising repetitious content, they did no harm to the essential content of the service, while actually enhancing the quality of the prayer experience precisely because the service had been abridged.

This principle of length is crucial for understanding the approach most liberal prayer books have taken toward the *P'sukei D'zimrah*. Most non-Orthodox authors of prayer books have expressed few theological problems with or objections to Psalms 145–150, the biblical writings that compose the basic content of this service. Nor did the other psalms and biblical citations in the *P'sukei D'zimrah* bother liberal prayer book composers. They generally treated biblical material with greater affection and regard anyway than they did rabbinic and medieval compositions. Here, in particular, after all, the material in question offered poetic praise of the divine while declaring the wonders of the universe that God fashioned.

To be sure, some Reconstructionist liturgists have raised objections to a literalist understanding of these prayers, since the psalms project an anthropomorphic view of a personal creator God that runs counter to a Reconstructionist naturalistic theology. However, as religious poetry, these passages are easily subject to metaphoric interpretations, and they are so rich and multidimensional that virtually all liberal liturgists, including Reconstructionist writers, have been able to find inspiration and meaning in them, despite the literal imagery that they have not necessarily accepted. The treatment of *P'sukei D'zimrah* in liberal liturgies has therefore been little informed by issues of manifest content.

Liberal liturgists have approached *P'sukei D'zimrah* principally in light of the classical function this rubric was intended to fulfill. The Talmud notes that the pious ones of old would prepare themselves for communal prayer through the recitation of psalms. The recital of these passages at this point in the service has therefore been instrumental for the act of communal worship in modern times no less than in the talmudic era. The psalms are intended to prepare people for prayer by creating a mood for personal and communal devotion.

Non-Orthodox liturgies have approached *P'sukei D'zimrah* with this concern in mind. Some liturgists — David Einhorn, for example — have removed the Hebrew altogether and composed vernacular renderings or translations of the psalms so that congregants can be inspired by the lofty sentiments contained in them in a language that these congregants understand. Others, such as Abraham Geiger (in his 1870 Siddur) and Isaac Mayer Wise (in his *Minhag America*), have shortened the number of psalms and passages to be recited so that worshipers can focus their thoughts on the few psalms that are retained without having to hurry through all the psalms that the traditional rite prescribes. The rationale for this is that it is better to recite a few psalms with genuine devotion than many psalms without proper intent. This approach has dominated the stance most liberal prayer books have adopted toward this service during the present century. Its application can be seen in the treatment accorded *P'sukei D'zimrah* in American Reform's *Gates of Prayer* (1975) and the newest Siddur of the British Liberal Movement, *Siddur Lev Chadash* (1995).

All this indicates that the problem that liberal liturgies have confronted in this section of the service, unlike elsewhere, is not one of manifest content. Rather, liberal liturgies have mostly tried to abbreviate the rubric in order to fulfill its talmudic purpose: establishing a mood for public prayer on the part of the community and the individual. My commentary on specific parts of the *P'sukei D'zimrah* is therefore sparse. Having emphasized that, in general, most Reform liturgies have simply abridged the amount of material that the traditional service contains, I have just a few specific notes regarding this or that prayer that was changed for ideological reasons.

Ashre

Psalm 145 and Its Rhetorical Structure

Reuven Kimelman

No psalm is recited more frequently than Psalm 145, known by its liturgical title *Ashre*. For well over a thousand years it has been recited thrice daily: twice in the morning and once to begin the afternoon service. Despite its frequency, however, its full meaning eludes readers who are unaware of its rhetorical structure. Rhetorical structure is the poetical form in which the psalm is composed.

THE POEM'S INTERNAL STRUCTURE

The whole liturgical piece is presented in chart form below. Psalm 145 itself is designated the body. The psalm verses that are prefixed and suffixed to it are designated prologue and epilogue. The psalm can be arranged into four stanzas, with verses 1 and 2 serving as prelude, verse 21 as postlude, and the middle verse (10) as interlude.

PROLOGUE

A. Happy are they who dwell in your house; they will ever praise You (Ps. 84:5).
B. Happy is the people like this. Happy is the people whose God is Adonai (Ps. 144:15).

Adapted from Reuven Kimelman, "Psalm 145: Theme, Structure, and Impact," *The Journal of Biblical Literature* 113 (1994): 23–44. A fuller version is slated to appear in Reuven Kimelman's forthcoming book, *The Rhetoric of Jewish Prayer: A Literary and Historical Commentary on the Prayerbook*.

BODY (PSALM 145)

PRELUDE: THE SINGLE AND SINGULAR PRAISE OF DAVID ALONE

David's Psalm:

1. *I* will exalt You, my God the king, and *praise your name for ever and ever.*
2. Every day *I* will *praise* You, and extol *your name for ever and ever.*

STANZA 1: GOD'S GREATNESS

3. *Great* is Adonai and highly praised. Endless is his greatness.
4. Generation upon generation will praise your deeds, and tell of your mighty acts.
5. I will speak of your wondrous acts, and your glorious majesty in its splendor.
6. People tell of your awe-inspiring might, and I proclaim your *greatness.*

STANZA 2: GOD'S GOODNESS

7. People spread your very great *goodness,* and sing of your righteousness.
8. Gracious and merciful is Adonai, endlessly patient and most kind.
9. Adonai is *good* to all, showering all his creatures with mercy.

INTERLUDE: PRAISE OF THE FAITHFUL

10. All your creatures will thank You, Adonai, and *your faithful will praise You.*

STANZA 3: GOD'S KINGSHIP

11. They will tell of the glory of your *kingdom,* and speak of your might.
12. Announce his greatness to humankind, and the majestic glory of his *kingdom.*
13. Your *kingdom* is a *kingdom* for all times, and your reign for every generation.

STANZA 4: GOD'S BENEVOLENCE IN MANY WAYS

14. Adonai *supports* all who fall, and *uprights* all who are bent over.
15. The eyes of all look to You, and You *give* them timely food.
16. You *open* your hand, and *satisfy* every living being.
17. Adonai is *righteous* in all his ways, and *gracious* in all his acts.
18. Adonai is *near* to all who call upon Him, to all who call upon Him in truth.
19. He *does the desire* of those who revere Him, and *hears their cry* and *saves* them.
20. Adonai *guards* all who love Him, and *destroys* all who are wicked.

POSTLUDE: UNIVERSAL ACKNOWLEDGMENT

21. Let my mouth speak Adonai's praise, and *all creatures praise his holy name for ever and ever.*

EPILOGUE

C. Let us praise Adonai from now and ever more. Halleluyah (Ps. 115:18).

The psalm's theme of divine sovereignty is announced in the first line by addressing God as "my God the king." Although there are other psalms that proclaim "my king and my God," (Ps. 5:3 and 84:4), only Ps. 145:1 uses the definite article ("*the* king"), thereby underscoring the exclusivity of divine rule. Opening with "my God the king" serves as a royal acclamation. According to the psalmist, awareness of such sovereignty evokes the desire to share it with others. This desire is regularly encountered in psalms that present God as king, such as Psalms 47, 93, 96, and 99.

Psalm 145 extends this message of divine sovereignty in three stages to successively broader circles. Each stage is marked by the word "praise" (Hebrew: *b.r.kh*), which crops up strategically in the second half of lines 1, 10, and 21, the very lines that serve as prelude, interlude, and postlude. The prelude starts: "I praise your name forever"; the interlude continues: "your faithful will praise You"; and the postlude climaxes: "all creatures praise his holy name for ever and ever."

The correspondence between the psalmist's "I" blessing God's name at the outset and the expectation of all creatures doing so in the end animates the whole psalm. In the interlude, "the faithful" appear as an intermediate step between "I" and "all." The drive toward inclusiveness is reinforced by what is known as an "envelope structure" — composing a poem such that the end echoes the beginning. In this case, the poem is "enclosed" in an envelope consisting of phrases of praise: the "I praise" of the prelude and the "all creatures shall praise" of the postlude; both "for ever and ever."

Stanzas 1 (lines 3–6) and 2 (lines 7–9) are also formally framed by envelope-like inclusion marking out their thematic fields. The topic of stanza 1 is God's greatness, so line 3 (its first line) opens with "Great is Adonai…Endless is his greatness," and line 6 (its last line) concludes, "I proclaim your greatness." Similarly, stanza 2, on the theme of God's goodness, features the word "good" or "goodness" in its first and last lines. By opening and closing with "great" and "good," the two stanzas converge to say it is precisely the link between divine greatness and goodness that evokes our praise.

What is implicit in stanzas 1 and 2 becomes explicit in 3 and 4. Sovereignty, for instance, though intimated in stanza 1, is made graphic in stanza 3, which is fairly filled with references to divine majesty.

Similarly, stanza 4 cites cases of God's goodness that are only intimated in stanza 2, but in the wake of the emphasis on divine kingship in stanza 3, these acts of goodness (especially "guards all who love Him, and destroys the wicked") dramatize signs of divine reign. Hoping that perceiving God as a great but caring king will trigger the universal desire to recognize God, the psalmist anticipates all humanity eventually joining in such an acclamation.

Each of the four stanzas forms a step in the escalation of praise. The first (lines 3–6) underscores the inadequacy of only the psalmist praising every day. God's "greatness" is "endless"; his "majesty" is "glorious." Such a compounding of synonyms, found only here in the whole Psalter, implies that even the loftiest encomium is an understatement.

Aside from forming the necessary halfway stop between the "I" who praises God at the poem's outset and the "all creatures" who do so as the psalm ends, the interlude (line 10) links up with the end of stanza 2, which it follows. Thus, on the heels of line 9, where God is pictured as "showering *all his creatures* with mercy," line 10 states, "*All your creatures* will thank You." Yet, so far, only "your faithful" are moved to "praise You"; the universal acclamation of praise that occurs at the poem's end is only anticipated here.

Stanza 3, on the theme of kingship, follows from the interlude. Anxious to praise God, the faithful now seek to "announce his greatness to humankind" (line 12). The universal thrust of the line is underscored if we compare it with the only other time the Bible expresses the desire "to announce his mighty acts," Ps. 106:8, where, however, there is no mention of the targeted audience, "humankind." What in Psalm 106 was for Israel's sake becomes in Psalm 145 for the sake of all. Stanza 3 thus heightens consciousness of God's presence in the world as majestic ruler throughout all time and space, a theme that becomes specified in the numerous acts of God's beneficence contained in stanza 4.

By stanza 4, we see a deliberate shift from cosmic ruler to daily nourisher. Regal power is mobilized in care of the downtrodden. And although, as line 17 proclaims, God is beneficent to all, there remains a correlation between the order of intimacy and the intensity of divine providence. Lines 16–20 progress on an axis of increasing closeness to God.

He feeds — all living (16);
He is close — to all who call Him (18);
He does the desire — of those who revere Him (19);
and preserves — all who love Him (20).

The stanza reaches closure by noting God's special solicitude for his devotees, confirming their faith in him.

Above, we saw the use of the "envelope" strategy for the poem as a whole. It appears also in three of the four stanzas. Stanza 1 begins (line 3) with "Great [is Adonai]" and ends (line 6) with "[I proclaim your] greatness"; stanza 2 starts (line 7) by celebrating "[your very great] goodness" and ends (line 9) by affirming, "[Adonai is] good"; stanza 3 begins and ends (lines 11 and 13) with "kingdom." Stanza 4 is not as clear, but there too we have a partial envelope insofar as God's "support" (line 14) is expressed by the fact that he "guards all who love him, and destroys all who are wicked" (line 20).

The movement of the stanzas from God's greatness to God's goodness to God's kingship to God's benevolence also uncovers the alternating pattern of (1) transcendence, (2) immanence, (3) transcendence, (4) immanence, agreeing with Heschel that "the dichotomy of transcendence and immanence is an oversimplification," for "God remains transcendent in His immanence, and related in His transcendence."

The postlude follows from the realization that God is this immanent but transcendent universally caring king. The "I" of the prelude ("I will exalt You") returns in the postlude ("Let *my* mouth speak Adonai's praise"), but now it is extended to a crescendo of all humanity everywhere and forever ("all creatures praise his holy name for ever and ever"). From beginning to end, the whole composition is ringed together by the theme of praise, and praise alone. Unmarred by any request, only Psalm 145 merited the superscription "David's Psalm."

The following diagram sums up the prayer's structural integrity:

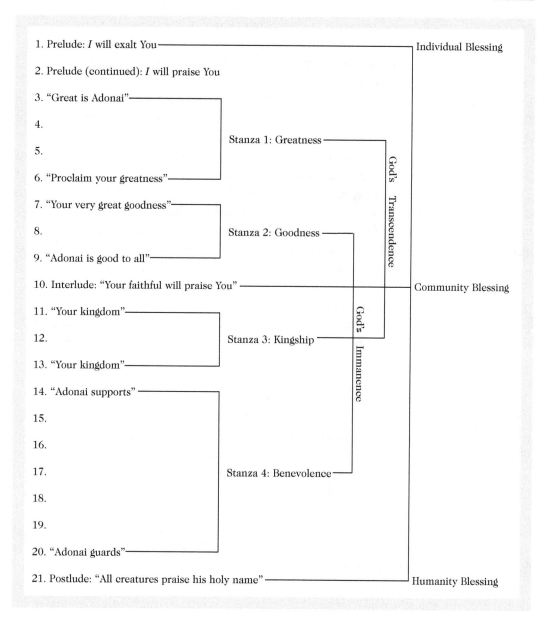

THE ACROSTIC

Beyond internal features, Psalm 145 is unified by the use of a Hebrew acrostic. Opinions differ on what role, if any, this structural device plays. Some deny it any significance, holding that acrostic poems are by their nature artificial.

Others see the full alphabet as a metaphor for totality or as a reflection of the full range of human expression, and still others see it as a memory aid or as relating to the enumerative character of Semitic poetry. The explanation most apropos to its use in Psalm 145 is metonymy, a rhetorical use of one thing in place of another with which it is closely associated. Professor Adelle Berlin explains, "The entire alphabet, the source of all words, is marshalled in praise of God. One cannot actually use all of the words in a language, but by using the alphabet one uses all potential words."

The psalmist deliberately omits the anticipated *nun* verse between lines 13 and 14. Such incomplete acrostics (known as lipograms) are common to the Bible and to other ancient literature. In fact, other acrostic psalms ascribed to David such as Psalms 25, 34, and 37 are also missing a letter or two, whereas those lacking ascriptions such as 111, 112, and 119 are all perfect acrostics.

Unable to leave matters alone, the Greek, Latin, and Syriac versions of the Bible, as well as the Dead Sea Scroll version from Qumran, insert a *nun* verse. The Qumran version, for instance, reads, "Faithful is God in his words and pious in all his deeds" *(ne'eman elohim bidvarav v'chasid b'khol ma'asav)*. But the authenticity of these verses is highly questionable. Among other things, the first few words of the Qumran example, "Faithful is God in his words" *(ne'eman elohim bidvarav)*, are suspiciously like those of the post-*Haftarah* blessing that reads, "the God who is faithful in all his words" *(ha'el hane'eman b'khol d'varav)*, and thus may very well have been a stock liturgical phrase that was commonplace and could be used to complete the acrostic.

Content-wise, there is no indication of anything missing. On the contrary, it has been speculated that the absence of the *nun* line is part of the message; namely, as all human praise of God is theologically inadequate, so the psalm is alphabetically imperfect.

The deliberate absence of a *nun* verse is consistent with other rhetorical devices with which the poem has been carefully constructed. The word *kol*, for example, translated as "all" or "every," threads its way through the psalm seventeen times. Its virtual ubiquity highlights the unending and universal chorus of praise to a God whose sovereignty and solicitude transcend temporal and spatial frontiers. So, for example, God, who is praised "every day" (line 2) and by "all creatures" (line 21) is "good to all" (line 9).

Another carefully crafted feature is that several times we have verses that constitute actual praise rather than talk about it. Line 2, for instance, says, "I will praise You," and line 3 performs the praise, saying, "Great is Adonai and highly praised." Stanza 2 provides two lines of performance, one for each of the previous half-sentences that constitute the prior line where the performance is announced, thus giving us an "a-b-b-a" structure, as follows:

7. (a) People spread your very great *goodness*, (b) and sing of your righteousness.
8. (b) Gracious and merciful is Adonai, endlessly patient and most kind.
9. (a) Adonai is *good* to all, showering all his creatures with mercy.

Line 9 ("Adonai is good to all") performs the intention of 7a ("People spread your very great goodness"), as line 8 ("Gracious and merciful is Adonai, endlessly patient and most kind") expresses the beneficence of 7b ("sing of your righteousness"). In stanza 3, line 13 ("Your kingdom is a kingdom for all times, and your reign for every generation") is the performance of line 11 ("They will tell of the glory of your kingdom").

Psalm 145 and Jewish Liturgy

There is even some indication that the structure of Psalm 145 left traces on the standard Jewish blessing formula (the *b'rakhah*). The prelude begins with the self's relation to God, the interlude expands to include the faithful, and the postlude encompasses all humanity. Each stage contains a form of the verb *b.r.kh* ("to praise") whence we get the Hebrew word for blessing *(b'rakhah)*, and taken together, they even parallel successive verbal units in the rabbinic blessing — as can be seen in the following chart:

"Blessed are You" — prelude	=	self–God relationship
"O Lord our God" — interlude	=	community–God relationship
"King of the universe" — postlude	=	humanity–God relationship

When the Talmud mandates the inclusion of a reference to God's kingship in every blessing, it cites Ps. 145:1 ("I will exalt You, my God the king, and praise your name for ever and ever") as justification. In fact, this verse (and only this verse) contains all four rabbinic requirements of the blessing: praise of God *(barukh)*, address of the divine name *(shem)*, God's kingship *(melekh)*, and an expression that God rules the whole world, or eternity *(melekh ha'olam)*:

"I will exalt You" = praise of God
"my God" = God's name
"the king" = God's kingship
"for ever and ever" = the whole world, or eternity

The six-word tripartite structure of the blessing corresponds to the six-word tripartite structure of Deut. 6:4, the familiar *Sh'ma yisra'el* statement of Jewish faith:

Sh'ma yisra'el / Adonai eloheinu / Adonai echad
Barukh atah / Adonai eloheinu / melekh ha'olam

We should therefore view the blessing formula, the *Sh'ma,* and Psalm 145 as all reflecting the same triple shift from self through community to humanity, all peaking in the realization and extension of divine sovereignty over everyone.

By placing Psalm 145 at the head of the series of psalms that precede the recitation of the *Sh'ma* and Its Blessings in the morning liturgy (see Volume 1, *The Sh'ma and Its Blessings*), Psalm 145 anticipates the *Sh'ma's* theme of the realization of divine sovereignty. Professor Shlomo Goitein has even designated Psalm 145 as "the *Sh'ma* of the Psalter."

PROLOGUE AND EPILOGUE

In the medieval period, a prologue and epilogue became staples of the liturgical rendition of Psalm 145. The prologue consists of Ps. 84:5 and 144:15; the epilogue is Ps. 115:18. By prefixing this prologue to Psalm 145, the psalm is introduced with a threefold repetition of the word *ashre*. Whatever external factors may account for the addition of the prologue (such as the medieval practice of reciting it thrice daily), the fact is that the liturgical role for Psalm 145 is enhanced by the *ashre* verses that are added. The first one (Ps. 84:5), "Happy [*ashre*] are they who dwell in your house…," is assumed to refer to the Temple of old and the synagogue now. It establishes a positive mood for synagogue prayer comparable to that of the introductory morning prayer *Mah Tovu*, wherein the worshiper (upon crossing the threshold of the synagogue) proclaims, "How goodly are your tents, O Jacob, your dwelling places, O Israel" *(Mah tovu ohalekha ya'akov mishk'notekha yisra'el)* (Num. 24:5). Note how parallel they are:

Mah tovu / ohalekha ("How goodly / are your tents")
Ashre / yoshvei veitekha ("Happy / are they who dwell in your house")

Indeed, some suggest the use of both introductory verses: *Mah tovu* upon entering, and *Ashre* upon sitting down. Both underscore the enviable position of those who frequent the house of God. Both are also inclusive. Unlike other ancient entrance liturgies, biblical or otherwise, neither excludes by stipulating ritual or even moral requirements for entrance.

The meaning of the second *ashre* verse (Ps. 144:15), "Happy [*ashre*] is the people like this, happy [*ashre*] is the people whose God is Adonai," is metamorphosed by its new context. As the final line of Psalm 144, it already introduced Psalm 145 in the Psalter. There, however, the "like this" *(kakha lo)* refers back to the prosperity portrayed in Psalm 144. In its new liturgical setting, divorced as it is from the rest of Psalm 144, which it used to end, "like this" refers to the enviable opportunity for dwelling in God's house.

The epilogue, "Let us praise Adonai from now and ever more. Halleluyah" (Ps. 115:18), also serves a dual function. On the one hand, the "us" is particularistic: a reference to the "I" of the prelude and the "faithful" of the interlude. Whether or not "all creatures" join us in God's praise, as the postlude anticipates, we intend doing so. On the other hand, all of the psalms that follow this one in the morning *Hallel* (Psalms 146–150) satisfy the postlude's universalistic demand. To begin with, Psalm 145 is rhetorically linked to these other psalms, not just numerically in that it happens to come first, but structurally, because of the device known as *anadiplosis,* that is, the conscious use of the same verbal element to end one line and to begin the line immediately following. In this case, the element in common is the explosive shout "Halleluyah," meaning "Praise God." It is the last word of the epilogue and the first word of all five of the psalms that follow. Finally, the universal praise for which the postlude calls is reached at the end of the very last psalm (150): "Let every breath praise

God! Halleluyah" *(Kol han'shamah t'hallel yah, hall'luyah)*. As worshipers work their way through the central psalms of the *P'sukei D'zimrah,* "David's Psalm" becomes the psalm of all the world, anticipating the glorious end of days when God will be acknowledged by one and all.

Introduction to the Commentaries

How to Look for Meaning in the Prayers

Lawrence A. Hoffman

THE ART OF JEWISH READING

I remember the day I looked at a manuscript of a prayer book that no one could identify. It had been smuggled out of Russia, then the Soviet Union, and was obviously the liturgy for Rosh Hashanah, but who had written it, and when? It was handwritten, so the style told us much, but in addition, someone had written marginal notes in another handwriting, and yet a third person had written comments to the comments — a third unknown scholar of years gone by whose name we wanted to rescue from oblivion.

Standing before the massive volume, I reflected on the sheer joy of studying a traditional Jewish text. I had seen printed versions before, but never a handwritten instance. What a wonderful habit we Jews developed once upon a time: writing a text in the middle of the page and then filling up the margins with commentaries. Every page becomes a cross-cut through Jewish history. Jewish Bibles come that way; so does the Talmud, the Mishnah, and the codes. We never read just the text. We always read it with the way other people have read it.

To be a Jewish reader, then, is to join the ranks of the millions of readers who came before us, leaving their comments in the margins, the way animals leave tracks in the woods. Go deep into the forest, and you will come across deer runs, for example: paths to water sources, carved out by hundreds of thousands of deer over time. The deer do not just inhabit the forest; they are part of the forest; they change the forest's contours as they live there, just as the forest changes them, by offering shelter, food, and water. There is no virgin forest, really; it is an ecosystem, a balance between the vegetation and the animals who live there.

So, too, there are no virgin texts. They too are ecosystems, sustaining millions of readers over time. When we read our classic texts, we tread the paths of prior readers, in search of spiritual nourishment. *My People's Prayer Book* is therefore not just the Siddur text; it is the text as read by prominent readers from among the people. You are invited to share our path and even to break new ground yourself, passing on to others your own marginal notes, should you wish.

THE HEBREW TEXT AND TRANSLATION

For the Hebrew text, we have chosen the Ashkenazi edition favored by the renowned historian of the liturgy, the late E. D. Goldschmidt, perhaps the greatest master of liturgical text who ever lived. Born in Germany, later a refugee from the Nazis, Goldschmidt moved to Israel, where he assiduously collected and compared thousands of manuscripts for the Siddur, to arrive at an authoritative version as free of scribal and printing error as possible.

The Goldschmidt text was then translated by Joel Hoffman, who consulted regularly and at length with Marc Brettler, so as to reproduce not only the content of the original Hebrew, but also its tone, register, and style, and to bring to modern readers the same experience (to the greatest extent possible) that the original authors would have conveyed with their words. In terms of content, we assume that, by and large, words have meaning only to the extent that they contribute to sentences and concepts — as, for example, "by and large," which has nothing to do with "by" or "large."

We try to reproduce a tone and register similar to the original text: formal, but not archaic; prose or poetry, depending on the Hebrew. Where the Hebrew uses obscure words, we try to do the same, and where it uses common idiom, we try to use equally common idiom. The current volume, for instance, contains the Song of the Sea (Exod. 15:1–18), one of the oldest poems in the Hebrew Bible. It would already have been read as archaic literature by the people who selected it for inclusion in the liturgy. Instead of the modern English usage that characterizes our translation generally, The Song (as it is customarily known) is deliberately cast in archaic style, so that reading it has the same flavor for us as it must have had for the Rabbis of old.

In addition, as much as possible, parallel structure and other similar literary devices found in the Hebrew are replicated in the English translation. We have not doctored the text to make it more palatable to modern consciousness. Blatant sexisms are retained, for instance, wherever we think the author intended them. We depend upon our commentaries to bridge the gap between the translation of the original and our modern sensibilities.

THE COMMENTARIES

The heart and soul of *Minhag Ami* is its choice of commentaries that surround the prayerbook text. Translator Joel Hoffman explains his choice of words, provides alternatives, and compares his own translation with a selection of the most popularly used prayer books in the English-speaking world. Marc Brettler comments particularly on the way the Bible is embedded in the Siddur. Elliot Dorff and Ellen Frankel provide theological reflections on what the prayers might mean, should mean, could mean, cannot mean, or have to mean (even if we wish they didn't). Judith Hauptman adds insight from the world of the Talmud and the rabbinic tradition that it spawned. Daniel Landes gives us the Halakhah of prayer, the rules and traditions by which this sacred liturgical drama has traditionally been carried out. Lawrence Kushner and Nehemia Polen supply a kabbalistic commentary, adding wisdom from the world of Chasidic masters. David Ellenson surveys liberal prayer books of the last 200 years to see how their writers agonized over attempts to update this book of Jewish books for modern times. Reuven Kimelman supplies an extensive and up-to-date analysis of Psalm 145 (the *Ashre*), perhaps the best-known and most important prayer in the *P'sukei D'zimrah*. My own contribution is a summary of what we know about the historical development of the liturgy: when prayers were written, what they meant in the context of their day — and to some extent, what later generations saw in them. I also provide some of the interesting textual variants between one tradition and another, especially between Sefardi tradition and Ashkenazi tradition (as represented here).

Some of the commentaries require some comments in advance.

Translator Joel Hoffman had to make a judicious selection of translations to compare with his own. For an Orthodox version, he relied on Philip Birnbaum's classic (1949) *Daily Prayer Book: Hasiddur Hashalem* ("Birnbaum") but looked also at *Siddur Kol Ya'akov* ("Artscroll," 1984). American Reform was represented by the *Gates of Prayer* ("GOP," 1975) and revisions since; Conservative Jews will find their *Siddur Sim Shalom* ("SSS," 1985), and Reconstructionists will see their *Kol Haneshamah* ("KH," 1994) cited. He compared British liturgy too: *Forms of Prayer* ("FOP," 1977) from the Reform Synagogues of Great Britain; and both *Service of the Heart* ("SOH," 1967) and *Siddur Lev Chadash* ("SLC," 1995) from the Union of Liberal and Progressive Synagogues. For biblical citations, he consulted the Jewish Publication Society Bible ("JPS"), but compared it with the New Revised Standard Version of 1989 ("NRSV"), and *The Five Books of Moses*, by Everett Fox ("Fox," 1995).

My own historical commentary had to deal with the fact that the Goldschmidt translation is only for Ashkenazi Jews — more specifically, the Ashkenazi version common in eastern Europe, often under the influence of Elijah ben Solomon of Vilna, known as the Vilna Gaon (1720–1797). To balance the picture, I cite Sefardi practice also.

But the word "Sefardi" has two distinct meanings.

Nowadays, it usually describes Jews whose liturgy was influenced by Chasidism and the specific brand of Kabbalah initiated by Isaac Luria (the "Ari"), in sixteenth-century Palestine. Goldschmidt compiled a scientific edition of this variant too, and I used that to represent "Sefardi practice." But "Sefardi" can also mean the old Spanish-Portuguese custom carried by Jews from Spain in 1492 and then brought to the Netherlands, whence it moved to England (among other places) and eventually to America as well. When I want to draw attention to this Spanish-Portuguese custom, I call it that, using as my guide the standard work published in England at the turn of the century by Moses Gaster, *The Book of Prayer and Order of Service According to the Custom of the Spanish and Portuguese Jews*. I try also to cite early prayer books of our tradition and commentators from the Middle Ages, as well as the Genizah fragments, manuscripts telling us how Jews prayed in Eretz Yisrael prior to the Crusades.

David Ellenson was asked to fill in the gap caused by the fact that even the standard Ashkenazi and Sefardi versions hardly represent the majority of Jews today. As Jews have evolved, so have our modern movements, each with its own version of what our forebears once considered normative. The last two hundred years have witnessed the composition of countless Jewish prayer books, and Ellenson surveys the most prominent of these for instances where the traditional text evoked debate.

For historical reasons, many are Reform, beginning with the *Hamburg Temple Prayer Books* of 1819 and 1841, the very first efforts to make the content of the classical liturgy comport with modern ideas. Ellenson's survey of the nineteenth century also included *Seder T'filah D'var Yom B'Yomo* (1854; republished, 1870) by Rabbi Abraham Geiger, the preeminent leader of German Reform.

For early American liturgies, he turned to Rabbis Isaac Mayer Wise and David Einhorn. Wise's *Minhag America* (1857) was the most popular prayer book of its day, and Einhorn's *Olath Tamid* (1856) became the prototype for the *Union Prayer Book*, which was adopted in 1895 as the official liturgy for North American Reform Jews. In 1975, *Gates of Prayer* replaced the *Union Prayer Book*, and in 1996 the latest in a series of gender-inclusive editions of *Gates of Prayer* appeared. All three of these official movement books are cited here.

Among the non-American prayer books of the late 1900s, Ellenson made extensive use of *Ha'avodah Shebalev*, adopted by the Israeli Progressive Movement in 1982, and *Siddur Lev Chadash*, published by the Union of Progressive and Liberal Synagogues in London in 1995.

These Reform prayer books are supplemented by several Conservative and Reconstructionist volumes. The former include various prayer books produced since 1958 by the Rabbinical Assembly of the Conservative Movement, but especially the 1985 *Siddur Sim Shalom*, along, now, with its revised version of 1998. Since Conservative worship is in Hebrew, however, and since the Hebrew is generally unchanged while the vernacular equivalent is usually a literal translation of it, Ellenson has less to say about Conservative books than he does of Reform volumes, where both Hebrew and English tend to vary widely. However, he has made careful use of the latest Conservative Siddur to appear in Israel: *Siddur Va'ani T'filati* (1998). Precisely because

Hebrew *is* the vernacular in Israel, this prayer book offers insight into contemporary issues of belief within Israeli Conservative Judaism. The Reconstructionist Movement, which, like Reform, has tended toward considerable liturgical creativity, is represented primarily by *Kol Haneshamah,* published in 1996, but from time to time Ellenson discusses earlier work, especially by Mordecai Kaplan, the founder of the movement.

Ellenson gives priority to denominationally associated prayer books because they have been most widely disseminated, but does include some others, notably *The Book of Blessings,* authored in 1996 by Jewish feminist Marcia Falk. He uses liberal prayer books more than he does Orthodox ones, because liberal books were changed more, as their authors tried to remain true to their liturgical heritage, without doing an injustice to modern ideas about God, the universe, and human nature. Orthodox volumes are cited here, but references to them are limited.

The halakhic commentary was included not just to explain how prayers should be said. Even without that abiding practical concern, it would have found its way here because Halakhah (Jewish law) is essential to Judaism. Frequently misunderstood as mere legalism, it is actually more akin to Jewish poetry, in that it is the height of Jewish writing, the pinnacle of Jewish concern, sheer joy to create or to ponder. It describes, explains, and debates Jewish responsibility, yet is saturated with spiritual importance. Jewish movements can be differentiated by their approach to Halakhah, but Halakhah matters to them all.

A short overview of its history and some of its vocabulary will be helpful in advance.

The topic of Halakhah is the proper performance of the commandments, said to number 613, and divided into positive and negative ones, numbering 248 and 365, respectively. Strictly speaking, commandments derived directly from Torah *(mid'ora'ita)* are of a higher order than those rooted only in rabbinic ordinance (called *mid'rabbanan*), but all are binding.

The earliest stratum of Halakhah is found primarily in the Mishnah, a code of Jewish practice promulgated about 200 C.E., The Mishnah is the foundation for further rabbinic discussion in Palestine and Babylonia, which culminated in the two Talmuds, one from each center, and called the Palestinian Talmud (or the Yerushalmi), and the Babylonian Talmud (or the Babli). While dates for both are uncertain, the former is customarily dated to about 400 C.E., and the latter between 550 and 650.

With the canonization of the Babli, Jewish law developed largely by means of commentary to the Talmuds and of responsa, applications of talmudic and other precedents to actual cases. These are still the norm today, but they were initiated by authorities in Babylonia called Geonim (sing., Gaon) from about 750 to shortly after 1000. By the turn of the millennium, other schools had developed in North Africa particularly, but also in western Europe. Authorities in these centers are usually called Rishonim ("first" or "early" [ones]) until the sixteenth century, when they become known as Acharonim ("last" or "later" [ones]).

The first law code is geonic (from about 750), but it was the Rishonim who really inaugurated the trend toward codifying, giving us many works, including three major ones that are widely cited here: the *Mishneh Torah*, by Maimonides (Moses ben Maimon, 1135–1204), born in Spain, but active most of his life in Egypt; the *Tur*, by Jacob ben Asher (1275–1340), son of another giant, Asher ben Yechiel, who had moved to Spain from Germany, allowing Ashkenazi and Sefardi practice to intertwine in his son's magnum opus; and the *Shulchan Arukh*, by Joseph Caro (1488–1575), who is technically the first generation of the Acharonim, but who wrote influential commentaries on both the *Mishneh Torah* and the *Tur* before composing what would become the most widely used legal corpus ever.

The halakhic commentary in this volume draws on all of the above. References to the *Tur* and the *Shulchan Arukh* usually are to the section called *Orach Chayim*, "The Way of Life," which contains most of the Halakhah on prayer and is shortened here to "O. Ch." The other references are either to standard halakhic works or to the authorities who authored them. In keeping with Jewish tradition, we refer to the authorities by acronyms that are formed by combining their title (usually, Rabbi) and their names, or by other titles that history has bestowed upon them. A list of the books and authorities follows:

Abudarham (David Abudarham [late 13th–14th century], Spain)

Bach (short for Bayit Chadash, commentary to the *Tur* by Joel Sirkes [1561–1640], Poland)

Ben Ish Chai (The Chakham Joseph Chaim [1832–1909], Baghdad)

Chida (Chaim Joseph David Azulai [1724–1806], Jerusalem)

Gra (The Vilna Gaon, Rabbi Elijah of Vilna [1720–1797], Lithuania)

Har Zvi (Zvi Pesach Frank [d. 1961], Jerusalem)

Iggrot Moshe (Moshe Feinstein [1895–1986], Russia and New York)

Maharil (Jacob ben Moses Moelin [1360–1427], Germany)

Magen Avraham (commentary to the *Shulchan Arukh* by Abraham Gombiner [1637–1683], Poland)

Mishnah B'rurah (by Israel Meir HaCohen Kagan [1838–1933], Poland)

Rashi (Solomon ben Isaac [1040–1105], France)

Rashba (Solomon ben Abraham Adret [1235–1310], Spain)

R'ma (Moses Isserles [1530–1575], Poland)

Riva (Isaac ben Asher [d. 1130], Germany)

Rivash (Isaac ben Sheshet Perfet [1326–1408], Spain)

Sefer Charedim (R. Eleazar ben Moses Azikri (1533–1600), Safed, Israel)

Sefer Chasidim (Judah Hachasid [d. 1217] Germany)

Taz (short for *Turei Zahav*, commentary to the *Shulchan Arukh* by David ben Samuel Halevi [1586–1667], Poland)

Torat Habayit (commentary by Moses ben Nachman, better known as Nachmanides [1194–1270], Spain)

We have gone out of our way to provide a panoply of scholars, all students of the prayerbook text, and all committed to a life of prayer, but representative of left, right, and center in the Jewish world. They represent all of us, all of *Am Yisrael,* all of those God had in mind when God said to Ezekiel (34:30), "They shall know that I, Adonai their God, am with them, and they, the House of Israel, are my people." Unabashedly scholarly and religious at one and the same time, *Minhag Ami,* "A Way of Prayer for My People," will be deemed a success if it provides the spiritual insight required to fulfill yet another prophecy (Isa. 52:6), that through our prayers,

> My people [*ami*] may know my name
> That they may know, therefore, in that day,
> That I, the One who speaks,
> Behold! Here I am.

1 | *Opening Blessing*

Barukh She'amar ("Blessed is the One by whose speech…")

1 With this do I prepare my mouth to thank, praise, and glorify my creator.

2 Blessed is the One by whose speech the world came to be. Blessed is He.

3 Blessed is the One who creates everything.

4 Blessed is the One who creates by speaking.

5 Blessed is the One who sustains by decreeing.

6 Blessed is the One who has mercy on the Earth.

7 Blessed is the One who has mercy on all creatures.

8 Blessed is the One who rewards those who fear Him.

9 Blessed is the One who lives forever and endures for all eternity.

10 Blessed is the One who saves by redeeming. Blessed is his name.

11 Blessed are You, Adonai our God, ruler of the world, fatherly merciful God, who is praised by the mouth of his

¹הֲרֵינִי מְזַמֵּן אֶת פִּי לְהוֹדוֹת וּלְהַלֵּל וּלְשַׁבֵּחַ אֶת בּוֹרְאִי.

²בָּרוּךְ שֶׁאָמַר וְהָיָה הָעוֹלָם. בָּרוּךְ הוּא.

³בָּרוּךְ עוֹשֶׂה בְרֵאשִׁית.

⁴בָּרוּךְ אוֹמֵר וְעוֹשֶׂה.

⁵בָּרוּךְ גּוֹזֵר וּמְקַיֵּם.

⁶בָּרוּךְ מְרַחֵם עַל הָאָרֶץ.

⁷בָּרוּךְ מְרַחֵם עַל הַבְּרִיּוֹת.

⁸בָּרוּךְ מְשַׁלֵּם שָׂכָר טוֹב לִירֵאָיו.

⁹בָּרוּךְ חַי לָעַד וְקַיָּם לָנֶצַח.

¹⁰בָּרוּךְ פּוֹדֶה וּמַצִּיל. בָּרוּךְ שְׁמוֹ.

¹¹בָּרוּךְ אַתָּה, יְיָ אֱלֹהֵינוּ, מֶלֶךְ הָעוֹלָם, הָאֵל, הָאָב הָרַחֲמָן, הַמְהֻלָּל בְּפִי עַמּוֹ, מְשֻׁבָּח וּמְפֹאָר בִּלְשׁוֹן חֲסִידָיו וַעֲבָדָיו. ¹²וּבְשִׁירֵי דָוִד עַבְדְּךָ נְהַלֶּלְךָ, יְיָ אֱלֹהֵינוּ. בִּשְׁבָחוֹת וּבִזְמִרוֹת נְגַדֶּלְךָ וּנְשַׁבֵּחֲךָ וּנְפָאֶרְךָ, וְנַזְכִּיר שִׁמְךָ

49

people, glorified and exalted by the tongue of his faithful and his servants. [12] By the songs of David your servant, we will praise You, Adonai our God; with glory and song, we will magnify and glorify and exalt You, and announce your name and proclaim You ruler, our ruler and our God. [13] The One, living to all eternity, praised and glorified ruler, his great name is never-ending. [14] Blessed are You, Adonai, our ruler who is praised in songs of glory.

וְנַמְלִיכְךָ, מַלְכֵּנוּ, אֱלֹהֵינוּ. [13]יָחִיד, חֵי הָעוֹלָמִים, מֶלֶךְ מְשֻׁבָּח וּמְפֹאָר עֲדֵי עַד שְׁמוֹ הַגָּדוֹל. [14]בָּרוּךְ אַתָּה, יְיָ, מֶלֶךְ מְהֻלָּל בַּתִּשְׁבָּחוֹת.

BRETTLER (BIBLE)

[1] *"With this do I prepare my mouth"* This relatively late addition to the liturgy was inserted as an introduction to *P'sukei D'zimrah,* which is composed of hymns, mostly from the Hebrew Bible, praising God. It is as if the individual needs to "psyche him/herself up" before reciting these hymns. Though such preparation is not common in biblical hymns, we do find it on occasion. It is found, for instance, in Psalms 103 and 104, which begin "Bless Adonai, my entire being."

[2] *"Blessed is"* The *barukh,* or "blessed is," formula is extremely common within the Bible, though the *(p. 54)*

DORFF (THEOLOGY)

[1] *"With this do I prepare my mouth"* Before we can enter into meditation "about" God *(the Sh'ma)* and dialogue "with" God (the *Amidah*), we must prepare ourselves for the encounter — just as we would if we were about to meet an important person. God deserves no less.

[2] *"Blessed is the One by whose speech"* This begins the section of the Siddur known as *P'sukei D'zimrah,* verses of song. Its purpose is to get us in the mood to pray. The liturgy does that by having us recite effusive, emotional materials from the Bible.

While there is good reason to engage in such preparation, *(p. 57)*

[1] With this do I prepare my mouth to thank, praise, and glorify my creator.

[2] Blessed is the One by whose speech the world came to be. Blessed is He.

[3] Blessed is the One who creates everything.

[4] Blessed is the One who creates by speaking.

[5] Blessed is the One who sustains by decreeing.

ELLENSON (MODERN LITURGIES)

[1] *"With this do I prepare my mouth to thank, praise, and glorify my creator"* Technically, this line that introduces the *P'sukei D'zimrah* is a *kavvanah* (see L. Hoffman, "With this do I prepare"). No liberal liturgist has included it here, possibly because of their more general objection to the kabbalistic tradition from which the line is derived. *(p. 59)*

FRANKEL (A WOMAN'S VOICE)

[6] *"Blessed is the One who has mercy on the Earth"* Who but the powerful can have mercy on others? Mercy emerges only from restraint, from the decision *not* to render judgment when judgment is due. An act of mercy transforms power into love.

In this prayer, we acknowledge God's *(p. 61)*

HAUPTMAN (TALMUD)

[1] *"With this do I prepare my mouth"* One question that seems to have preoccupied the Rabbis of the Talmud was how to put oneself in the mood for prayer. Since a Jew was required to pray at least twice a day, it was not a simple matter to achieve the right mind-set on a regular basis. R. Eliezer talks about the problem of maintaining one's *kavvanah* ("intent") when prayer becomes *keva* ("fixed" or "standardized"), just another regularized part of one's day (M. Ber. 4:4). One way suggested by the *(p. 61)*

KUSHNER & POLEN (CHASIDISM)

"*When You hid your face, I was terrified.*" This line from Ps. 30:8 precedes the *P'sukei D'zimrah* and so is not found in this volume; in *Nusach Sfarad* (the Sefardi rite), however, it is closely associated with *P'sukei D'zimrah* and has attracted considerable Chasidic commentary.

Consider this in the light of Deut. 31:18, where God says, "I will surely hide my face...." The Hebrew here employs a common biblical construction for emphasis by using two forms of the *same* verb, "*hestayer asteer.*" In English, this double verb is customarily rendered as "surely hide." But this repetition might also imply that there are *two* kinds of hiding going on. The first is that God is *(p. 63)*

L. HOFFMAN (HISTORY)

THE ENTIRE RUBRIC CALLED P'SUKEI D'ZIMRAH IS MOSTLY BIBLICAL CITATIONS, SO IT IS BRACKETED BY BLESSINGS, A TYPICAL PRACTICE OF THE RABBIS, WHO GENERALLY INTRODUCED AND FOLLOWED BIBLICAL READINGS WITH A BENEDICTION. BARUKH SHE'AMAR ("BLESSED IS THE ONE BY WHOSE SPEECH...") INTRODUCES THE RUBRIC, BUT IT, IN TURN, IS NOWADAYS PRECEDED BY AN INTRODUCTORY MEDITATION, HIN'NI MUKHAN ("WITH THIS DO I PREPARE...").

[1] "*With this do I prepare*" This meditative introduction from the Sefardi rite is not, technically, *(p. 66)*

---

¹הֲרֵינִי מְזַמֵּן אֶת פִּי לְהוֹדוֹת וּלְהַלֵּל וּלְשַׁבֵּחַ אֶת בּוֹרְאִי.

²בָּרוּךְ שֶׁאָמַר וְהָיָה הָעוֹלָם. בָּרוּךְ הוּא.

³בָּרוּךְ עוֹשֶׂה בְרֵאשִׁית.

⁴בָּרוּךְ אוֹמֵר וְעוֹשֶׂה.

⁵בָּרוּךְ גּוֹזֵר וּמְקַיֵּם.

J. HOFFMAN (TRANSLATION)

[1] "*With this do I*" Hebrew, *hareni*, literally, "Behold, I...." This formulaic term has no equivalent in English. Artscroll opts for simply "I now...." We try to mimic at least the formulaic tone of this introduction.

[1] "*To thank*" Hebrew, *l'hodot*, translated elsewhere in these volumes (and more accurately) as "gratefully acknowledge." But here the term appears as part of a series of single verbs, and to introduce so long a phrase would destroy the pattern.

[2–10] "*Blessed is*" Hebrew, alas, often does not distinguish between *(p. 68)*

LANDES (HALAKHAH)

[1] "*With this do I prepare my mouth*" As one begins the *P'sukei D'zimrah,* one should have in mind the various regulations that Halakhah prescribes for it:

1. It is to be said quietly and with deep intensity.
2. It is to be said deliberately, without rushing through it.
3. One should not interrupt it to speak or to greet someone. Necessary announcements, however, like the page number, may *(p. 64)*

6 Blessed is the One who has mercy on the Earth.

7 Blessed is the One who has mercy on all creatures.

8 Blessed is the One who rewards those who fear Him.

9 Blessed is the One who lives forever and endures for all eternity.

10 Blessed is the One who saves by redeeming. Blessed is his name.

11 Blessed are You, Adonai our God, ruler of the world, fatherly merciful God, who is praised by the mouth of his people, glorified and exalted by the tongue of his faithful and his servants. 12 By the songs of David your servant, we will praise You, Adonai our God; with glory and song, we will magnify and glorify and exalt You, and announce your name and proclaim You ruler, our ruler and our God. 13 The One, living to all eternity, praised and glorified ruler, his great name is never-ending. 14 Blessed are You, Adonai, our ruler who is praised in songs of glory.

בָּרוּךְ מְרַחֵם עַל הָאָרֶץ. ⁶

בָּרוּךְ מְרַחֵם עַל הַבְּרִיּוֹת. ⁷

בָּרוּךְ מְשַׁלֵּם שָׂכָר טוֹב לִירֵאָיו. ⁸

בָּרוּךְ חַי לָעַד וְקַיָּם לָנֶצַח. ⁹

בָּרוּךְ פּוֹדֶה וּמַצִּיל. בָּרוּךְ ¹⁰ שְׁמוֹ.

בָּרוּךְ אַתָּה, יְיָ אֱלֹהֵינוּ, מֶלֶךְ ¹¹ הָעוֹלָם, הָאֵל, הָאָב הָרַחֲמָן, הַמְהֻלָּל בְּפִי עַמּוֹ, מְשֻׁבָּח וּמְפֹ־ אָר בִּלְשׁוֹן חֲסִידָיו וַעֲבָדָיו. וּבְשִׁירֵי דָוִד עַבְדֶּךָ נְהַלֶּלְךָ, יְיָ ¹² אֱלֹהֵינוּ. בִּשְׁבָחוֹת וּבִזְמִרוֹת נְגַדֶּלְךָ וּנְשַׁבֵּחֲךָ וּנְפָאֶרְךָ, וְנַזְכִּיר שִׁמְךָ וְנַמְלִיכְךָ, מַלְכֵּנוּ, אֱלֹהֵינוּ. יָחִיד, חֵי הָעוֹלָמִים, מֶלֶךְ ¹³ מְשֻׁבָּח וּמְפֹאָר עֲדֵי עַד שְׁמוֹ הַגָּדוֹל. בָּרוּךְ אַתָּה, יְיָ, מֶלֶךְ ¹⁴ מְהֻלָּל בַּתִּשְׁבָּחוֹת.

BRETTLER (BIBLE)

structure of the first half of this prayer, where *barukh* is followed by a litany of epithets of God ("Blessed is the one who creates...who sustains...who has mercy..."), is unparalleled in biblical literature. We do have a series of *barukh* statements in Deut. 28:3–6, but there, humans, not God, are the recipients of blessing. (On God as the recipient of the blessing, see the comments in Volume 1, *The Sh'ma and Its Blessings,* pp. 29–30.)

"Blessed is the one" is thus a post-biblical prayer with a form that is not found in the Bible. But it uses many biblical phrases. The rubric will end also with a post-biblical blessing, *Yishtabach* ("Let your name be forever praised"), and its midpoint (after Psalm 150) displays a similar string of biblical verses also beginning with *barukh* (see Brettler, "Blessed be Adonai forever. Amen and Amen!" p. 152). The result is a very strong sense of overall balance. Given the preponderance of blessing as a theme in the entirety of *P'sukei D'zimrah,* it is not surprising that classical sources call this unit a *Hallel* ("praise").

[2–4] *"By whose speech...by speaking"* The very first words introduce a reference to the first creation story in Genesis 1, where the world is created through divine speech. This creation story ultimately becomes more canonical than the alternative from Genesis 2, which depicts God in a more anthropomorphic fashion. The theme of divine speech is then continued in the next line ("the One who creates by speaking"). Thereafter, however, the prayer will move forward chronologically, from a God who creates, to a God who sustains creation and, ultimately, who rewards and who redeems us. A somewhat similar progression is found in Psalm 136, which begins with a reference to creation but then moves on to God's delivering us from Egypt. This prayer's use of a set of short, staccato phrases all opening with the same word has biblical precedents as well, as, for instance (again), in Psalm 136, which punctuates a list of God's actions with "For his mercy endures forever":

> Give thanks to Adonai
> for his mercy endures forever.
> Give thanks to the God of gods
> for his mercy endures forever.
> Give thanks to the Lord of lords
> for his mercy endures forever.

[2] *"Blessed is He"* Used twice of people in the Bible (Num. 22:12; Ruth 2:20), but never of God. In such cases it is unclear if the liturgy is extending biblical usages or is preserving a usage that existed in the biblical period, but was not preserved for one reason or another in biblical texts.

[5] *"Blessed is the One who sustains by decreeing"* As observed in the notes on the translation (see J. Hoffman, "Blessed is," p. 53), this phrase is quite difficult to interpret accurately. It may continue the preceding theme of creation, or equally it may introduce the following theme of God's continued supervision over the world. The lack of biblical precedents for the phrase makes it particularly difficult to decide how it should be understood.

[6, 7] *"Blessed is the One who has mercy on the Earth. Blessed is the One who has mercy on all creatures"* God's mercy is a fundamental biblical theme, particularly in prophetic literature. The idea is presented here in typical biblical parallelistic style, where the second half mirrors and explicates the first, noting more specifically that God's mercy

extends not just to the earth in general, but to earth's inhabitants, people, in particular. This couplet serves as a literary bridge to the next sentence, which will also have people as its subject.

⁸ *"Blessed is the One who rewards"* Although the grammatical focus of this sentence is the one God, its real focus is on humans. Its intent seems to be to use the "standard" rabbinic retribution theology to encourage people to follow God's ways. That theology is referred to elsewhere, as, for instance, Ezekiel 18, which comments on the proverb "Fathers eat sour grapes and their children's teeth are blunted" by promising, "Only the person who sins will die" (v. 4), whereas those "who have kept my rules and acted honestly...shall live" (v. 9). Retribution theology allows above all for repentance, again a common theme in both Bible and post-biblical literature. Ezekiel 18 concludes by assuring us, "It is not my desire that anyone shall die — declares the Lord God. Repent, therefore, and live."

Those who fear or love God are mentioned also in many psalms, which similarly note God's providence over such individuals (e.g. Ps. 34:10, "Fear Adonai...for there is no want to them that fear Him"; Ps. 115:11, "You who fear Adonai, trust in Adonai. He is their help and shield"; Ps. 145:19–20, "He will fulfill the desire of those who fear Him.... Adonai preserves all those who love Him, but He will destroy the wicked").

^{9, 10} *"Blessed is the One who lives forever and endures for all eternity...who saves by redeeming"* God's eternal endurance is a common biblical idea. Deuteronomy 32:40–41, for instance, has God say, "As I live forever...I'll mete out retribution to my foes." As the introduction of this prayer moves toward its conclusion, it notes the most significant reason to bless God — his eternal life, which is directly related to the final clause here, "God who saves by redeeming." Ultimate redemption will occur only "ultimately," but God, being eternal, is sure to be around to bring it about.

¹⁰ *"Blessed is his name"* Our blessing is actually made of two distinct and originally separate literary units. The blessing proper begins with our verse 6, "Blessed are You, Adonai our God...." Verses 2–5 (from "Blessed is the One..." to "Blessed is his name") constitute an introductory litany of praise. The final verse, "Blessed is his name," is an obvious attempt to balance the introductory "Blessed is He." Nominal sentences like "Blessed is his name" are often ambiguous, in that it is unclear whether they express a fact, a wish, or a command. In this context, all of these are likely — God as creator and sustainer is blessed, should be blessed, and even must be blessed.

¹¹ *"Fatherly merciful God...his servants"* This sentence typifies biblical poetic style: it may be divided into two sections of approximately equal length ("fatherly...people" and "glorified...servants"), with many of the words in the second section echoing those of the first (e.g., "his people" and "his faithful and his servants"). The idea that God is merciful as a father (rather than mother!) mirrors Ps. 103:13: "As a father has compassion for his children, so Adonai has compassion for those who fear Him." In Mesopotamian prayers, the merciful deities may be evoked as both father and mother.

It is possible that the Bible here uses the image of a compassionate father because it is trying to avoid applying female imagery to God.

[12] *"By the songs of David your servant, we will praise you, Adonai our God"* This announced intent introduces a series of scriptural quotations that will fill up the bulk of the material in the *P'sukei D'zimrah*. Most of these are from sections of the Bible attributed to David. David's poetic compositions were considered the most exquisite ever composed, so by repeating them in what follows, worshipers would properly be acknowledging God's sovereignty.

The Bible often calls David God's servant (e.g., 1 Kings 11:38; Isa. 37:35; Ps. 132:10), despite the fact that he is depicted in 2 Samuel as far from an ideal king. It is possible that the epithet "servant" emphasizes the close relationship between God and David. Other special individuals are called "servant" also, especially Moses (Exod. 14:31; Josh. 1:1; Mal. 3:22). If this is correct, then calling David a servant singles him out as particularly significant and, perhaps, even expresses incipient notions of Davidic messianism.

God's servant, of course, has a significantly close (though subservient) relationship with God. This aspect of "servanthood" explains the interest in deciphering the identity of the "suffering servant" in the second half of Isaiah 53. It is also interesting to see that some sections of the Bible democratize the notion, stating that all Israel are God's servants (e.g., Lev. 25:42, 55).

[13] *"The One, living to all eternity, praised and glorified ruler, his great name is never-ending"* As the prayer moves to its conclusion, it uses a tricolon (a poetic line divided into three sections) for climactic effect: (1) the One, living to all eternity, (2) praised and glorified ruler, (3) his great name is never-ending. All of its ideas and phrases are found earlier in the paragraph, making it suitable for a closing. The line begins and ends by describing God's eternity, while the main implication of that eternity, that God should be praised and glorified, is sandwiched in between.

[14] *"Praised in songs of glory [m'hulal batishbachot]"* A perfect segue into the following hymns. Indeed, the early post-biblical word *tishbachot* ("songs of glory") really means "hymns."

———◆———

DORFF (THEOLOGY)

Jewish law does not actually *require* that any of this section be recited. Thus those in a real hurry on a given morning may begin with the morning blessings *(Birkhot Hashachar)*, then proceed directly to the two blessings before the *Sh'ma*, the *Sh'ma* and the blessing after it, the *Amidah*, and the *Alenu*. Those who have some but not a lot of time for preparation should say the blessings that mark off this section — *Barukh she'amar* and *Yishtabach*—and include at least something (if not everything) in between. If you must choose just one of the psalms, the Talmud's preference is *Ashre,* Psalm 145, along with the two verses from Pss. 84:5 and 144:15 that introduce it. Beyond that, you may recite as many or as few of the materials included in *P'sukei D'zimrah* as you like — or add some of your own! The point is to get you into the mood to pray; what will effectively do that will vary with the individual and, frankly, even with the day.

Still, the Rabbis did not choose the materials of this section randomly; this is, after all, part of the Siddur, the ordered liturgy. We shall therefore examine below the reasons for their choices and the way they organized what they chose. Those considerations might convince you, as they have persuaded most of our ancestors, that unless there is a pressing need to shorten the process of preparation or to express something specific, this section of the Siddur might do just fine. In fact, its themes and moods might be just what we need on an average morning to get us into the proper frame of mind to pray.

How do we prepare for dialogue with God? The liturgy has us utter a multitude of praises of God — so many, in fact, that it borders on sycophancy. Why this unrelenting repetition of God's praises? Surely, if God is as powerful as we say, God does not need this flattery.

God does not need these praises; *we* do. We need to bless God this incessantly in order to extricate our focus from ourselves. We are, by nature, egocentric. If we are going to be able to get out of ourselves sufficiently to have a relationship with God, we must learn to put aside our self-centered feelings and thoughts. In the early morning, when this is said, we are often barely awake, let alone in a frame of mind to think about God. The liturgy, therefore, goes overboard in its praises of God in trying to get us to focus on God rather than ourselves. In the process, it also points out to us just how awesome God actually is — someone worthy of our notice and appreciation!

The first line of this section ("Blessed is the One by whose speech") clearly refers to the opening chapter of the Torah, in which God creates the universe by *saying,* "Let there be *x,*" and there was *x*. As Saadiah Gaon (882–942, Babylonia) and others point out, this is one way in which God's creation is radically different from ours: God creates out of nothing through speech, while human beings can create only by fashioning what already exists into a new pattern or form (see Saadiah's *Book of Doctrines and Beliefs,* chapter 1, section 3).

And yet our speech creates too. We may not be able to create physical things through speaking, as God does, but through what we say, we surely create thoughts, feelings, desires, and relationships — indeed, entire realms of human experience. Just as surely we can destroy worlds by what we say if we are not careful. Thus even though our mode of creation is not God's, we can have a sense of how God creates through the power of our own speech to create and destroy.

[6, 7] *"Blessed is the One who has mercy on the Earth. Blessed is the one who has mercy on all creatures"* The Rabbis maintain that God could only create the world by mixing

justice with mercy. It may be likened to a king who had empty vessels. The king said: "If I put hot water into them, they will crack; if I put ice water into them, they will contract." What did the king do? He mixed the hot water with the cold and poured the mixture into the vessels, and they endured. Similarly, the Holy One, blessed be He, said: "If I create the world only with the attribute of mercy, sins will multiply beyond all bounds; if I create it only with the attribute of justice, how can the world last? Therefore I will create it with both attributes; would that it might endure!" (Genesis Rabbah 12:15).

[10] *"Blessed is his name"* That is, "Blessed is God's reputation." Because God does all these good things, when the name of God comes to mind, people think of blessing. May the same thing happen when people think of our names!

[12] *"We will praise You"* Just as God was praised in the past by his people, his faithful, his servants, and by David, so we too will praise God now, using some of the same praises David and others of our ancestors created. We thus join in the chain of our people in acknowledging and appreciating God. This means two things. First, we do not praise God as a new act, for our people have done this for generations, and we are hereby joining with them. That should give us a sense of continuity as well as reassurance that what we are doing is appropriate. On the other hand, we do not depend on the praises of the past to suffice for us; we too must join in this chorus for the awareness of God to have impact on us.

———◆———

ELLENSON (MODERN LITURGIES)

Interestingly enough, however, Isaac Mayer Wise replaced it with the instruction that "Ten adults, males or females" constitute a *minyan*. In offering such a directive prior to the morning service for public prayer, Wise was displaying his conviction that "the principle of justice and the law of God inherent in every human being demand that woman be admitted to membership in the congregation and be given equal rights with man; that her religious feelings be allowed scope for the sacred cause of Israel." In principle, Reform rabbis had declared women to be equal with regard to performing all the *mitzvot* as early as 1845. But that ruling had not yet been institutionalized in any liturgies. Wise's declaration in *Minhag America* (1872 edition) probably marks the first time in Jewish history that women were explicitly counted as members of the prayer quorum required for Jewish public worship.

[2] *"Blessed is the one by whose speech the world came to be"* Many liberal prayer books include this rabbinic composition that introduces *P'sukei D'zimrah*, which praises God for the power of creation. The few that do omit it seldom base their decision on theological grounds. After all, numerous Reform theologians and liturgists have regularly affirmed the notion of a personal God who, in some way, created the universe.

The removal is more probably based on the principle of length. In the interests of shortening the service, a rabbinic introduction to the more important biblical material was deemed expendable.

But this has not always been the case. Some liberal liturgists do reject the doctrine of a supernatural God of creation, and these writers have employed either commentary or original composition to resolve their difficulties with the traditional view that is so obvious in the manifest content of this paragraph. The Reconstructionist *Kol Haneshamah* (1994) adds a marginal commentary upon this passage to let worshipers know that it is not comfortable with the anthropomorphic description of a personal God that this prayer presents. *Kol Haneshamah* interprets this prayer in an "abstract manner" that expresses "our basic trust in life." This same sensibility leads Marcia Falk (*The Book of Blessings,* 1996) to excise this composition altogether. She omits the traditional psalms as well, but offers in their place a very free adaptation of Psalm 150 that, she says, "is not even an approximate translation of the Hebrew" but is "inspired" by the original psalm and intended to complement the Hebrew adaptation. She notes also that in the Hebrew, "references to the power of the (male) creator have been eliminated, and, in some lines, replaced by references to the beauty of creation."

Falk's English accompaniment reads:

> *Praise the world—*
> *praise its fullness*
> *and its longing,*
> *its beauty and its grief.*
>
> *Praise stone and fire,*
> *lilac and river,*
> *and the solitary bird*
> *at the window.*
>
> *Praise the moment*
> *when the whole*
> *bursts through pain*
>
> *and the moment*
> *when the whole*
> *bursts forth in joy.*
>
> *Praise the dying beauty*
> *with all your breath*
> *and, praising, see*
>
> *the beauty of the world*
> *is your own.*

FRANKEL (A Woman's Voice)

creative power and our dependence as creatures upon that power. At the beginning, God spoke the world into being, and the Holy One has continued to sustain that creation by fiat, by royal decree. Why then, if God is committed to sustaining the world, the need for divine mercy?

The Latin root of "mercy" is *merces*, from which we derive the French word *merci*, meaning both "thanks" and "compassion," but also the English words "merchant," "mercenary," and "commerce," which hark back to the word's ancient sense of "pay" or "reward." Mercy was thus originally regarded as a quid pro quo: in exchange for the king's leniency, the subject vowed allegiance to the throne. That idea is expressed in another phrase in this prayer: "Blessed is the One who rewards those who fear [God]."

But when we consider together the complementary phrases "Blessed is the One who has mercy on the Earth" and "Blessed is the One who has mercy on all creatures," we discover that something else is going on. The Hebrew verb *m'rachem* has a very different etymology than "mercy." It derives from *rechem*, the Hebrew word for "womb." God's mercy thus does not emerge from an act of clemency, of noblesse oblige, but from motherly love. Having given birth to the world and all its creatures, God remains concerned with the world's welfare and stays involved in the well-being of all those who live upon the earth.

Then, in a brilliant oxymoron, this prayer expands this notion of God's nurturance to include fathers as well as mothers. For we pray to God as *av harachaman*, "merciful father," literally, the father who acts *as though* he had a womb, whose fatherhood emerges from acts of nurture. No wonder we "magnify and glorify and exalt" such a God!

As we move through this prayer, we encounter a hierarchy of divine caring that deepens our gratitude for the many levels of God's love manifest in the world. God not only sustains creation as a whole, but also brings a maternal solicitude to each one of its creatures. God not only rewards the God-fearing, but ultimately redeems us all. That is the miracle of a mother's love: it endures, *adei ad*, "for all eternity."

———◆———

HAUPTMAN (Talmud)

Mishnah to reach the requisite spiritual state is to face toward the Temple's Holy of Holies (4:5). An additional benefit of every Jew's turning to Jerusalem, expressed in metaphorical terms, is that the prayers that arrive at this sacred space from all over the world can then ascend to heaven together and make a stronger plea to be heard.

Yet another technique for concentration in prayer was developed by the pious people of the Mishnaic period, known as Chasidim. They would prepare themselves for prayer by having time elapse — by "tarrying" — between the pursuit of their daily activities and the beginning of their prayers (M. Ber. 5:1). We do not know what they did during this wait — sit silently, sing, study, or meditate upon God's attributes, perhaps. All the Mishnah says is that they tarried for a period of time. We can glean a little more information from the statement of R. Yosi b. Chalafta (second century C.E.), "May it be my lot to finish *Hallel* every day" (Shab. 118b). He was referring, the Gemara says, not to the *Hallel* that we recite on festivals (Psalms 113–118) but to *P'sukei D'zimrah* (lit., "Verses of Song"), other hymns from the Book of Psalms. This passage teaches us, therefore, that already in the Mishnaic period some individuals were reciting selected psalms before praying.

Several centuries later it became standard practice to recite Psalms 145–150, now called *P'sukei D'zimrah*, in order to prepare for *Shacharit*, the morning prayer. Only Psalm 145 is recited prior to *Minchah*, the afternoon prayer. Several verses introduce the evening prayer of *Ma'ariv*.

In commenting on the practice of the Chasidim, the Gemara (Ber. 30b) cites yet other opinions of what it means to prepare for prayer. One Rabbi says, "Serve God in awe, rejoice [before Him] while trembling (Ps. 2:11)," apparently demanding a mood of levity and seriousness at the same time. The Gemara further says that in order to enter into prayer, one cannot be sad, lazy, lightheaded, or occupied with trivial matters. The ideal way to enter into prayer is to have just experienced the joy of performing a *mitzvah* (31a). Both of these statements describe a high-spirited mood tempered by the solemnity of the occasion. This is a state that is not easy to achieve. Finally, the Gemara relates that when R. Akiba would lead the prayers for others he would try to keep them short. But when he would pray on his own, he would pray so fervently and bow and prostrate himself so many times that if one left the academy when R. Akiba was in one corner, and returned several hours later, he would find R. Akiba in a different corner, still praying. This suggests that true or heartfelt prayer is intense, protracted, and physical.

^{2} *"Blessed is the One by whose speech the world came to be [Barukh she'amar]"* Two lengthy blessings, *Barukh she'amar* and *Yishtabach* ("Let your name be forever praised" — see p. 177) frame the *P'sukei D'zimrah*. They are similar in that they praise God many times over. *Barukh she'amar* describes God as having created the world by verbal fiat, but God does not then withdraw from creation and let it fend for itself. Instead, God maintains an active interest in what transpires on earth and gives a person his or her just deserts. The paragraph eventually maintains, "Blessed are You...who is praised...by the songs of David your servant," a clear reference to the Psalms that follow and that constitute the heart of this rubric.

Bracketing a set of verses with blessings is standard prayer practice, as already seen in the *Sh'ma*, and even in the practice of reading the Torah in the synagogue service, where people called for an *aliyah* recite a blessing prior to the reading and then another one after it. The *Haftarah* also receives opening and closing blessings. The point of surrounding biblical texts with blessings is to dedicate them to the purpose of prayer, to state explicitly why these chapters are being recited and what the worshiper hopes to accomplish by them. The blessings also serve as punctuation, marking the beginning and the end of the unit.

[14] *"Ruler who is praised in songs of glory [melekh m'hullal batishbachot]"* These closing words of our opening blessing reappear with slight variation in *Yishtabach*, the closing blessing *(el melekh gadol batishbachot),* and in the blessing following Psalms 113–118, the *Hallel* that we say on festivals and at the Passover Seder. They suggest that God is dependent on human beings for praise, even as human beings have the urge to praise God — a rather counterintuitive idea of mutual need, developed in detail by Abraham Joshua Heschel.

———◆———

KUSHNER & POLEN (CHASIDISM)

hiding and therefore life seems hard or painful or even worse. The second kind of hiding is that the hiddenness itself is concealed from us. The hiding is itself hidden. We don't even know, in other words, that God is hiding. And that is the source of our terror and dismay! This is because we are more frightened by the fact that we don't realize that God is hiding (*Siddur Baal Shem Tov*, p. 71).

The first kind of hiding is tolerable. We remain convinced that even though we don't understand what's going on, even though God's face, as it were, seems concealed from us, still we remain convinced of God's presence. Indeed, if we understand that God is present but only hidden, that the hiddenness, in other words, has a purpose, then our present sadness is mitigated. But when the hiddenness is itself concealed, then the terror of meaninglessness overwhelms us. Our goal, therefore, is a faith in and an abiding trust that the world is working out the way it's supposed to. And we are summoned to find the hidden meaning we trust is already there.

We have a similar teaching in the name of Dov Baer of Mezritch: Once Rabbi Dov Baer was walking on the street accompanied by his disciples and saw a little girl hiding in an alcove, weeping.

"Why are you crying, little girl?" asked the rabbi.

"I was playing hide-and-seek with my friends," replied the girl, "but they didn't come looking for me!"

Rabbi Dov Baer sighed and said to his students, "In the answer and the tears of that little girl I heard the weeping of the *sh'khinah,* "'…And I will surely hide My face…" (Deut. 31:18). I, God, have hidden Myself too, as it were, but no one comes to look for Me!'" (*Itturay Torah,* ed. Aaron Jacob Greenberg [Jerusalem: Yavneh, 1987], vol. VI, 198–99).

[5] *"Blessed is the One who sustains by decreeing"* The Hebrew literally says, *gozer um'kayem,* "the One who decrees and fulfills" or "the One who decrees and causes [the decree] to endure."

In Rabbinic Hebrew, the word *gozer* ("decree") has a harsh, even punitive connotation. In the Yom Kippur liturgy, for example, we ask God to "avert the stern decree," or we speak in Hebrew of an anti-Semitic edict or persecution using the same verbal root, *gozer!* It is surprising therefore, notes Abraham Jacob Friedmann, the Sadagora Rebbe (1819–1883), that this morning prayer should begin by using a word with such bitter connotations and then — to make matters even worse — to follow it immediately by requesting inflexibility, "...and causes [the decree] to endure"!

Perhaps the solution depends on how we read the second word, *um'kayem*, "and causes [the decree] to endure." Perhaps the referent here is *not* the decree but the worshiper! Yes, the business of living is often inescapably contorted by one "stern decree" after another; from that there is simply no escape. The question is, can we make it through the pain of the present moment and survive? Can we endure? Whenever we receive a harsh life decree, suggests the Sadagora Rebbe, God simultaneously also gives us the power to prevail over it and to endure.

The Chasidim of Eliezer Zusya Portugal, the Skulener Rebbe, imprisoned for his religious teaching by the Communist Romanian government, tell the story of how he arrived at this same insight independently. Put into solitary confinement, he was compelled to find some way to maintain his sanity and spiritual compass. He devised a daily liturgical regimen. Each morning he would recite the service by focusing on each individual phrase, one phrase at a time. He would not permit himself to move on to the next phrase in the prayer until he felt he had found some personal message of hope and redemption. The result, not surprisingly, even for a mind of such enormous creativity and imagination, was that the morning service lasted throughout the entire day. And during his prayers he too came to the identical insight that while God might impose difficult decrees on us, God also grants us the spiritual stamina and resilience to endure and prevail. The Skulener's Chasidim recount that soon after attaining this insight, their rebbe was freed from prison and returned to his community.

———◆———

LANDES (HALAKHAH)

be made, but only if absolutely necessary.

4. One can put on *tallit* and *t'fillin* between the psalms if there is no opportunity to do so before.

5. In many prayers, it is customary that when worshipers hear the prayer leader recite the first three words of a blessing's conclusion (the *chatimah*), *Barukh atah A-donai* ("Blessed are You, A-donai..."), they respond, *Barukh hu uvarukh sh'mo* ("Blessed is He and blessed is his name"). One does not, however, respond in that way during the *P'sukei D'zimrah*, although it is permitted to answer *amen* upon hearing the prayer leader complete its opening and closing blessings.

6. In order to join the community in reciting the *Sh'ma* and Its Blessings and the *Amidah*, someone who arrives too late to say the whole *P'sukei D'zimrah* may say an abridgment consisting of the opening and closing benedictions and Psalm 145 (the *Ashre*).

7. If such a latecomer has the time for adding more, the following priorities are to be honored:

   a. *Hall'luy-ah! Hall'lu e-l b'kodsho* ("Halleluy-ah! Praise God in his sanctuary," Psalm 150 [see p. 142]).

   b. *Hall'luy-ah! Hall'lu et A-donai min hashamayim* (Praise God! Praise Adonai from the heavens...," Psalm 148 [see p. 134]).

   c. The rest of the *Hall'lu* psalms (Psalms 146, 147, and 149 [see pp. 124, 128, 138]).

   d. *Vay'varekh david* ("So David blessed A-donai..." [see p. 156]).

   e. *Hodu* ("Acknowledge A-donai with thanks..." [see p. 78]).

8. If one arrives late, and does not have enough time to say even an abridged *P'sukei D'zimrah* because of the need to catch up with the congregation, it is better to wait for a later minyan in which to pray or even to pray by oneself.

² *"Blessed is the One by whose speech"* The importance of this introductory blessing to the *P'sukei D'zimrah* can be seen from a ruling of the Vilna Gaon (the Gra). The prayer in question follows Psalm 30, the end of the prior rubric known as "Morning Blessings" (not reproduced here, but see future volume in this series, *Birkhot Hashachar: Morning Blessings*). The Gra excluded Psalm 30 from his worship because, as a psalm, it looked the same as the psalms that make up the bulk of the *P'sukei D'zimrah,* and he held that no such psalms of praise may be recited without this blessing to introduce them (*Ma'aseh Rav,* 20).

It is customary to stand for the entire paragraph, although opinion is divided here. The Gra allows worshipers to sit throughout the entire *P'sukei D'zimrah,* including its opening and closing blessings (*Ma'aseh Rav,* 27).

One holds the two *tsitsit* (fringes of the *tallit*) in front of oneself during the recitation of this paragraph and then kisses them when the recitation is ended.

¹¹ *"Blessed are You"* It helps to label the material from here until the end of the paragraph as "B," and the lines that come before it in the paragraph as "A." Quite clearly, from a stylistic point of view, the actual blessing (the *b'rakhah*) is B: it begins with the expected "Blessed are You" formula and ends with a *chatimah* (concluding sentence), beginning with "Blessed are You." This format is typical of blessings. In form, it is a *b'rakhah arikhta* ("a long blessing"), meaning a blessing that is a sort of theological essay — it has sentences between the opening and the closing lines that expand upon its theme. By contrast, "short blessings" are one-liners that begin and end with a simple "Blessed are You" statement (like the blessings for food or for performing commandments).

Nonetheless, for halakhic purposes, the material in A is considered to be an integral part of B, since tradition attributes it to the *anshei k'nesset hag'dolah* ("The Men of the

Great Assembly"), a group said to have bridged the period between Ezra (c. 450 B.C.E.) and the first Rabbis (c. 167 B.C.E.). They are said to have instituted it "according to a note that fell [to them] from heaven."

[14] *"Blessed...songs of glory"* The concluding formula of the blessing, known as its *chatimah,* or "seal." Worshipers who finish it in time to hear the prayer leader's conclusion of the blessing should answer *amen* to the prayer leader's blessing. Though interruptions in the rubric are in general prohibited, answering *amen* to the blessings of others is regarded as an exception to the rule.

———◆———

L. HOFFMAN (HISTORY)

part of the Ashkenazi or the Spanish Portuguese rite, but it has become a common addition to many prayer books today, so we have chosen to include it. It is a remnant of what was once a longer introduction to the *P'sukei D'zimrah* called a *kavvanah* (plural: *kavvanot*) and derived from the particular brand of Jewish mysticism that we call Kabbalah. The Rabbis of antiquity used *kavvanah* to mean the "spontaneous and creative" aspect of prayer, as opposed to *keva,* the fixed aspect of the service (see Volume 1, *The Sh'ma and Its Blessings,* "The Way It All Began: The Jazz of Worship," p. 3). Nowadays, we use the word to denote the inner concentration that we direct toward a prayer while we say it, to avoid just reciting the words merely by rote.

The kabbalists had yet a third meaning. The Kabbalah assumed that every prayer has both an obvious and outer (exoteric) meaning and a hidden and inner (esoteric) meaning. Only the hidden meaning matters. Some kabbalists went so far as to say that reciting a prayer without keeping in mind the esoteric meaning is tantamount to not saying the prayer at all, so that worshipers unfamiliar with the secrets behind the prayers should not even bother praying. Kabbalistic prayer books, therefore, prescribed meditations like this one to remind worshipers of the secret meaning that they were to be thinking about while they recited the mere outward form of the words.

Though the specifics of each prayer's secret message varied, they all amounted to the same thing. Kabbalistic doctrine taught that during the process of creation, the unity of God had been torn apart, so that the masculine and the feminine side of God were now in exile from one another — like two lovers seeking reunion. Ultimate deliverance, they said, will arrive only when God's unity is restored. In one way or another, then, every prayer alluded to some aspect of the ultimate reunification of God's male and female sides. These two aspects of God are known by a variety of names, including "the holy One blessed be He" for the male and the *Sh'khinah* for the female.

For a long time, different *kavvanot* were called for, depending on the prayer and the specific aspect of God's unity to which the prayer was believed to point. In 1662, however, Nathan of Hanover, a kabbalist, published a book with a single standardized *kavvanah* that could be used for every prayer. Over time, the formula was added to or otherwise altered, but eventually, one version became well-known. By then, the Kabbalah had spread throughout the Muslim countries around the Land of Israel and north to Poland, where, a century later, the Jews whom we call Chasidim had arisen and were formulating their own prayer books with the Kabbalah as their basis. The standardized *kavvanah* was thus incorporated into Chasidic ritual as well as the Sefardi rite that developed in Arab lands like Syria and Yemen. The full version is, "With this, do I prepare my mouth to thank, praise and glorify my creator for the sake of the unification of the holy One blessed be He and his *Sh'khinah* by means of the hidden and concealed One, in the name of all Israel."

The version in most prayer books, and the one we use here, drops the last half of the formula, since these books are produced for Jews who do not actively subscribe to the Kabbalah in its entirety. Ironically, of course, for kabbalists, the part that is now missing is the only part that really matters, since it alone expresses the secret message of the prayer. The part remaining, however, can be said without regard for any esoteric meaning. It serves as a nice way of focusing attention on the content of the entire *P'sukei D'zimrah* section: praise of God.

Kabbalistic practice still calls for the worshiper to recite the entire formula, then to grasp in one hand all the *tsitsit* (the tassels) of the *tallit* (as a sign of uniting the four letters of God's name), and to stand while reciting *Barukh she'amar* ("Blessed is the One by whose speech..."), the prayer that follows.

[2] *"Blessed is the One by whose speech the world came to be. Blessed is He"* The introductory blessing for the whole rubric, announcing its theme: praise of God by psalms. the opening line is a reference to the rabbinic doctrine that the universe was actually spoken into being. But the last three words, "Blessed is He [God]," could equally as well mean "Blessed is it," referring back to "the world." Commentators suggest, therefore, that the moment the world was created, it existed in a state of blessing. According to the Midrash, God said at the time, "I have created the universe in a blessed state. If only it will remain that way!" Despite the fact that human sin pollutes the universe all the time, Judaism insists nonetheless that the universe is still sacred.

[2] *"Blessed is He"* The Babylonian Jewish community in the geonic period (c. 750–1034) was ruled by religious authorities called the Geonim and by a secular authority called the exilarch, akin to the British crown or French royalty. He took office according to a lavish coronation ceremony, which included special Shabbat worship in his honor. A tenth-century account of the service mentions our prayer and observes that the cantor would sing, "Blessed is the One by whose speech the world came to be," and the congregation would respond, "Blessed is He." The same "Blessed is He" phrase would then serve as a response to all the following "Blessed is..." lines in this prayer, which would be sung antiphonally to the continued chant of the congregation, affirming over and over again, "Blessed is He."

The thirteenth-century law code, the *Tur*, prescribes, "'Blessed is He...' must be sung to a pretty melody, for it is a beautiful and charming song." It sets the tone for this entire rubric, which provides psalms and songs in praise of God prior to the formal beginning of communal prayer that follows.

[11] *"Blessed are You, Adonai our God, ruler"* Blessings customarily end with a summarizing sentence that begins "Blessed are You..." and they often begin also with that phrase. A close look at this entire paragraph suggests that the original blessing began only here, halfway through the paragraph, where the telltale introductory "Blessed are You" is found. Many variant versions, like the rite used once by Jews in the Balkans and the Palestinian medieval Genizah fragments, do not have the first half.

When and why the first half got added is a mystery, but the phrases in it are largely taken from the Mishnah (Ber. 9), where they are part of independent blessings that are to be said upon seeing a variety of natural phenomena in God's world. We know that the Mishnah does not contain all the blessings that once were current among the Rabbis, and one tantalizing possibility is that even the phrases here that are not found in the Mishnah were once independent blessings in their own right. Our prayer would then have been produced by an anonymous author who plundered the large store of blessings that Jews once used to greet the universe, making them into a lavish litany of praise to greet the new day.

———◆———

J. HOFFMAN (TRANSLATION)

describing reality and expressing a wish. So rather than a statement about God ("Blessed is the One...") this might be a statement about what should be: "Blessed be the One..." While context will sometimes solve this problem, often we can but guess at the best translation of the Hebrew.

[2] *"By whose speech the world came to be"* It is exceedingly difficult to convey the poetic beauty of this prayer. The opening line, in iambic pentameter, contains but four words, creating an elegance we cannot hope to capture in translation. Substituting "Praised" for "Blessed" would yield a line that scans slightly better, but at the cost of not starting this blessing with the same word in English that starts all the others. Literally, the line reads, "Blessed is the One who spoke and the world was," but Hebrew commonly uses conjunction ("and") where English requires subordination ("by whose speech," in this case).

[5] *"Sustains"* Others, "fulfills." But probably this is a continuation of previous themes. God's speech created the world, God creates [the world] by speaking, and God sustains [the world] by decreeing.

[7] *"All creatures"* Literally, "the creatures," but in context, with no creatures previously mentioned here, "the creatures" lacks any prior referents and is, in fact, barely English.

[10] *"Who saves by redeeming"* Literally, "saves and redeems," but we assume, as above, that the Hebrew "and" has more than mere conjunctive force, even though here, unlike above, we have less semantic evidence.

[11] *"His faithful and his servants"* Or perhaps, as in Birnbaum, "his faithful servants."

[12] *"David your servant"* The transition back to second person here is odd, but we remain faithful to the Hebrew by using it.

[12] *"With glory and song"* Both "glory" and "song" are plural in Hebrew, but the English "glories" is not what we want.

[12] *"Announce [nazkir] your name [shimkha]"* Artscroll's "mention" and Birnbaum's "call upon" both seem too bland. The notion is probably something like "highlight," but that, too, is inappropriate in context. Hence, we choose "announce," treating the verb *nazkir* as a form of mentioning. Another possibility is that the entire Hebrew phrase *(nazkir shimkha)* is a technical term for a type of verbal act that praises God.

[13] *"The One [yachid], living to all eternity [chei ha'olamim]...His great name is never-ending [adei ad sh'mo]"* For *chei ha'olamim,* Birnbaum offers the more literal "life of the universe," but it is not clear what this means. We translate it in parallel with ending of the line immediately after it *(adei ad sh'mo),* "His name is never-ending." The two lines are meant to go together as alternative ways of expressing God's eternality. "Never-ending" is the right meaning for *adei ad,* but it does not do justice to the evocative nature of the Hebrew.

◆ ◆ ◆

2 | *Biblical Interlude I: Medieval Additions*

A. 1 Chronicles 16:8–36

¹ Acknowledge Adonai with thanks; call upon his name; announce his acts among the nations. ² Sing to Him, play instruments to Him, discuss all his wonders. ³ Revel in his holy name; be glad of heart all who seek Adonai. ⁴ Search out Adonai in his might. ⁵ Seek his presence always. ⁶ Remember the wonders He has done, the wonders and judgments of his mouth. ⁷ Descendants of Israel, his servants, children of Israel, his chosen: He is Adonai our God, whose judgments fill the earth. ⁸ Remember his covenant forever, the word He commanded for a thousand generations, which He established with Abraham, his oath to Isaac. ⁹ He set it as a law to Jacob, as an everlasting covenant to Israel, with these words: "To you I give the land of Canaan, your pledged inheritance," when you were few in number and barely living there. ¹⁰ When people would walk from nation to nation and from one kingdom to another people, He permitted no one to oppress them and warned kings about them: "Do not touch my anointed ones, and do not harm my prophets." ¹¹ Sing to Adonai, all the earth, and announce his

¹ הוֹדוּ לַיָי, קִרְאוּ בִשְׁמוֹ, הוֹדִיעוּ בָעַמִּים עֲלִילוֹתָיו. ²שִׁירוּ לוֹ, זַמְּרוּ לוֹ, שִׂיחוּ בְּכָל נִפְלְאוֹתָיו. ³הִתְהַלְלוּ בְּשֵׁם קָדְשׁוֹ. יִשְׂמַח לֵב מְבַקְשֵׁי יְיָ. ⁴דִּרְשׁוּ יְיָ וְעֻזּוֹ. ⁵בַּקְּשׁוּ פָנָיו תָּמִיד. ⁶זִכְרוּ נִפְלְאֹתָיו אֲשֶׁר עָשָׂה, מֹפְתָיו וּמִשְׁפְּטֵי פִיהוּ. ⁷זֶרַע יִשְׂרָאֵל עַבְדּוֹ, בְּנֵי יַעֲקֹב בְּחִירָיו. הוּא יְיָ אֱלֹהֵינוּ, בְּכָל הָאָרֶץ מִשְׁפָּטָיו. ⁸זִכְרוּ לְעוֹלָם בְּרִיתוֹ, דָּבָר צִוָּה לְאֶלֶף דּוֹר, אֲשֶׁר כָּרַת אֶת אַבְרָהָם, וּשְׁבוּעָתוֹ לְיִצְחָק. ⁹וַיַּעֲמִידֶהָ לְיַעֲקֹב לְחֹק, לְיִשְׂרָאֵל בְּרִית עוֹלָם, לֵאמֹר. לְךָ אֶתֵּן אֶרֶץ כְּנָעַן, חֶבֶל נַחֲלַתְכֶם. בִּהְיוֹתְכֶם מְתֵי מִסְפָּר, כִּמְעַט וְגָרִים בָּהּ. ¹⁰וַיִּתְהַלְּכוּ מִגּוֹי אֶל גּוֹי, וּמִמַּמְלָכָה אֶל עַם אַחֵר. לֹא הִנִּיחַ לְאִישׁ לְעָשְׁקָם, וַיּוֹכַח עֲלֵיהֶם מְלָכִים. אַל תִּגְּעוּ בִּמְשִׁיחָי, וּבִנְבִיאַי אַל תָּרֵעוּ. ¹¹שִׁירוּ לַיָי כָּל הָאָרֶץ, בַּשְּׂרוּ מִיּוֹם אֶל יוֹם יְשׁוּעָתוֹ. ¹²סַפְּרוּ בַגּוֹיִם אֶת כְּבוֹדוֹ, בְּכָל הָעַמִּים נִפְלְאוֹתָיו. כִּי גָדוֹל יְיָ וּמְהֻלָּל

71

salvation day by day. [12] Tell of his glory among the nations, of his wonders among all the peoples. [13] For Adonai is great and most praised, revered above all gods, for all the nations' gods are false gods, while Adonai created the heavens, with majesty and glory before Him, might and joy in his abode. [14] To Adonai, you families of various peoples, ascribe honor and might to Adonai! [15] Ascribe the honor of his name to Adonai, bring an offering and come before Him; bow down before Adonai in holy beauty. [16] Tremble before Him, all the earth; let the world be firm, so that it not falter. [17] Let the heavens rejoice and let the earth be glad, and let it be said among the nations that Adonai is king. [18] Let the sea roar along with all its fullness, and let the field exult along with all that is in it. [19] Then the trees of the forest will sing before Adonai, for He comes to judge the earth. [20] Acknowledge Adonai with thanks, for He is good, for his kindness is everlasting. [21] So say, "Redeem us, our God of redemption, and gather us together and save us from the nations, to acknowledge your holy name with thanks, to glory in your praise. [22] Blessed is Adonai, Israel's God, from time immemorial and to the ends of time." [23] Then the entire nation voiced *amen* and praise to God.

B. MIXTURE OF PSALM VERSES

[1] Exalt Adonai our God, and bow down before his footstool—holy is He! (Ps. 99:5).

מְאֹד, וְנוֹרָא הוּא עַל כָּל אֱלֹהִים. ¹³כִּי כָּל אֱלֹהֵי הָעַמִּים אֱלִילִים, וַיְיָ שָׁמַיִם עָשָׂה. הוֹד וְהָדָר לְפָנָיו, עֹז וְחֶדְוָה בִּמְקוֹמוֹ. ¹⁴הָבוּ לַיְיָ מִשְׁפְּחוֹת עַמִּים, הָבוּ לַיְיָ כָּבוֹד וָעֹז. ¹⁵הָבוּ לַיְיָ כְּבוֹד שְׁמוֹ, שְׂאוּ מִנְחָה וּבֹאוּ לְפָנָיו, הִשְׁתַּחֲווּ לַיְיָ בְּהַדְרַת קֹדֶשׁ. ¹⁶חִילוּ מִלְּפָנָיו כָּל הָאָרֶץ, אַף תִּכּוֹן תֵּבֵל בַּל תִּמּוֹט. ¹⁷יִשְׂמְחוּ הַשָּׁמַיִם וְתָגֵל הָאָרֶץ, וְיֹאמְרוּ בַגּוֹיִם יְיָ מָלָךְ. ¹⁸יִרְעַם הַיָּם וּמְלֹאוֹ, יַעֲלֹץ הַשָּׂדֶה וְכָל אֲשֶׁר בּוֹ. ¹⁹אָז יְרַנְּנוּ עֲצֵי הַיָּעַר, מִלְּפְנֵי יְיָ, כִּי בָא לִשְׁפּוֹט אֶת הָאָרֶץ. ²⁰הוֹדוּ לַיְיָ כִּי טוֹב, כִּי לְעוֹלָם חַסְדּוֹ. ²¹וְאִמְרוּ, הוֹשִׁיעֵנוּ אֱלֹהֵי יִשְׁעֵנוּ, וְקַבְּצֵנוּ וְהַצִּילֵנוּ מִן הַגּוֹיִם, לְהוֹדוֹת לְשֵׁם קָדְשֶׁךָ, לְהִשְׁתַּבֵּחַ בִּתְהִלָּתֶךָ. ²²בָּרוּךְ יְיָ אֱלֹהֵי יִשְׂרָאֵל מִן הָעוֹלָם וְעַד הָעֹלָם. ²³וַיֹּאמְרוּ כָל הָעָם אָמֵן וְהַלֵּל לַיְיָ.

¹רוֹמְמוּ יְיָ אֱלֹהֵינוּ, וְהִשְׁתַּחֲווּ לַהֲדֹם רַגְלָיו, קָדוֹשׁ הוּא.

²Exalt Adonai our God, and bow down before his holy mountain, for holy is Adonai our God (Ps. 99:9).

³And He is merciful, forgives iniquity, does not destroy, is quick to turn away his ire, and keeps his anger in check (Ps. 78:38).

⁴You, Adonai, do not hold back your mercy from me, your kindness and your faithfulness will always protect me (Ps. 40:12).

⁵Remember your mercy, Adonai, and your kindness, for they are eternal (Ps. 25:6).

⁶Acknowledge God's strength, for his majesty is upon Israel, his strength in the skies. ⁷Feared is God from your abode. ⁸The God of Israel is the One who gives strength and power to the nation— blessed is God! (Ps. 68:35–36).

⁹Adonai is a God of vengeance; present yourself, God of vengeance. ¹⁰Rise up, judge of the land, and bring a just reward to the arrogant (Ps. 94:1–2).

¹¹Salvation is Adonai's, let your blessing forever be your people's (Ps. 3:9).

¹²The Lord of Hosts is with us, the God of Jacob is forever our stronghold (Ps. 46:8).

¹³Lord of Hosts, happy is the one who trusts in You (Ps. 84:13).

¹⁴Adonai, save us! May our king answer us when we cry out (Ps. 20:10).

¹⁵Save your people and bless your heritage. ¹⁶Tend them and raise them up forever (Ps. 28:9).

²רוֹמְמוּ יְיָ אֱלֹהֵינוּ, וְהִשְׁתַּחֲווּ לְהַר קָדְשׁוֹ, כִּי קָדוֹשׁ יְיָ אֱלֹהֵינוּ.

³וְהוּא רַחוּם, יְכַפֵּר עָוֹן וְלֹא יַשְׁחִית, וְהִרְבָּה לְהָשִׁיב אַפּוֹ, וְלֹא יָעִיר כָּל חֲמָתוֹ.

⁴אַתָּה, יְיָ, לֹא תִכְלָא רַחֲמֶיךָ מִמֶּנִּי, חַסְדְּךָ וַאֲמִתְּךָ תָּמִיד יִצְּרוּנִי.

⁵זְכֹר רַחֲמֶיךָ יְיָ, וַחֲסָדֶיךָ, כִּי מֵעוֹלָם הֵמָּה.

⁶תְּנוּ עֹז לֵאלֹהִים, עַל יִשְׂרָאֵל גַּאֲוָתוֹ, וְעֻזּוֹ בַּשְּׁחָקִים. ⁷נוֹרָא אֱלֹהִים מִמִּקְדָּשֶׁיךָ. ⁸אֵל יִשְׂרָאֵל, הוּא נֹתֵן עֹז וְתַעֲצֻמוֹת לָעָם. בָּרוּךְ אֱלֹהִים.

⁹אֵל נְקָמוֹת יְיָ, אֵל נְקָמוֹת, הוֹפִיעַ. ¹⁰הִנָּשֵׂא, שֹׁפֵט הָאָרֶץ, הָשֵׁב גְּמוּל עַל גֵּאִים.

¹¹לַיְיָ הַיְשׁוּעָה, עַל עַמְּךָ בִרְכָתֶךָ סֶּלָה.

¹²יְיָ צְבָאוֹת עִמָּנוּ, מִשְׂגָּב לָנוּ אֱלֹהֵי יַעֲקֹב סֶלָה.

¹³יְיָ צְבָאוֹת, אַשְׁרֵי אָדָם בֹּטֵחַ בָּךְ.

¹⁴יְיָ, הוֹשִׁיעָה. הַמֶּלֶךְ יַעֲנֵנוּ בְיוֹם קָרְאֵנוּ.

¹⁵הוֹשִׁיעַ אֶת עַמֶּךָ וּבָרֵךְ אֶת נַחֲלָתֶךָ. ¹⁶וּרְעֵם וְנַשְּׂאֵם עַד הָעוֹלָם.

¹⁷נַפְשֵׁנוּ חִכְּתָה לַיָי, עֶזְרֵנוּ וּמָגִנֵּנוּ הוּא, כִּי בוֹ יִשְׂמַח לִבֵּנוּ, כִּי בְשֵׁם קָדְשׁוֹ בָטָחְנוּ. ¹⁸יְהִי חַסְדְּךָ יְיָ עָלֵינוּ, כַּאֲשֶׁר יִחַלְנוּ לָךְ.

¹⁹הַרְאֵנוּ יְיָ חַסְדֶּךָ, וְיֶשְׁעֲךָ תִּתֶּן־לָנוּ.

²⁰קוּמָה עֶזְרָתָה לָּנוּ, וּפְדֵנוּ לְמַעַן חַסְדֶּךָ.

²¹אָנֹכִי יְיָ אֱלֹהֶיךָ הַמַּעַלְךָ מֵאֶרֶץ מִצְרָיִם. ²²הַרְחֶב פִּיךָ וַאֲמַלְאֵהוּ.

²³אַשְׁרֵי הָעָם שֶׁכָּכָה לּוֹ. ²⁴אַשְׁרֵי הָעָם שֶׁיְיָ אֱלֹהָיו.

²⁵וַאֲנִי בְּחַסְדְּךָ בָטַחְתִּי. ²⁶יָגֵל לִבִּי בִּישׁוּעָתֶךָ. ²⁷אָשִׁירָה לַיָי, כִּי גָמַל עָלָי.

C. Psalm 100

[Omitted on Erev Yom Kippur, Erev Pesach, and Chol Hamo'ed Pesach]

¹מִזְמוֹר לְתוֹדָה.

²הָרִיעוּ לַיָי כָּל הָאָרֶץ. ³עִבְדוּ אֶת יְיָ בְּשִׂמְחָה, בֹּאוּ לְפָנָיו בִּרְנָנָה. ⁴דְּעוּ כִּי יְיָ הוּא אֱלֹהִים, הוּא עָשָׂנוּ, וְלוֹ אֲנַחְנוּ, עַמּוֹ וְצֹאן מַרְעִיתוֹ. ⁵בֹּאוּ שְׁעָרָיו בְּתוֹדָה, חֲצֵרוֹתָיו בִּתְהִלָּה. ⁶הוֹדוּ לוֹ, בָּרְכוּ שְׁמוֹ. ⁷כִּי טוֹב יְיָ, לְעוֹלָם חַסְדּוֹ, וְעַד דֹּר וָדֹר אֱמוּנָתוֹ.

---

¹⁷Our soul waits for Adonai; He is our help and protector, for our heart rejoices in Him, for we trust in his holy name. ¹⁸Shower us with your kindness, as we wait for You (Ps. 33:20–22).

¹⁹Show us your kindness, Adonai, and grant us your salvation (Ps. 85:8).

²⁰Arise as our help, and redeem us for the sake of your kindness (Ps. 44:27).

²¹I am Adonai your God, who brought you out of the land of Egypt. ²²Open your mouth and I will fill it (Ps. 81:11).

²³Happy is the people like this. ²⁴Happy is the people whose God is Adonai (Ps. 144:15).

²⁵I trust in your kindness. ²⁶My heart will rejoice in your salvation. ²⁷I will sing to Adonai, because He has rewarded me (Ps. 13:6).

C. Psalm 100

[Omitted on Erev Yom Kippur, Erev Pesach, and Chol Hamo'ed Pesach]

¹A psalm in grateful acknowledgment:

²Shout praise to Adonai, all the earth! ³Serve Adonai in joy; come before Him in happiness. ⁴Know that Adonai is God: He made us and we are his, his nation and the flock of his pasture. ⁵Enter his gates with grateful acknowledgment, his courts with praise. ⁶Gratefully acknowledge Him, praise his name. ⁷For Adonai is good, his mercy is everlasting, and his faithfulness spans all generations.

D. Mixture of Biblical Verses

[1] May Adonai's glory last forever. [2] May Adonai rejoice in his works (Ps. 104:31).

[3] Blessed be Adonai's name from now and ever more! [4] Let Adonai's name be praised from the rising of the sun to its setting. [5] Adonai rises above all nations. [6] His presence lies above the heavens (Ps. 113:2–4).

[7] Adonai, your name is eternal. [8] Adonai, your renown lasts from generation to generation (Ps. 135:13).

[9] Adonai established his throne in the heavens, and his kingdom rules over all (Ps. 103:19).

[10] Let the heavens rejoice and the earth be glad, and let it be said among the nations that Adonai is king (1 Chron. 16:31).

[11] Adonai was, Adonai is, and Adonai will always be king. [12] Adonai is king for ever and ever. [13] The nations perished from his earth (Ps. 10:16).

[14] Adonai brings to naught the plans of nations, foils the schemes of peoples (Ps. 33:10).

[15] Many plans lie in one's heart, but Adonai's plan is the one that will arise (Prov. 19:21).

[16] Adonai's plan will stand forever; his thoughts span all generations (Ps. 33:11).

[17] For by his speech it came to be, by his command it stood firm (Ps. 33:9).

[18] For Adonai chose Zion, there to live (Ps. 132:13).

[1] לְהִי כְבוֹד יְיָ לְעוֹלָם. [2] יִשְׂמַח יְיָ בְּמַעֲשָׂיו.

[3] יְהִי שֵׁם יְיָ מְבֹרָךְ מֵעַתָּה וְעַד עוֹלָם. [4] מִמִּזְרַח שֶׁמֶשׁ עַד מְבוֹאוֹ, מְהֻלָּל שֵׁם יְיָ. [5] רָם עַל כָּל גּוֹיִם יְיָ. [6] עַל הַשָּׁמַיִם כְּבוֹדוֹ.

[7] יְיָ, שִׁמְךָ לְעוֹלָם. [8] יְיָ, זִכְרְךָ לְדֹר וָדֹר.

[9] יְיָ בַּשָּׁמַיִם הֵכִין כִּסְאוֹ, וּמַלְכוּתוֹ בַּכֹּל מָשָׁלָה.

[10] יִשְׂמְחוּ הַשָּׁמַיִם וְתָגֵל הָאָרֶץ, וְיֹאמְרוּ בַגּוֹיִם יְיָ מָלָךְ.

[11] יְיָ מֶלֶךְ, יְיָ מָלָךְ, יְיָ יִמְלֹךְ לְעֹלָם וָעֶד. [12] יְיָ מֶלֶךְ עוֹלָם וָעֶד. [13] אָבְדוּ גוֹיִם מֵאַרְצוֹ.

[14] יְיָ הֵפִיר עֲצַת גּוֹיִם, הֵנִיא מַחְשְׁבוֹת עַמִּים.

[15] רַבּוֹת מַחֲשָׁבוֹת בְּלֶב-אִישׁ, וַעֲצַת יְיָ הִיא תָקוּם.

[16] עֲצַת יְיָ לְעוֹלָם תַּעֲמֹד, מַחְשְׁבוֹת לִבּוֹ לְדֹר וָדֹר.

[17] כִּי הוּא אָמַר וַיֶּהִי, הוּא צִוָּה וַיַּעֲמֹד.

[18] כִּי בָחַר יְיָ בְּצִיּוֹן, אִוָּהּ לְמוֹשָׁב לוֹ.

¹⁹ For God chose Jacob to be his, Israel to be his prized possession (Ps. 135:4).

²⁰ For Adonai will not abandon his people, nor leave his heritage (Ps. 94:14).

²¹ He is merciful, forgives iniquity, does not destroy, is quick to turn away his ire, and keeps his anger in check (Ps. 78:38).

²² Adonai, save us! ²³ May our king answer us when we cry out (Ps. 20:10).

¹⁹כִּי יַעֲקֹב בָּחַר לוֹ יָהּ, יִשְׂרָאֵל לִסְגֻלָּתוֹ.

²⁰כִּי לֹא יִטֹּשׁ יְיָ עַמּוֹ, וְנַחֲלָתוֹ לֹא יַעֲזֹב.

²¹וְהוּא רַחוּם, יְכַפֵּר עָוֹן וְלֹא יַשְׁחִית, וְהִרְבָּה לְהָשִׁיב אַפּוֹ, וְלֹא יָעִיר כָּל חֲמָתוֹ.

²²יְיָ, הוֹשִׁיעָה. ²³הַמֶּלֶךְ יַעֲנֵנוּ בְיוֹם קָרְאֵנוּ.

BRETTLER (BIBLE)

[1]*"Acknowledge Adonai with thanks"* The first section of this prayer (through "Then the entire nation voiced *amen* and praise to God") is taken from 1 Chron. 16:8–36, a prayer recited when David brought the ark to Jerusalem. The choice of this prayer to head up the scriptural section of *P'sukei D'zimrah* is somewhat surprising — a psalm would have been expected. But this passage from Chronicles is, in fact, based on psalms and introduces the rubric extremely well because of its imperative style: the opening five verses contain together a total of ten imperatives commanding us to praise God *(p. 81)*

DORFF (THEOLOGY)

[1]*"Acknowledge Adonai with thanks"* Within the bookends that the beginning and ending blessings create, *P'sukei D'zimrah* can be divided into four major sections, each using selections from the Bible: (1) the joyous hymn that Asaph and his kinsmen created at King David's behest to celebrate the arrival and emplacement of the ark of the covenant in Jerusalem; (2) a selection of biblical verses, including Psalm 100; (3) Psalms 145–150; and (4) a brief version of the story of the Exodus, culminating in the triumphant song sung by the Israelites after crossing the Red Sea. We thus begin this section (1) with a reenactment of what our *(p. 84)*

ELLENSON (MODERN LITURGIES)

[13]*"For all the nations' gods are false gods"* Even when they retained large sections of the traditional text, most non-Orthodox prayer books have omitted this line, feeling that it expresses a noxious notion of gentiles as "idolaters" — an unfitting *(p. 87)*

FRANKEL (A WOMAN'S VOICE)

[1]*"Acknowledge Adonai with thanks; call upon his name"* How grateful we are when those who have come before us leave behind them a legacy in their names. Whether it is wealth, fame, wisdom, or a good name, we appreciate that we do not have to start from scratch. In a very real sense, this is how we experience "chosenness"

A. 1 CHRONICLES 16:8–36

[1] Acknowledge Adonai with thanks; call upon his name; announce his acts among the nations. [2] Sing to Him, play instruments to Him, discuss all his wonders. [3] Revel in his holy name; be glad of heart all who seek Adonai. [4] Search out Adonai in his might. [5] Seek his presence always. [6] Remember the wonders He has done, the

in our individual lives. We cannot freely choose our ancestors. We are chosen by their choices.

In this prayer, as in so many others in the Siddur, we connect ourselves with the founders of the Jewish people, the patriarchs Abraham, Isaac, and Jacob. We acknowledge that we are bound to them by a covenant stretching back "for a thousand generations." We take pride in our difference from the nations, our specialness as God's anointed ones.

How does that "most-favored nation status" feel to us today in *(p. 87)*

KUSHNER & POLEN (Chasidism)

[13]*"Might and joy in his abode"* In tractate Hagigah 5b, we have a discussion of sadness and joy in the divine precincts. The Talmud points to a verse in Jeremiah 13 that speaks of God weeping in a secret chamber. Rav Papa then points to our verse in Chronicles, "…might and joy are in his abode!" which seems to disagree with the passage in Jeremiah. This apparent contradiction is then resolved when we realize that Jeremiah's weeping refers to the outer chambers, while Chronicle's joy refers to the inner chambers. In other words, in the innermost divine chamber there is always joy. In this way presumably God can respond anthropopathically to the human condition without compromising an *(p. 88)*

LANDES (Halakhah)

[13]*"For [ki] (pause) all [kol] the nations' gods [elohei ha'amim] (pause) are false gods [elilim] (pause), while A-donai [va'a-donai] created the heavens [shamayim (pause) asah]"* Why the pauses? Traditional practice regularly asks us to pause between certain words to emphasize their meaning or to prevent a misunderstanding that might result from merging words into each other by garbling them together unthoughtfully. Such sloppy recitation, labeled talmudically "swallowing *(p. 88)*

L. HOFFMAN (History)

ORIGINALLY, THE INTRODUCTORY BLESSING LED DIRECTLY TO PSALM 145, THE FIRST PSALM IN THE DAILY HALLEL. MEDIEVAL JEWS, HOWEVER, INSERTED HERE 1 CHRON. 16:8–36 AND PSALM 100, ALONG WITH TWO SETS OF BIBLICAL VERSES — ALL ON THE THEME OF SINGING GOD'S PRAISE.

[1]*"Acknowledge Adonai with thanks"* 1 Chron. 16:8–36. Only the Ashkenazi rite includes it. All other rites move directly from the prior blessing to psalms, an apt design, given the purpose of this whole rubric: to offer God praise by means of a *Hallel*, that is, a group of psalms. The logic of moving from the last *(p. 89)*

¹הוֹדוּ לַיָּי, קִרְאוּ בִשְׁמוֹ, הוֹדִיעוּ בָעַמִּים עֲלִילוֹתָיו. ²שִׁירוּ לוֹ, זַמְּרוּ לוֹ, שִׂיחוּ בְּכָל נִפְלְאוֹתָיו. ³הִתְהַלְלוּ בְּשֵׁם קָדְשׁוֹ. יִשְׂמַח לֵב מְבַקְשֵׁי יְיָ. ⁴דִּרְשׁוּ יְיָ וְעֻזּוֹ. ⁵בַּקְּשׁוּ פָנָיו תָּמִיד. ⁶זִכְרוּ נִפְלְאוֹתָיו אֲשֶׁר עָשָׂה,

J. HOFFMAN (Translation)

[1]*"Acknowledge Adonai with thanks"* Again, the lyric beauty of this text is not reflected in our English translation, which barely captures the meaning of the original. The biblical original that is transported here has been composed with great care as to the way verbs are arranged. The verbs that begin each line form a staccato-like series: "acknowledge," "call upon," "announce," "sing," "play," "discuss," and so forth. The collective impact of the series as a whole is more important than the nuances of any of the individual words that make it up. *(p. 89)*

wonders and judgments of his mouth. [7] Descendants of Israel, his servants, children of Israel, his chosen: He is Adonai our God, whose judgments fill the earth. [8] Remember his covenant forever, the word He commanded for a thousand generations, which He established with Abraham, his oath to Isaac. [9] He set it as a law to Jacob, as an everlasting covenant to Israel, with these words: "To you I give the land of Canaan, your pledged inheritance," when you were few in number and barely living there. [10] When people would walk from nation to nation and from one kingdom to another people, He permitted no one to oppress them and warned kings about them: "Do not touch my anointed ones, and do not harm my prophets." [11] Sing to Adonai, all the earth, and announce his salvation day by day. [12] Tell of his glory among the nations, of his wonders among all the peoples. [13] For Adonai is great and most praised, revered above all gods, for all the nations' gods are false gods, while Adonai created the heavens, with majesty and glory before Him, might and joy in his abode. [14] To Adonai, you families of various peoples, ascribe honor and might to Adonai! [15] Ascribe the honor of his name to Adonai, bring an offering and come before Him; bow down before Adonai in holy beauty.

מִפְתָיו וּמִשְׁפְּטֵי פִיהוּ. [7] זֶרַע יִשְׂרָאֵל עַבְדּוֹ, בְּנֵי יַעֲקֹב בְּחִירָיו. הוּא יְיָ אֱלֹהֵינוּ, בְּכָל הָאָרֶץ מִשְׁפָּטָיו. [8] זִכְרוּ לְעוֹלָם בְּרִיתוֹ, דָּבָר צִוָּה לְאֶלֶף דּוֹר, אֲשֶׁר כָּרַת אֶת אַבְרָהָם, וּשְׁבוּעָתוֹ לְיִצְחָק. [9] וַיַּעֲמִידֶהָ לְיַעֲקֹב לְחֹק, לְיִשְׂרָאֵל בְּרִית עוֹלָם, לֵאמֹר. לְךָ אֶתֵּן אֶרֶץ כְּנָעַן, חֶבֶל נַחֲלַתְכֶם. בִּהְיוֹתְכֶם מְתֵי מִסְפָּר, כִּמְעַט וְגָרִים בָּהּ. [10] וַיִּתְהַלְּכוּ מִגּוֹי אֶל גּוֹי, וּמִמַּמְלָכָה אֶל עַם אַחֵר. לֹא הִנִּיחַ לְאִישׁ לְעָשְׁקָם, וַיּוֹכַח עֲלֵיהֶם מְלָכִים. אַל תִּגְּעוּ בִּמְשִׁיחָי, וּבִנְבִיאַי אַל תָּרֵעוּ. [11] שִׁירוּ לַיְיָ כָּל הָאָרֶץ, בַּשְּׂרוּ מִיּוֹם אֶל יוֹם יְשׁוּעָתוֹ. [12] סַפְּרוּ בַגּוֹיִם אֶת כְּבוֹדוֹ, בְּכָל הָעַמִּים נִפְלְאֹתָיו. כִּי גָדוֹל יְיָ וּמְהֻלָּל מְאֹד, וְנוֹרָא הוּא עַל כָּל אֱלֹהִים. [13] כִּי כָּל אֱלֹהֵי הָעַמִּים אֱלִילִים, וַיְיָ שָׁמַיִם עָשָׂה. הוֹד וְהָדָר לְפָנָיו, עֹז וְחֶדְוָה בִּמְקֹמוֹ. [14] הָבוּ לַיְיָ מִשְׁפְּחוֹת עַמִּים, הָבוּ לַיְיָ כָּבוֹד וָעֹז. [15] הָבוּ לַיְיָ כְּבוֹד שְׁמוֹ, שְׂאוּ מִנְחָה וּבֹאוּ לְפָנָיו, הִשְׁתַּחֲווּ לַיְיָ

¹⁶Tremble before Him, all the earth; let the world be firm, so that it not falter. ¹⁷Let the heavens rejoice and let the earth be glad, and let it be said among the nations that Adonai is king. ¹⁸Let the sea roar along with all its fullness, and let the field exult along with all that is in it. ¹⁹Then the trees of the forest will sing before Adonai, for He comes to judge the earth. ²⁰Acknowledge Adonai with thanks, for He is good, for his kindness is everlasting. ²¹So say, "Redeem us, our God of redemption, and gather us together and save us from the nations, to acknowledge your holy name with thanks, to glory in your praise. ²²Blessed is Adonai, Israel's God, from time immemorial and to the ends of time." ²³Then the entire nation voiced amen and praise to God.

¹⁶חִילוּ מִלְּפָנָיו בְּהַדְרַת קֹדֶשׁ. כָּל הָאָרֶץ, אַף תִּכּוֹן תֵּבֵל בַּל תִּמּוֹט. ¹⁷יִשְׂמְחוּ הַשָּׁמַיִם וְתָגֵל הָאָרֶץ, וְיֹאמְרוּ בַגּוֹיִם יְיָ מָלָךְ. ¹⁸יִרְעַם הַיָּם וּמְלֹאוֹ, יַעֲלֹץ הַשָּׂדֶה וְכָל אֲשֶׁר בּוֹ. ¹⁹אָז יְרַנְּנוּ עֲצֵי הַיָּעַר, מִלְּפְנֵי יְיָ, כִּי בָא לִשְׁפֹּט אֶת הָאָרֶץ. ²⁰הוֹדוּ לַיְיָ כִּי טוֹב, כִּי לְעוֹלָם חַסְדּוֹ. ²¹וְאִמְרוּ, הוֹשִׁיעֵנוּ אֱלֹהֵי יִשְׁעֵנוּ, וְקַבְּצֵנוּ וְהַצִּילֵנוּ מִן הַגּוֹיִם, לְהוֹדוֹת לְשֵׁם קָדְשֶׁךָ, לְהִשְׁתַּבֵּחַ בִּתְהִלָּתֶךָ. ²²בָּרוּךְ יְיָ אֱלֹהֵי יִשְׂרָאֵל מִן הָעוֹלָם וְעַד הָעוֹלָם. ²³וַיֹּאמְרוּ כָל הָעָם אָמֵן וְהַלֵּל לַיְיָ.

BRETTLER (BIBLE)

(e.g., "Acknowledge... with thanks," "call upon," "revel," "remember") — a fitting, even a perfect, opening for a section of the service given over to praising God. Additionally, the prayer itself in Chronicles is a pastiche of various biblical Psalms (especially 96 and 105) — again, a fitting prelude for a liturgical section that itself combines various biblical verses and chapters, much as this Chronicles citation does. Finally, Chronicles is one of the latest biblical books, probably dating from the fourth pre-Christian century. It is thus closer to the rabbinic period than most other biblical literature, including the bulk of Psalms, and as such is closer to rabbinic ideology as well. It should, therefore, not be surprising that the classical liturgists felt "comfortable enough" with the notions embedded within it to use its words in significant places in the liturgy.

¹*"Announce his acts among the nations"* This expression of biblical universalism assumes that God should be acknowledged not only by Israel, but by all other nations

as well. Many biblical texts, however, assume only that God must be acknowledged by Israel, but not necessarily by other nations, which are free to follow their own gods. The notion expressed here becomes predominant in the exilic and post-exilic period, as we see, for example, from Isaiah 40–66, an exilic and post-exilic work in its own right that was tacked on to the first part of the book of Isaiah even though it is not by the same author. Rabbinic theology inherited this universalism from the post-exilic biblical era.

³*"Revel… be glad"* These are not isolated thoughts but are intrinsically connected to the contents of Psalm 105, from which the Chronicler quotes: God is a powerful God ("his might"), who has performed "wonders" for Israel. We may assume that these will continue, giving us reason to revel and to be glad.

⁷*"Descendants of Israel, his servants, children of Israel, his chosen"* A typical parallel bicolon (phrase divided into two parallel thoughts), which is also a vocative (it calls on Israel), giving Israel two seemingly contradictory reasons to follow God: they are his servants but also the one he has chosen. The first attribute ("servants") is normally negative, implying that we follow God because we must, the way a servant obeys a master. The second, however, is just the reverse, in that we are God's "chosen," not God's "enslaved." We follow God out of love and gratitude for being chosen. These contradictory attributes work together throughout biblical and rabbinic texts, expressing the complicated relationship between God and Israel, which is at various times harsh or loving, compulsory or voluntary.

⁸*"Remember his covenant forever, the word He commanded for a thousand generations"* "A thousand generations" is used here, as elsewhere in the Bible, as a stereotyped expression for "forever," the word that it mirrors in the parallel first half of the line on which it comments. The imperative "remember" returns us to the ten imperatives that began this prayer ("Acknowledge," etc.), though the psalm from which the Chronicler draws (105:8) reads "He remembers," with God as the subject, understanding the verse as referring to God's recollection of the unbreakable nature of the covenant rather than Israel's obligation to uphold it. The word's reference was changed from God to Israel, because the law became more significant in the period of the Chronicler; Israel now had to be reminded to keep it. The same impetus led to the psalm being incorporated in its Chronicles form liturgically.

⁹*"To Israel"* That is, Jacob, who was renamed "Israel" in Gen. 32:29.

⁹*"With these words"* This sounds like the introduction to a quotation, but the following phrase appears nowhere in extant biblical literature. The idea of giving Canaan to Israel is found often (e.g., Gen. 17:8), but nowhere is the land called "your pledged inheritance." The Chronicler and psalmist either had access to a tradition that was subsequently lost or had a different notion of what it meant to "quote" a text or tradition.

⁹*"When you were few in number and barely living there"* According to the biblical tradition, Israel began to multiply only after they arrived in Egypt (Exod. 1:7). This

psalm recognizes the fact that until then, little land beyond the Machpelah Cave in Hebron actually belonged to the Israelites.

[10]"*When people would walk*" The context makes it quite clear that this refers to the patriarchs wandering to places like Gerar or Aram, and not to the wanderings after the Exodus from Egypt. In fact, the Chronicler will soon stop quoting from Psalm 105, which continues with an account of the plagues and Exodus. He deliberately deemphasizes the Egypt story in order to create an impression of Israel's unbroken land tenure in Eretz Yisrael from the patriarchal period onward.

[10]"*Do not touch my anointed ones, and do not harm my prophets*" This is the final quotation of Psalm 105 (v. 15) here. The verse is remarkable, since context suggests that the referents are the patriarchs, who are never called "anointed ones," while of them, only Abraham is once called a prophet (Gen. 20:7). This is a remarkable case of the "creative historiography" that characterizes late biblical as well as post-biblical historiographical tradition.

[11]"*Sing to Adonai*" This section, through "for He comes to judge the earth," is a variant or modified version of Psalm 96, one of the "enthronement psalms" celebrating God's power as king that were later incorporated into the *Kabbalat Shabbat* liturgy. God as king was a major theme throughout the biblical period, including the post-exilic period (cf., e.g., Zech. 14:9, "Adonai shall be king over all the earth; on that day Adonai shall be one and his name shall be one," incorporated into the *Alenu*). Stylistically, its opening ("Sing to Adonai") parallels the language from Psalm 105 with which the Chronicler began his prayer ("Sing to Him"), reiterating the universalistic message that some day all nations will praise the one true God.

[11–13]"*Sing...announce....Tell.... For Adonai is great...all the nations' gods are false idols...Adonai created the heaven, with majesty and glory...his abode*" Three imperatives ("sing," "announce" "tell"), mirroring those used above, in verses 13 and 14, are followed by three "motive clauses" that justify the urge to praise God. These three sentences express a progression: "Adonai is great," "all the nations' gods are false idols," and "Adonai created the heaven, with majesty and glory.... his abode." The reference to God's abode is what led the Chronicler to include this psalm. It perfectly described what David would have said when he brought the ark back from the Philistines, the context in which Chronicles inserts it. The Chronicler changes "his Temple" *(mikdasho)* to "his abode" *(m'komo)* to fit the context in which Solomon's Temple has yet to be built.

[14]"*To Adonai...ascribe honor and might*" This new subunit, introduced by this set of seven imperatives, combines the themes found earlier. All nations should come to praise God at the Temple ("bow down...in holy beauty"). Much of the terminology used here is also found in the ancient Israelite coronation ritual, so the nations are coming not just to serve God, but to acknowledge God's sovereignty.

[16]"*Tremble before him all the earth; let the world be firm, so that it not falter*" The alternative translation noted here, "for He fashioned and steadied the world" (see J. Hoffman, "Tremble before Him...let the world be firm," p. 90), does not agree with the Hebrew text that we have, but does agree with some manuscripts of the Greek Septuagint and is preferable. Instead of "let the world be firm...," which (as J. Hoffman notes) seems to have nothing to do with "Tremble before Him," the alternative provides, "Let all on earth tremble before Him, for He fashioned and steadied the world" — an illustration of God's might, as a motive clause to explains why the nations should honor him.

[17]"*Let the heavens rejoice...for He comes to judge the earth*" The various depictions here are directly connected to God's role as king ("and let it be said among the nations that Adonai is king"): the rejoicing of heaven and earth parallels the joy of the public upon the coronation, and God's role as judge reflects a royal role. However, God is a superlative king, so it is not only mortals, but also heaven and earth who rejoice, and He judges not a single nation, but "the earth." With this revised quotation from Psalm 96, the quotation of large blocks of material by the Chronicler has ended — the next three sentences are biblical verses from different places in Psalms.

[20]"*Acknowledge Adonai with thanks, for He is good*" From Ps. 118:1, 29. This frames the unit by its similarity to the opening verse, "Acknowledge Adonai with thanks." This formula, "Acknowledge Adonai with thanks," was probably a common liturgical refrain in the post-exilic period (cf. 2 Chron. 20:21).

[21-23]"*So say...and praise to God.*" Psalm 106:47–48. Verse 48 is noteworthy. The biblical Book of Psalms is actually divided into five smaller books, each of which ends with a doxology, an exuberant invitation to praise God eternally. "Blessed is Adonai, Israel's God from time immemorial to the ends of time" is the doxology that ends Book Four and therefore offers proper climax to this section of the prayer. This suggests that the prayer now found in the Siddur also once ended here, with the doxology.

Verse 47 looks like a realistic pulling back from the optimistic universalism that characterized the heady universalism of the prayer so far. Far from worshiping God, the nations are oppressing Israel, who calls on God for salvation so at least they, Israel, if not the nations, may praise God. Adding this verse mutes the consistent universalistic theology thus far, but is more realistic and demonstrates the multiplicity of canonical views about the relation between Israel and the nations.

———◆———

DORFF (THEOLOGY)

ancestors said and how they felt at that triumphant moment when Jerusalem became not only the capital of the Jewish people, but the center of Judaism. We then move (2) through a selection of biblical verses that express moods of awe of God, reconciliation with God after sinning, hope for salvation from enemies, and trust in God's enduring love. That is followed (3) by the last six psalms of the Book of Psalms; it is as if, in completing that book, we were reciting it in its entirety in praise of God each day. Finally (4), the liturgy uses selections from Chronicles, Nehemiah, and Exodus to tell the story of the Exodus in a short form to remind us of what led up to the triumphant march through the Red Sea and the song our ancestors sang then. We thus begin and end this section with recollections of moments of triumph and the feelings of joy, thanksgiving, and awe we felt then, and in between we express many of the other feelings we have in interacting with God each day.

By including the *P'sukei D'zimrah* in the liturgy, two things are accomplished. First, words are actually placed in our mouths, so that if we are not particularly awake on a given morning, a set of prescribed words can coax us into greater awareness of what God means to us and how we should respond to the manifold manifestations of God in our lives. Also, we are given not just any words, but biblical words to express our own feelings, which, on any given day, may be different from what they were the day before. In that way, the emotive words of *P'sukei D'zimrah* enable our dumb mouths to sing.

6–8 *"Remember the wonders He has done...Remember his covenant forever"* The juxtaposition of God's creation of nature with his establishing a covenant with us declares that God is *both* the universal God of nature *and* the specific God of the Jewish covenant. Psalm 19, a psalm used in the expanded *P'sukei D'zimrah* on Sabbaths and Festivals, also contains this juxtaposition. Even though gorgeous sunsets are often the easiest way to become aware of God, He is to be found not just in the wonders of nature, but also in the duties of learning and living by the Torah. The Rabbis, in fact, maintain that God created the world only so that there would be an opportunity for the People Israel to accept the covenant:

> What is the meaning, they ask, of the words, "The earth feared and was still" (Ps. 76:9)? Before Israel accepted the Torah, the earth was afraid; after they accepted the Torah, it was still. For the Holy One, praised be He, stipulated a condition with the earth: If Israel accepts the Torah, you may exist, but if not, I will return you to the state of being unformed and void [as before Creation, according to Genesis 1:2] (Shab. 88a).

Rabbi Samson Raphael Hirsch (1808–1888, Germany), the founder of modern Orthodoxy, maintains that since God created the earth, scientific investigation of the world is an important way of learning about God and his purposes. The revelation of the Torah, for Hirsch, takes precedence over what we learn from science, for the former is the word of God and the latter is the product of human beings. Therefore, if there is any apparent contradiction between them, the Torah must prevail over science. Most moderns, including me, would not privilege the Torah over science on matters within the purview of science. There is ample precedent within the Jewish tradition for that view, for biblical texts have often been interpreted to reflect the science of the times. Philo (c. 20 B.C.E.–c. 50 C.E.), for example, reads Plato's *Timaeus* into the opening chapter of Genesis, and Maimonides (1135–1204) makes that chapter fit Aristotle's *Metaphysics*. Even for Hirsch, though, science is to be pursued by Jews, not only for its own sake or for what it can do for us pragmatically, but as an avenue to God. We are, as the liturgy says here, to remember *both* the wonders that God has created *and* the covenant He has established with us forever.

[9] *"To you I give the land of Canaan, your pledged inheritance"* Precisely because God created the entire earth, He has a right to apportion some of it to his chosen people, Israel. This is also the point of the very first comment of Rashi (Rabbi Sh'lomo Yitz'haki (1040–1105, France) on the Torah: even though the Torah was meant for the Jewish people, it begins with a description of all of creation to explain why God, as creator, has the right to bestow the Land of Israel on the People Israel.

[13] *"Revered above all gods, for all the nations' gods are false gods, while Adonai created the heavens"* Other nations' gods were often the personification of particular forces in nature, while God created the heavens, the earth, the sea, and all contained therein. Moreover, other nations' gods could not ultimately control the natural forces that they were supposed to be, but God can "judge all the earth."

[20] *"Acknowledge Adonai with thanks, for He is good, for his kindness is everlasting"* This is a favorite line of the liturgy. It appears here, from the Book of Chronicles, and, as such, is recited as part of the Daily *Hallel*, but it also appears in Ps. 118:1 and so is part of the Egyptian *Hallel* recited on the New Moon, the Pilgrimage Festivals (Passover, Shavuot, and Sukkot), Chanukah, and, nowadays, Israel's Day of Independence. (For the various *Hallels*, see above, p. 7.) The liturgical use of Psalm 118 in *Hallel* emphasizes this line by repeating it five times at the beginning and twice again as the final summary verse, so that we actually say it seven times in all there. All that liturgical usage indicates how central this theological tenet is in our understanding of God.

What does it affirm? First, we are to acknowledge God for his goodness, rather than to take all of life's bounties for granted. That includes not only the special boons we are granted, but the everyday gifts as well — a body that functions reasonably well for much of life, a mind to think and to recognize the manifold aspects of life, emotional faculties enabling us to respond to the world with all our being, family and friends, the Jewish people and its heritage, and so forth.

Second, God is good. We may not always fathom God's goodness, but we are to have faith that ultimately God is not mean, capricious, or even apathetic; God is positively good. That characteristic sharply distinguishes Israel's God from other gods of the ancient world; Israel's God is inherently good — and demands goodness from us.

Third, God is trustworthy. The Hebrew word here, *chasdo,* literally means faithfulness, trustworthiness. God's fidelity is forever, and because He is good, his kindness lasts forever.

These tenets establish a foundation for how we are to think of God and of ourselves in God's world. Being just and good, God demands justice and goodness from us. God also imposes upon us duties that we are expected to fulfill. In the end, though, since God is personally and morally good, we may have confidence that this world that God created is not intended to be a mean or unfriendly place, and we may perceive in God's goodness the ideal of moral goodness toward which we ourselves should aspire.

[21] *"Redeem us, our God of redemption, and gather us together and save us from the nations"* The nation, celebrating the establishment of the ark of the covenant in David's city, Jerusalem, asks God to use his power to protect its national sovereignty from the other nations. For even the heavens, the earth, the sea, the fields, and the trees proclaim God's sovereignty; the other nations of the earth should certainly also acknowledge that Adonai is king and will therefore ensure his people's continued existence in its land. This national dimension of redemption, in which the People Israel hopes for salvation from the oppression and the threats of other nations, appears often in the liturgy.

———◆———

ELLENSON (MODERN LITURGIES)

concept for a modern worshiper to hold. Abraham Geiger, for example, purged this phrase from his 1870 *Gebetbuch*.

[21] *"Gather us together and save us from the nations"* Abraham Geiger omitted this sentence from both the 1854 and the 1870 versions of his prayer books, on the grounds that it expresses an unwanted Jewish nationalism and a xenophobic distrust of modern societies in which Jews found themselves during the era of emancipation and freedom. *Kibbutz Galuyot* ("Gathering of the Exiles" — see Volume 2, *The Amidah,* pp. 124–26) and its attendant ideal of a Jewish people living in exile under the yoke of gentile oppressors were notions that Geiger and others like him recognized as having some truth during the Middle Ages, but no longer appropriate for the modern age.

———◆———

FRANKEL (A WOMAN'S VOICE)

an ever-shrinking world" How does it feel to those who are excluded from that elite lineage, even from *within* the chosen people? Would there have been a thousand generations after Abraham had it not been for the matriarchs, Sarah, Rebekah, Rachel, and Leah; the concubines Bilhah and Zilpah; the midwives Shifra and Puah? Where would we be today had it not been for the foreign women who married and bore children to the men of Israel — Tamar, Zipporah, and Ruth? Would we not have died out as a people had we not borrowed from our neighbors and thus enriched our heritage?

We find hints of this inclusive strain later in this prayer when we invite the rest of the world to join in our songs of praise: "To Adonai, you families of various peoples, ascribe honor and might to Adonai!" As we struggle to open our tradition to new voices, especially those of women, let us listen for other strains that harmonize with our song, so that we may truly proclaim: "Let it be said among the nations that Adonai is king."

———◆———

KUSHNER & POLEN (CHASIDISM)

innermost divine joy. One can also easily understand how Chasidism, with its emphasis on joy, would find this teaching so attractive.

It is significant therefore that Rabbi Kalonymus Kalman Shapira of Piesetzna, who ministered in the Warsaw Ghetto and may have been the last Chasidic Polish rebbe to preach on Polish soil, inverted our verse yet again. (Nehemia Polen, *The Holy Fire* [Northvale, N.J.: Jason Aronson, 1994], pp. 119ff., 141). Read from within such a dark time, the Piesetzner understood that "...in His inner chambers, God grieves and weeps for the sufferings of Israel.... God is to be found in His inner chambers weeping...."

———◆———

LANDES (HALAKHAH)

the words," is forbidden. In this particular instance, we are asked to pause between the words *ki* and *kol*, in the phrase *ki* [pause] *kol elohei ha'amin elilim va'a-donai shamayim asah*. The reason for the pause is rooted in Hebrew grammar. The word *kol* begins with the letter *kaf* (pronounced k), which, however, is equivalent to *khaf* (pronounced kh) when a vowel precedes it. If we run the preceding word *ki* into the word *kol*, the word *kol* (now preceded by the final vowel *i* from *ki*) would become *khol*. So as to avoid that mispronunciation, we pause between *ki* and *kol*. Similarly, we pause between *ha'amim* and *elilim* so that the phrase does not become a meaningless *ha'amimelilim*, and between *shamayim* and *asah* so as not to say *shamayimasah*, again a meaningless combination of sound.

Sometimes the directive to avoid "swallowing" words derives from alternative meanings that such illicit vocal combinations would produce. Here, however, the issue is not alternative meanings but just the desire to say the words properly, rather than to slur them into meaningless gibberish.

We also pause between *elilim* [gods] and *A-donai*, so as to separate idolatry from the truly divine.

———◆———

L. HOFFMAN (HISTORY)

line of the blessing, "Blessed are You…who is praised in songs of glory," to the psalms is obvious. "Acknowledge Adonai with thanks" is not extraneous to the theme of praise, however. In its biblical context, it is the praise offered by King David when he managed to rescue the ark of the covenant from the Philistines and bring it into Jerusalem.

Those rites that go immediately to the psalms do not actually omit the section from Chronicles. They generally say it prior to the introductory blessing, so as not to interrupt the flow from blessing to psalms.

———◆———

J. HOFFMAN (TRANSLATION)

³ *"All who seek"* Literally, "those who seek."

⁴ *"Search out"* "Search out," like the prior "seek," may also be a technical term, representing a specific way of praising God.

⁴ *"Adonai in his might"* Literally, "and his might," but here, as elsewhere, the Hebrew "and" has more than mere conjunctive force.

⁵ *"His presence"* Literally, "his [God's] face."

⁷ *"Descendants [zera] of Israel, his servants [avdo], children of Israel, his chosen"* Avdo is literally "servant" (singular, not plural) to match the Hebrew *zera*, "seed," which is a collective singular noun used here for "descendants," like the English "progeny." English does not readily allow for describing all the Israelites as "his servant" (collectively), however, so we pluralize it as "servants."

Also, following standard translations, we assume that the entire phrase is a vocative ("O you descendants of Israel…"), but it could also be a simple statement of fact: "The descendants of Israel are his servants…"

⁹ *"He set it as a law"* Perhaps the sense here is akin to the English idiom "He set it in stone," the idea being that God first made an oral promise to Abraham and Isaac, then literally put the promise in stone later.

⁹ *"To you I give the land of Canaan, your pledged inheritance [chevel nachalatkhem]"* Birnbaum's "portion of your possession" may be literal, word for word, but it seems devoid of meaning. At issue is the first Hebrew word, *chevel,* which may come from the root "to pledge" (hence our translation). Although "to you" is singular in Hebrew, "your" is plural, suggesting that the latter phrase ("your pledged inheritance" *[chevel nachalatkhem]*) is a quotation from elsewhere. But the only other place it occurs is in Psalm 105, of which this text is an abridgment. A similar phrase occurs in Deut. 32:9, but there Jacob is God's "pledged inheritance" while here Canaan is ours.

[9]*"Few in number and barely living there [kim'at v'garim bah]"* Or perhaps the intention is something like "few (number-wise) and small (living-there-wise)." Birnbaum's translation,"…[you] were but a few men, very few, and strangers in it," seems to assume that the word *garim,* "dwell," is pointed *gerim,* "strangers," but the actual Hebrew text supports our translation.

[10]*"People"* Others, "they."

[13]*"Most praised [m'hulal m'od]"* This same word for "praised" *(m'hulal)* was used to end *Barukh she'amar.*

[13]*"Above all gods"* Presumably, "all other gods" is the idea.

[13]*"False gods"* The Hebrew, *elil* (sometimes translated as "idol"), is a diminutive form of "God" *(el).* Presumably the word play suggests something like "a little god," that is, "a lesser god," which, by virtue of not being really powerful, amounts in essence to "a false god."

[13]*"His abode"* Literally, "his place," but clearly implying the place where God dwells, hence, "abode."

[16]*"Tremble before Him…let the world be firm"* It is not clear how these two wishes ("Tremble…" and "let the world be firm…") relate. *Siddur Sim Shalom* translates, "Let all on earth tremble before Him, for He fashioned and steadied the world." This is not what the Hebrew means, but it does make more sense, and it accords with the Greek text of the Septuagint.

[19]*"To judge the earth"* Birnbaum suggests "rule the earth," presumably seeing God's judgment as an act of his ultimate rule.

[20]*"Acknowledge Adonai… for He is good"* Another reading, equally well supported by the Hebrew and adopted by *Siddur Sim Shalom,* is "Acknowledge Adonai because it is good [to do so.]" The implied subject of the predicate "good" is either "God" or "it."

[22]*"From time immemorial and to the ends of time"* Hebrew has two words for "forever": *me'olam,* literally "from the world," and *l'olam,* literally "to the world." The first means "forever in the past up until now" and the second "from now until forever." Variants of each of these appear here, a usage we try to mirror in our translation.

[23]*"Voiced amen and praise to God"* Other translations suggest, "said 'Amen,' and praised God," but it is more likely that "amen" and "praise to God" are two categories of things the people said. In the same way that "said Grace" might mean "said the word 'grace,'" but more likely means, "said the words of Grace," so too "voiced amen" might mean "said the words referred to by 'amen,'" perhaps in this case "said, 'amen and amen.'" "Amen and amen" was a common formulaic ending, appearing in our liturgy (in section 4, for example — see p. 147) as well as in the Dead Sea Scrolls. Saying it might be described as "saying Amen" (like saying Grace).

◆ ◆ ◆

BRETTLER (BIBLE)

1-2 *"Exalt Adonai our God"* (Ps. 99:5, 9) We now get a pastiche of psalm verses that share, in varying degrees, the themes of the previous verses from Chronicles, such as God's praise-worthiness, his compassion, his eternal nature, and his power. However, instead of the universalistic theme that foresees the nations all acknowledging God, these verses are Israel-centric, focusing on Israel's praising God and God's helping Israel.

Given the nature of the concluding section, there will be few comments on the individual verses beyond noting their biblical source. *(p. 96)*

B. MIXTURE OF PSALM VERSES

DORFF
(THEOLOGY)

3-10 *"And He is merciful, forgives iniquity, does not destroy, is quick to turn away his ire...a just reward to the arrogant"* God can be trusted to balance his justice with his mercy. That applies not only to the People Israel as a whole, but also to me as an individual. Thus God will not hold back his mercy from me, for "your kindness and faithfulness will always protect me." At the same time, God, as a God of vengeance, will destroy Israel's enemies and, as in Egypt, will save the People Israel from its enemies.

——◆——

1 Exalt Adonai our God, and bow down before his footstool—holy is He! (Ps. 99:5).

2 Exalt Adonai our God, and bow down before his holy mountain, for holy is Adonai our God (Ps. 99:9).

FRANKEL (A WOMAN'S VOICE)

20 *"Redeem us for the sake of your kindness"* Like the Hebrew word *rachamim* — translated as "compassion" or "mercy," but connoting something different from these English terms (see above, "Blessed is the One who has mercy on the Earth") — the Hebrew word *chesed,* usually translated as "kindness," differs from its English counterpart in significant ways. Even the Christian scholars who created the King James Bible in the sixteenth century understood that the Hebrew term was untranslatable; that is why they coined a new English word, "loving-kindness," instead of the simpler, commonplace word "kindness."

For what is the essence of kindness? As with mercy and charity, kindness often derives from a sense of superiority. We extend ourselves to others less fortunate; we make allowances for their shortcomings. What motivates us to do so? Is it a natural sympathy for our fellow creatures? Is it an act of grace? Is it (as the sociobiologists claim) a genetic predisposition, the evolutionary advantage of altruism?

The truth is that we do not have to *feel* kind to *act* kindly. When a parent says to a child, "Be kind to your sister," or "Say a kind word to the poor old man," she does not question the child's motivation or sympathies. *(p. 96)*

J. HOFFMAN (TRANSLATION)

[3] *"And He is"* The tenses in this paragraph are inconsistent, alternating between present, past, and future. Perhaps our translation should be likewise ill-formed, but we choose instead to stick to one tense. Since tenses function differently in Hebrew than they do in English, Hebrew sometimes allows for greater freedom in the choice of them.

[3] *"Keeps his anger in check"* A possible interpretation for the Hebrew, which literally says, "does not stir up all [or any of] his anger," as reflected in Birnbaum, for example.

[5] *"They are eternal [me'olam hemah]"* That is, having existed forever up until now, as in Birnbaum's "…they have been since eternity."

[6] *"Acknowledge God's strength [oz]"* Literally, "give strength to God." Birnbaum translates, "give honor to God," but there is little support for the Hebrew *oz* meaning "honor," and just a few words later he translates the same word as "glory."

[7] *"Feared is God from your abode"* So reads the Hebrew, with a shift from third person ("God") to second ("your").

[9] *"Adonai is a God of vengeance; present yourself, God of vengeance"* Hebrew regularly omits the word "is," which must be supplied in English. It may be, however, that the article ("the") should be omitted in the English, too. Then the line would be an impassioned vocative, "Adonai, O God of vengeance, present yourself, O God of vengeance." If that is the case, we suffer from a further problem: the lack of a modern vocative in English (such as the archaic "O God").

[10] *"A just reward"* In Hebrew, simply "reward," but in English, "reward" (with no modifying adjectives) represents only good rewards, while a "just reward" can be either good or (as in this case) bad, similar to the English "deal in kind with." Below, the same root is used for Adonai's (good) reward.

[11] *"Let your blessing forever be your people's"* Context suggests the shift from declarative ("Your blessing is forever your people's") to volitional ("Let your blessing be…"). The Hebrew might mean either.

Again, we see the shift from the third person ("Salvation is Adonai's") to "your people's."

This Hebrew for this line and for the last lacks verbs. This grammatical alternative in Hebrew adds a certain poetic feel, which we attempt to capture in English by the use of the genitives "Adonai's" and "your people's."

רוֹמְמוּ יְיָ אֱלֹהֵינוּ, וְהִשְׁתַּחֲווּ לַהֲדֹם רַגְלָיו, קָדוֹשׁ הוּא.¹

רוֹמְמוּ יְיָ אֱלֹהֵינוּ, וְהִשְׁתַּחֲווּ לְהַר קָדְשׁוֹ, כִּי קָדוֹשׁ יְיָ אֱלֹהֵינוּ.²

³And He is merciful, forgives iniquity, does not destroy, is quick to turn away his ire, and keeps his anger in check (Ps. 78:38).

⁴You, Adonai, do not hold back your mercy from me, your kindness and your faithfulness will always protect me (Ps. 40:12).

⁵Remember your mercy, Adonai, and your kindness, for they are eternal (Ps. 25:6).

⁶Acknowledge God's strength, for his majesty is upon Israel, his strength in the skies. ⁷Feared is God from your abode. ⁸The God of Israel is the One who gives strength and power to the nation—blessed is God! (Ps. 68:35–36).

⁹Adonai is a God of vengeance; present yourself, God of vengeance. ¹⁰Rise up, judge of the land, and bring a just reward to the arrogant (Ps. 94:1–2).

¹¹Salvation is Adonai's, let your blessing forever be your people's (Ps. 3:9).

¹²The Lord of Hosts is with us, the God of Jacob is forever our stronghold (Ps. 46:8).

¹³Lord of Hosts, happy is the one who trusts in You (Ps. 84:13).

וְהוּא רַחוּם, יְכַפֵּר עָוֹן וְלֹא
יַשְׁחִית, וְהִרְבָּה לְהָשִׁיב אַפּוֹ,
וְלֹא יָעִיר כָּל חֲמָתוֹ.

אַתָּה, יְיָ, לֹא תִכְלָא רַחֲמֶיךָ
מִמֶּנִּי, חַסְדְּךָ וַאֲמִתְּךָ תָּמִיד
יִצְּרוּנִי.

זְכֹר רַחֲמֶיךָ יְיָ, וַחֲסָדֶיךָ, כִּי
מֵעוֹלָם הֵמָּה.

תְּנוּ עֹז לֵאלֹהִים, עַל יִשְׂרָאֵל
גַּאֲוָתוֹ, וְעֻזּוֹ בַּשְּׁחָקִים. נוֹרָא
אֱלֹהִים מִמִּקְדָּשֶׁיךָ. אֵל יִשְׂרָאֵל,
הוּא נוֹתֵן עֹז וְתַעֲצֻמוֹת לָעָם.
בָּרוּךְ אֱלֹהִים.

אֵל נְקָמוֹת יְיָ, אֵל נְקָמוֹת,
הוֹפִיעַ. הִנָּשֵׂא, שֹׁפֵט הָאָרֶץ,
הָשֵׁב גְּמוּל עַל גֵּאִים.

לַיְיָ הַיְשׁוּעָה, עַל עַמְּךָ בִרְכָתֶךָ
סֶלָה.

יְיָ צְבָאוֹת עִמָּנוּ, מִשְׂגָּב לָנוּ
אֱלֹהֵי יַעֲקֹב סֶלָה.

יְיָ צְבָאוֹת, אַשְׁרֵי אָדָם בֹּטֵחַ
בָּךְ.

¹⁴Adonai, save us! May our king answer us when we cry out (Ps. 20:10).

¹⁵Save your people and bless your heritage. ¹⁶Tend them and raise them up forever (Ps. 28:9).

¹⁷Our soul waits for Adonai; He is our help and protector, for our heart rejoices in Him, for we trust in his holy name. ¹⁸Shower us with your kindness, as we wait for You (Ps. 33:20–22).

¹⁹Show us your kindness, Adonai, and grant us your salvation (Ps. 85:8).

²⁰Arise as our help, and redeem us for the sake of your kindness (Ps. 44:27).

²¹I am Adonai your God, who brought you out of the land of Egypt. ²²Open your mouth and I will fill it (Ps. 81:11).

²³Happy is the people like this. ²⁴Happy is the people whose God is Adonai (Ps. 144:15).

²⁵I trust in your kindness. ²⁶My heart will rejoice in your salvation. ²⁷I will sing to Adonai, because He has rewarded me (Ps. 13:6).

¹⁴יְיָ, הוֹשִׁיעָה. הַמֶּלֶךְ יַעֲנֵנוּ בְיוֹם קָרְאֵנוּ.

¹⁵הוֹשִׁיעָה אֶת עַמֶּךָ וּבָרֵךְ אֶת נַחֲלָתֶךָ. ¹⁶וּרְעֵם וְנַשְּׂאֵם עַד הָעוֹלָם.

¹⁷נַפְשֵׁנוּ חִכְּתָה לַיְיָ, עֶזְרֵנוּ וּמָגִנֵּנוּ הוּא, כִּי בוֹ יִשְׂמַח לִבֵּנוּ, כִּי בְשֵׁם קָדְשׁוֹ בָטָחְנוּ. ¹⁸יְהִי חַסְדְּךָ יְיָ עָלֵינוּ, כַּאֲשֶׁר יִחַלְנוּ לָךְ.

¹⁹הַרְאֵנוּ יְיָ חַסְדֶּךָ, וְיֶשְׁעֲךָ תִּתֶּן־לָנוּ.

²⁰קוּמָה עֶזְרָתָה לָּנוּ, וּפְדֵנוּ לְמַעַן חַסְדֶּךָ.

²¹אָנֹכִי יְיָ אֱלֹהֶיךָ הַמַּעַלְךָ מֵאֶרֶץ מִצְרָיִם. ²²הַרְחֶב פִּיךָ וַאֲמַלְאֵהוּ.

²³אַשְׁרֵי הָעָם שֶׁכָּכָה לּוֹ. ²⁴אַשְׁרֵי הָעָם שֶׁיְיָ אֱלֹהָיו.

²⁵וַאֲנִי בְּחַסְדְּךָ בָטָחְתִּי. ²⁶יָגֵל לִבִּי בִּישׁוּעָתֶךָ. ²⁷אָשִׁירָה לַיְיָ, כִּי גָמַל עָלָי.

BRETTLER (BIBLE)

[17-18] *"Our soul...as we wait for you"* Ps. 33:20–22. Biblical theology does not believe in a bipartite human being composed of body and soul; this notion entered Judaism most likely from the Greeks. The word translated as "soul," *nefesh,* represents the animating or life force of the individual — to lose a *nefesh* is to die. Thus, the psalmist who says, "Our soul waits for Adonai," means that the community wholeheartedly awaits God's salvation.

[25-27] *"I trust...has rewarded me"* Ps. 13:6. The prayer suddenly switches to the singular, as if reminding us that prayer is ultimately a personal thing. Instead of requests or entreaties phrased in the imperative, as before, we get a declaration of faith in God's ability to save, which motivates hymns to God. Ending the prayer on the motif of confidence follows biblical models, including Psalm 13, from which this, its concluding verse, is taken.

———◆———

FRANKEL (A WOMAN'S VOICE)

What matters is the behavior. And truly, how much better the world would be if we all were kind to each other, whether or not we felt like it.

But *chesed* goes further. It finds its source in empathy. It emerges out of the impulse to love others as ourselves. When the Chasidim of eastern Europe chose this name for themselves, derived from the Hebrew root word *chesed,* they understood that to be a *chasid,* a pious person, meant to live a holy life in all its dimensions — in prayer, in communal relations, in physical activities, in solitude. Performing acts of *chesed* was part of the *chasid's* spiritual practice, like keeping kosher or studying Torah. It was a way of serving God.

When we pray here for God's *chesed,* we remind God that this quality is part of God's essential being, an attribute as central as power, judgment, and wisdom. Divine *chesed* does not depend upon our actions or our merits. Rather it is for "your [God's] sake" that *chesed* manifests itself in the world. It flows down from heaven like the rain or dew. It is not the kindness of kingly beneficence, but the loving-kindness of the overflowing heart.

———◆———

J. HOFFMAN (TRANSLATION)

[12] *"The Lord [Adonai] of Hosts is with us"* Until now we have used "Adonai" without translation. But "Adonai of Hosts" doesn't seem to mean anything, and so we are forced to translate.

[18] *"Shower us with your kindness [y'hi chasd'kha adonai alenu]"* A poetic rendering of poetic Hebrew.

◆ ◆ ◆

BRETTLER (BIBLE)

[1] *"A psalm in grateful acknowledgment"* The liturgy continues with Psalm 100, which is quoted in its entirety. It follows nicely in that it shares the same themes as the previous prayer from Chronicles: all nations' worshiping God, God alone as king, worship at the Temple, and God's eternal nature. It even shares the phrase *hodu lo,* "gratefully acknowledge him," with that unit. As observed in the notes to the translation, it is quite unclear in what sense the word *todah* is used in the psalm's superscription (introductory verse): it may refer to the *todah* offering, a subtype of the *sh'lamim* (peace?) offering, whose purpose is not entirely clear (cf. Lev. 7:11–15), or it may refer to the nations' acknowledgment *(todah)* of God, which is commanded later in the psalm. If the first scenario is correct, this would be one of the few cases where spoken words accompany a sacrifice according to the Bible.

[7] *"For Adonai is good, his mercy [chesed] is everlasting"* It is extremely difficult to capture the nuance of the term *chesed,* translated here as "mercy." *Chesed* is a quality possessed by the more powerful entity in a relationship, which that individual is not obligated to bestow on the less powerful entity. Often, it is associated with *b'rit* ("covenant"): by entering into *(p. 100)*

FRANKEL (A WOMAN'S VOICE)

[1] *"A psalm in grateful acknowledgment [mizmor l'todah]"* This prayer-poem calls upon us to assume an attitude of thanksgiving by "serv[ing] Adonai in joy" and "com[ing] before God in happiness." Twice more within these five verses, we encounter the word *todah,* which in modern Hebrew means "thank you." We are charged to "enter his [God's] gates *b'todah*" and to "gratefully acknowledge [*hodu*]" God and bless God's name. (Is it purely coincidental that the Hebrew word for turkey, the American Thanksgiving sacrifice, also happens to be *hodu?*)

For what are we to be thankful? For our special connection to God, for an unbreakable bond that "spans all generations." Our gratitude emerges from our understanding that we have done nothing to deserve such everlasting mercy and faithfulness; it is ours simply because God made us and claims us as "the flock of his pasture." What better reason for gratitude than knowing that we are loved unconditionally? What a small price to pay for eternal watchfulness!

———◆———

C. PSALM 100

[Omitted on Erev Yom Kippur, Erev Pesach, *and* Chol Hamo'ed Pesach]

[1] A psalm in grateful acknowledgment:

[2] Shout praise to Adonai, all the earth! [3] Serve Adonai in joy; come before Him in happiness.

KUSHNER & POLEN (CHASIDISM)

[3] *"Serve Adonai in joy; come before Him in happiness"* Ps. 100:2. The Hebrew for "in joy" is *b'simchah*. And its prefix, *bet*, here translated as "in," can also be understood in this context to mean "through." Thus, *b'simchah* could mean either "in joy" or "through joy." Both offer sound spiritual advice. To "serve God *in* happiness" suggests that one should be joyous while serving God. According to the Baal Shem Tov and subsequent Chasidism, however, joy is more than merely an ideal state in which to perform religious acts. The joy itself becomes a necessary ingredient for all religious life, a primary religious category.

In the same way, sadness is also dangerous, for it is a confabulation of our evil side. *(p. 100)*

LANDES (HALAKHAH)

[1] *"A psalm in grateful acknowledgment"* This psalm is omitted on Shabbat and holidays, days on which the thanksgiving sacrifice was omitted from the temple cult service. It is similarly omitted on the day before Passover and the intermediate days of Passover, when the sacrifice was not offered because it had a *chametz* ("leaven") component in the form of the ten leavened rolls. Also, it is omitted on the day before Yom Kippur, when the sacrifice was passed over for fear that it would not *(p. 101)*

L. HOFFMAN (HISTORY)

[1] *"A psalm in grateful acknowledgment"* Psalm 100. Tradition associates this psalm with the general act of offering God grateful acknowledgment but also with the specific offering in the ancient temple called the *todah,* the "thanksgiving offering." Because of this latter tradition, a Sefardi custom is to say this psalm earlier in the service, prior to "Blessed is the One by whose speech the world came to be," because other readings about sacrifices are said there. Sefardi sources cite a midrash to the effect that the thanksgiving offering is greater than all the others, *(p. 101)*

[1] מִזְמוֹר לְתוֹדָה.

[2] הָרִיעוּ לַיָי כָּל הָאָרֶץ. [3] עִבְדוּ אֶת יָי בְּשִׂמְחָה, בֹּאוּ לְפָנָיו בִּרְנָנָה. [4] דְּעוּ כִּי יָי הוּא אֱלֹהִים,

J. HOFFMAN (TRANSLATION)

[1] *"A psalm in grateful acknowledgment [l'todah]"* Birnbaum gives us, "a psalm for the thank-offering," suggesting that *todah* here refers to the *todah* offering of old. Even so, neither "thank offering" nor *"todah* offering" means anything to a modern English reader, whereas "grateful acknowledgment" at least represents what the offering was for.

[4] *"We are his [lo anachnu]"* The traditional written version of the Torah (the masoretic text, as it is known, after the Masoretes, a group of medieval Palestinian scholars who established the text as we have it) is almost always the proper version both for writing and for reading purposes, but sometimes tradition recognizes "official" *(p. 101)*

⁴Know that Adonai is God: He made us and we are his, his nation and the flock of his pasture. ⁵Enter his gates with grateful acknowledgment, his courts with praise. ⁶Gratefully acknowledge Him, praise his name. ⁷For Adonai is good, his mercy is everlasting, and his faithfulness spans all generations.

הוּא עָשָׂנוּ, וְלוֹ אֲנַחְנוּ, עַמּוֹ
וְצֹאן מַרְעִיתוֹ. ⁵בֹּאוּ שְׁעָרָיו
בְּתוֹדָה, חֲצֵרוֹתָיו בִּתְהִלָּה. ⁶הוֹ-
דוּ לוֹ, בָּרְכוּ שְׁמוֹ. ⁷כִּי טוֹב
יְיָ, לְעוֹלָם חַסְדּוֹ, וְעַד דֹּר וָדֹר
אֱמוּנָתוֹ.

BRETTLER (BIBLE)

a relationship with someone of inferior status, you may help them by bestowing *chesed* upon them.

"Mercy," "faithfulness," "goodness," and "graciousness" all express aspects of *chesed* that God bestows on Israel.

◆

KUSHNER & POLEN (CHASIDISM)

When you are depressed, you are not only unhappy, your will is weakened, you are unable to act. You have literally lost the good fight. It is not surprising then that the second verse of Psalm 100 should attract the attention of Jewish spiritual teachers.

Sometimes your evil side leads you astray, convincing you that you have committed a grave sin when, in fact, you have done nothing seriously wrong or you may not even have sinned at all! The goal of the evil side is precisely this paralysis that results from sadness and depression. When you are sad, you quit serving your creator. You must therefore be alert to such (self) deception of your evil side and say to (that "other" side of) yourself: "With your trickery and chicanery you want me to stop serving God, but I will have none of it!"

Indeed, even if you *had* committed a minor sin, you should remember that God draws great pleasure from your joy. And the ultimate goal, even more than your own perfection, is to please God. Preoccupation with religious failures, mistakes, and sins only debilitates a person, rendering him or her incapable of serving and pleasing God. Only when your tears are "tears of joy" is weeping acceptable. Beware of sadness; in the words of our Psalm, serve God through joy (*Tsavat HaRibash*, 44, 45; 103:72; *Or HaEmet* 102:2).

◆

LANDES (HALAKHAH)

be eaten in full before the fast began, in which case it would have to be burned. Though allowable, and even necessary, under such conditions, such gratuitous burning of an offering was considered disrespectful and therefore to be avoided.

Because it replaces the thanksgiving offering that was once offered in the Temple, this psalm (Psalm 100) has special significance in Jewish tradition. In keeping with its special status, it is supposed to be sung, not just said (*Sha'arei T'shuvah to Shulchan Arukh*, O. Ch. 51:1 and *Kaf Hachayim* 48). The *Shulchan Arukh* holds that "all songs will be voided in the future time [the messianic era] except 'A psalm in grateful acknowledgment'" (*Shulchan Arukh*, O. Ch. 51:1).

———◆———

L. HOFFMAN (HISTORY)

so that a time will come in the messianic era when all the other sacrifices will cease, except for this one.

———◆———

J. HOFFMAN (TRANSLATION)

deviations from the written form. When two such versions exist, the written one is called *k'tiv*, but the official "real" meaning is called *k'ri*. Here we have such an instance. The written text has *lo anachnu*, with *lo* spelled *lamed alef*, meaning (literally) "not we." Oral tradition, however (the version we reproduce here), provides that the word be read as if it is *lamed vav*, meaning "We are his [God's]."

7 *"His faithfulness spans all generations [ad dor vador]"* The Hebrew is "from generation to generation," but that construction fails in English. The sense is not that God's faithfulness passes consecutively through the generations, but that it is "trans-generational," encompassing all generations simultaneously and equally. "Trans-generational," however, is the wrong register to use here, so we opt for "spans all generations."

———◆ ◆ ◆———

BRETTLER (BIBLE)

1-2 "May Adonai's glory last forever...works" Ps. 104:31, the beginning of a series of biblical verses known as a catena—a chain of verses connected to one another thematically. In this case, they all mention God's name, typically in the form *Adonai,* and praise God's greatness as sovereign. The first verse introduces the themes: God's wondrous *works,* which imply that his *glory* will last *forever.* The last three verses become petitionary, lauding God's compassion for Israel and requesting national salvation. The prior verses thus serve to introduce the petition, in essence "buttering up" God.

Stylistically, this prayer stands out as a unified composition, despite the fact that it is composed of diverse biblical verses adroitly sewn together. It is one of the finest examples within the liturgy of how a "composer" may reuse earlier material to compose a work that has its own integrity and beauty.

3-6 "Blessed be" These three verses, from Ps. 113:2–4, twice mention God's name, quite appropriately for a psalm that will repeat time after time the name *Adonai.* The biblical assumption is that by blessing or praising Adonai's name (as opposed to the name of a competing deity), the true God is being acknowledged.

7-8 "Adonai, your name...generation" From Ps. 135:13, a justification for acknowledging God—unlike other kings who die, God is eternal.

9 "Adonai established his throne... rules over all" From Ps. 103:19, using words such as throne and kingdom to suggest the central theme of God's sovereignty. Sovereignty is a concern of many psalms, which are frequently carried over to the liturgy, not only here, but also, for instance, as part of *Kabbalat Shabbat.*

10 "Let the heavens rejoice... is king" An anomalous verse from a psalm, but found in David's prayer in 1 Chron. 16:31, a psalm that served as the basis for the earlier prayer in *P'sukei D'zimrah,* "Acknowledge Adonai with thanks" (p. 78). Though from a psalm, citing it from Chronicles (rather than the more standard Ps. 96:10) shows that Chronicles was much better known in medieval times than it is to us.

11 "Adonai was [Pss. 93:1; 96:10; 97:1; 99:1; 1 Chron. 16:31], Adonai is [Pss. 10:16; 29:10], and Adonai will always be king (p. 105)

D. MIXTURE OF BIBLICAL VERSES

1 May Adonai's glory last forever. **2** May Adonai rejoice in his works (Ps. 104:31).

3 Blessed be Adonai's name from now and ever more! **4** Let Adonai's name be praised from the rising of the sun to its setting. **5** Adonai rises above all nations. **6** His presence lies above the heavens (Ps. 113:2–4).

KUSHNER & POLEN (CHASIDISM)

[7] *"Adonai, your name is eternal"* Ps. 135:13. In biblical Hebrew, *l'olam* means "eternal" (as translated here). But in Rabbinic Hebrew *l'olam* can be understood literally to mean "for the world." Noting this, Zev Wolf of Zhitomir (d. 1800) in his *Or HaMeir*, citing the Baal Shem Tov, asks the question: Why does the psalmist say, "God, your name is *for* the world"?

In order to appreciate his answer, we must remember that this four-letter divine name, the tetragrammaton, probably originally meant something like "the One who brings into being all that is." It is made from the root letters of the Hebrew verb "to be" and, like all names, mysteriously contains something of the inner nature of the one who bears it. For this reason we must be especially careful, warns Zev Wolf of Zhitomir, not to confuse the essential nature of God with any name, even if it is the *Shem Havaya* itself, the Name of Being. For even this most intimate, awesome, and essential of all God's names, which nourishes and vitalizes all creation, is nevertheless only an instrument of God's creative process. As we read in *Petach Eliyahu*, which begins *(p. 106)*

J. HOFFMAN (TRANSLATION)

[6] *"His presence lies"* Hebrew, "is."

[9] *"His throne"* Literally, "chair."

[15–16] *"Adonai's plan...will arise...will stand forever"* In Hebrew, as in English, the full metaphor is played out. First Adonai's plan "arises," and then it "stands" forever. If we were to ignore the extended metaphor, we might have translated the latter verb as "prevail," but "stand" correctly matches the Hebrew in its entirety.

[17] *"By his speech it came to be"* Presumably, "it," both here and immediately following, is "the world" — again the theme of speaking the world into being is emphasized (see "Blessed is the One by whose speech," p. 49).

[17] *"His command it stood firm"* Hebrew, just "stood."

[19] *"God [yah] chose Jacob to be his"* Hebrew *Yah* is one of the names for God, but unlike *Adonai,* it is not readily replicable in English, so we choose just to say "God."

The Hebrew is actually ambiguous, potentially meaning "Jacob chose God."

———◆———

¹¹יְהִי כְבוֹד יְיָ לְעוֹלָם. ¹²יִשְׂמַח יְיָ בְּמַעֲשָׂיו.

¹³יְהִי שֵׁם יְיָ מְבֹרָךְ מֵעַתָּה וְעַד עוֹלָם. ⁴מִמִּזְרַח שֶׁמֶשׁ עַד מְבוֹאוֹ, מְהֻלָּל שֵׁם יְיָ. ⁵רָם עַל כָּל גּוֹיִם יְיָ. ⁶עַל הַשָּׁמַיִם כְּבוֹדוֹ.

⁷Adonai, your name is eternal. ⁸Adonai, your renown lasts from generation to generation (Ps. 135:13).

⁹Adonai established his throne in the heavens, and his kingdom rules over all (Ps. 103:19).

¹⁰Let the heavens rejoice and the earth be glad, and let it be said among the nations that Adonai is king (1 Chron. 16:31).

¹¹Adonai was, Adonai is, and Adonai will always be king. ¹²Adonai is king for ever and ever. ¹³The nations perished from his earth (Ps. 10:16).

¹⁴Adonai brings to naught the plans of nations, foils the schemes of peoples (Ps. 33:10).

¹⁵Many plans lie in one's heart, but Adonai's plan is the one that will arise (Prov. 19:21).

¹⁶Adonai's plan will stand forever; his thoughts span all generations (Ps. 33:11).

¹⁷For by his speech it came to be, by his command it stood firm (Ps. 33:9).

¹⁸For Adonai chose Zion, there to live (Ps. 132:13).

¹⁹For God chose Jacob to be his, Israel to be his prized possession (Ps. 135:4).

⁷יְיָ, שִׁמְךָ לְעוֹלָם. ⁸יְיָ, זִכְרְךָ לְדֹר וָדֹר.

⁹יְיָ בַּשָּׁמַיִם הֵכִין כִּסְאוֹ, וּמַלְכוּתוֹ בַּכֹּל מָשָׁלָה.

¹⁰יִשְׂמְחוּ הַשָּׁמַיִם וְתָגֵל הָאָרֶץ, וְיֹאמְרוּ בַגּוֹיִם יְיָ מָלָךְ.

¹¹יְיָ מֶלֶךְ, יְיָ מָלָךְ, יְיָ יִמְלֹךְ לְעֹלָם וָעֶד. ¹²יְיָ מֶלֶךְ עוֹלָם וָעֶד. ¹³אָבְדוּ גוֹיִם מֵאַרְצוֹ.

¹⁴יְיָ הֵפִיר עֲצַת גּוֹיִם, הֵנִיא מַחְשְׁבוֹת עַמִּים.

¹⁵רַבּוֹת מַחֲשָׁבוֹת בְּלֶב-אִישׁ, וַעֲצַת יְיָ הִיא תָקוּם.

¹⁶עֲצַת יְיָ לְעוֹלָם תַּעֲמֹד, מַחְשְׁבוֹת לִבּוֹ לְדֹר וָדֹר.

¹⁷כִּי הוּא אָמַר וַיֶּהִי, הוּא צִוָּה וַיַּעֲמֹד.

¹⁸כִּי בָחַר יְיָ בְּצִיּוֹן, אִוָּה לְמוֹשָׁב לוֹ.

¹⁹כִּי יַעֲקֹב בָּחַר לוֹ יָהּ, יִשְׂרָאֵל לִסְגֻלָּתוֹ.

²⁰For Adonai will not abandon his people, nor leave his heritage (Ps. 94:14).

²¹He is merciful, forgives iniquity, does not destroy, is quick to turn away his ire, and keeps his anger in check (Ps. 78:38).

²²Adonai, save us! ²³May our king answer us when we cry out (Ps. 20:10).

²⁰כִּי לֹא יִטּוֹשׁ יְיָ עַמּוֹ, וְנַחֲלָתוֹ לֹא יַעֲזֹב.

²¹וְהוּא רַחוּם, יְכַפֵּר עָוֹן וְלֹא יַשְׁחִית, וְהִרְבָּה לְהָשִׁיב אַפּוֹ, וְלֹא יָעִיר כָּל חֲמָתוֹ.

²²יְיָ, הוֹשִׁיעָה. ²³הַמֶּלֶךְ יַעֲנֵנוּ בְיוֹם קָרְאֵנוּ.

BRETTLER (BIBLE)

[Exod. 15:18, from the conclusion of the Song of the Sea] " The only sentence in the entire prayer not found in the Hebrew Bible. It is, however, a compilation of parts of various biblical verses. The fact that it is a composed "verse" indicates its importance: unable to find a verse that expressed what he wanted about God's limitless sovereignty, our poet composed his own from snippets of verses here and there.

¹²⁻¹³ *"Adonai is king…his earth"* From Ps. 10:16, introducing the main theme of the second part of the prayer: the hope that God's kingship will be manifest through support of Israel.

¹⁵ *"Many plans…that will arise"* Prov. 19:21. Proverbs has the same biblical poetic structure as Psalms, so this verse, which thematically belongs here, can be introduced from that book without looking intrusive.

¹⁶ *"Adonai's plan"* Ps. 33:11. The juxtaposition of this verse with the previous one shows the skill by which this prayer was composed. The two verses in question come from different biblical books, but they cohere nicely because this verse begins with "Adonai's plan," the very idea with which the previous verse concluded.

¹⁷ *"By his speech it came to be"* Ps. 33:9. The first verse to refer to God not by name (*Adonai*), but with the third person pronoun *hu* ("he"). It is quite possible, however, that in early rabbinic times, this pronoun was understood as one of God's names. Ancient prayers for Sukkot, known already in the Mishnah and used while walking around the altar (nowadays, the synagogue sanctuary) while carrying the *lulav*, may refer to that name when they conclude, "*Ani vaho*, save us!" The Bible uses the pronoun *hu* in parallel with names for God within personal names, as, for example, in the variant names *Aviyah* (my [divine] father is *yah*) and *Avihu* (my [divine] father is he [*hu*]).

[20] *"For Adonai will not abandon...heritage"* Ps. 94:14. A typical biblical couplet, where the second half intensifies the first. Israel is God's heritage *(nachalah)*, a word that typically refers to land. Land can always be given away or sold. By contrast, this verse teaches, Israel, as God's *nachalah*, is inalienable. As a farmer tends his *nachalah*, so God will tend Israel, but will never "leave" Israel by giving it to another.

[21] *"He is merciful...in check"* From Ps. 78:38, adduced here to explain the previous verse: God can *never* abandon Israel, because of his great mercy. This sentiment is cited to counteract alternate biblical pictures of God as angry or vengeful.

[22–23] *"Adonai save us! May our king answer us [Adonai hoshi'a hamelekh ya'aneinu]"* The placement of the Hebrew *hamelekh*, "the king," allows it to be either the subject of the wish, "May our king answer us," or the object of the prior verb, "Save." In its original context, a royal psalm (Ps. 20:10), the verse probably meant, "Adonai save the king! May He answer us when we cry out!" The current prayer, however, was composed long after Jewish kingship ceased, so it means, "Adonai save us! May our king answer us."

———◆———

KUSHNER & POLEN (CHASIDISM)

Tikkunei HaZohar (a companion to the Zohar written in fourteenth-century Spain), "God, when you withdraw yourself from them, even your names become hollow!"

Perhaps the *real* meaning of our verse therefore is, "Lord, your name is only for *this* world (and those of us who dwell there), but your true God-ness is even beyond *all* your names" (Zev Wolf of Zhitomir, *Or HaMeir, Shofetim*).

[8] *"Your renown lasts from generation to generation"* According to the *Noam Elimelekh* of Rabbi Elimelekh of Lizhensk, each new spiritual level is called a "generation." And in order to ascend to the next level above, you must learn to sanctify the ordinary, physical deeds of your present level. In this way, our verse from Psalm 135 now means that our daily actions like eating and bathing must also become expressions of praising God. We thus expand our spiritual reach to encompass ever-increasing spheres of otherwise mundane activity. One by one they too are now revealed to be instruments of praise.

———◆ ◆ ◆———

3 | *The Daily* Hallel
(Hallel Sheb'khol yom)

PSALMS 145–150

A. PSALM 145 (*ASHRE*)

[1] Happy are they who dwell in your house; they will ever praise You (Ps. 84:5).

[2] Happy is the people like this. [3] Happy is the people whose God is Adonai (Ps. 144:15).

[4] David's Psalm:

[5] I will exalt You, my God the king, and praise your name for ever and ever.

[6] Every day I will praise You, and extol your name for ever and ever.

[7] Great is Adonai and highly praised. Endless is his greatness.

[8] Generation upon generation will praise your deeds, and tell of your mighty acts.

[9] I will speak of your wondrous acts, and your glorious majesty in its splendor.

[10] People tell of your awe-inspiring might, and I proclaim your greatness.

[11] People spread your very great renown, and sing of your righteousness.

אַ֯שְׁרֵי יוֹשְׁבֵי בֵיתֶךָ, עוֹד יְהַלְלוּךָ סֶּלָה. [1]

²אַשְׁרֵי הָעָם שֶׁכָּכָה לּוֹ. ³אַשְׁרֵי הָעָם שֶׁיְיָ אֱלֹהָיו.

⁴תְּהִלָּה לְדָוִד.

⁵אֲרוֹמִמְךָ אֱלוֹהַי הַמֶּלֶךְ, וַאֲבָרְכָה שִׁמְךָ לְעוֹלָם וָעֶד.

⁶בְּכָל יוֹם אֲבָרְכֶךָ, וַאֲהַלְלָה שִׁמְךָ לְעוֹלָם וָעֶד.

⁷גָּדוֹל יְיָ וּמְהֻלָּל מְאֹד, וְלִגְדֻלָּתוֹ אֵין חֵקֶר.

⁸דּוֹר לְדוֹר יְשַׁבַּח מַעֲשֶׂיךָ, וּגְבוּרֹתֶיךָ יַגִּידוּ.

⁹הֲדַר כְּבוֹד הוֹדֶךָ, וְדִבְרֵי נִפְלְאֹתֶיךָ אָשִׂיחָה.

¹⁰וֶעֱזוּז נוֹרְאֹתֶיךָ יֹאמֵרוּ, וּגְדֻלָּתְךָ אֲסַפְּרֶנָּה.

¹¹זֵכֶר רַב טוּבְךָ יַבִּיעוּ, וְצִדְקָתְךָ יְרַנֵּנוּ.

107

¹² Gracious and merciful is Adonai, endlessly patient and most kind.

¹³ Adonai is good to all, showering all his creatures with mercy.

¹⁴ All your creatures will thank You, Adonai, and your faithful will praise You.

¹⁵ They will tell of the glory of your kingdom, and speak of your might.

¹⁶ Announce his greatness to humankind, and the majestic glory of his kingdom.

¹⁷ Your kingdom is a kingdom for all times, and your reign for every generation.

¹⁸ Adonai supports all who fall, and uprights all who are bent over.

¹⁹ The eyes of all look to You, and You give them timely food.

²⁰ You open your hand, and satisfy every living being.

²¹ Adonai is righteous in all his ways, and gracious in all his acts.

²² Adonai is near to all who call upon Him, to all who call upon Him in truth.

²³ He does the will of those who revere Him, and hears their cry and saves them.

²⁴ Adonai guards all who love Him, and destroys all who are wicked.

²⁵ Let my mouth speak Adonai's praise, and all creatures praise his holy name for ever and ever.

²⁶ Let us praise Adonai from now and ever more. Halleluyah (Ps. 115:18).

חַנּוּן וְרַחוּם יְיָ, אֶרֶךְ אַפַּיִם וּגְדָל־חָסֶד. ¹²

טוֹב יְיָ לַכֹּל, וְרַחֲמָיו עַל כָּל מַעֲשָׂיו. ¹³

יוֹדוּךָ יְיָ כָּל מַעֲשֶׂיךָ, וַחֲסִידֶיךָ יְבָרְכוּכָה. ¹⁴

כְּבוֹד מַלְכוּתְךָ יֹאמֵרוּ, וּגְבוּרָתְךָ יְדַבֵּרוּ. ¹⁵

לְהוֹדִיעַ לִבְנֵי הָאָדָם גְּבוּרֹתָיו, וּכְבוֹד הֲדַר מַלְכוּתוֹ. ¹⁶

מַלְכוּתְךָ מַלְכוּת כָּל עֹלָמִים, וּמֶמְשַׁלְתְּךָ בְּכָל דּוֹר וָדֹר. ¹⁷

סוֹמֵךְ יְיָ לְכָל הַנֹּפְלִים, וְזוֹקֵף לְכָל הַכְּפוּפִים. ¹⁸

עֵינֵי כֹל אֵלֶיךָ יְשַׂבֵּרוּ, וְאַתָּה נוֹתֵן לָהֶם אֶת אָכְלָם בְּעִתּוֹ. ¹⁹

פּוֹתֵחַ אֶת יָדֶךָ, וּמַשְׂבִּיעַ לְכָל חַי רָצוֹן. ²⁰

צַדִּיק יְיָ בְּכָל דְּרָכָיו, וְחָסִיד בְּכָל מַעֲשָׂיו. ²¹

קָרוֹב יְיָ לְכָל קֹרְאָיו, לְכֹל אֲשֶׁר יִקְרָאֻהוּ בֶאֱמֶת. ²²

רְצוֹן יְרֵאָיו יַעֲשֶׂה, וְאֶת שַׁוְעָתָם יִשְׁמַע וְיוֹשִׁיעֵם. ²³

שׁוֹמֵר יְיָ אֶת כָּל אֹהֲבָיו, וְאֵת כָּל הָרְשָׁעִים יַשְׁמִיד. ²⁴

B. Psalm 146

[1] Praise God! Praise Adonai, my soul. [2] I will praise Adonai so long as I live and sing to my God so long as I exist. [3] Do not trust in princes, in mortals who offer no salvation, whose spirit leaves them and who will return to the earth. [4] On that day his designs perish. [5] Happy are those whose help is the God of Jacob, whose hope rests on Adonai their God, maker of heaven and earth, the sea, and all that they contain, keeper of truth forever, the grantor of justice to the oppressed, provider of bread to the hungry. [6] Adonai frees the captive. [7] Adonai opens the eyes of the blind. [8] Adonai uprights the bent over. [9] Adonai loves the righteous. [10] Adonai guards strangers, upholding the orphan and widow, but thwarting the way of the wicked. [11] Adonai will reign forever, your God, Zion, for all generations. Halleluyah.

C. Psalm 147

[1] Halleluyah. It is good to sing to our God and it is pleasant; praise is beautiful. [2] Adonai rebuilds Jerusalem; He will gather the dispersed among Israel. [3] The One who heals the broken-hearted will repair their sorrow. [4] The One who counts the stars will give each a name. [5] Great is our Lord and mighty; his wisdom is infinite. [6] Adonai raises the humble and casts the wicked down to earth. [7] Answer Adonai with grateful acknowledgment; play music for God with the harp. [8] He covers the sky with clouds, provides rain for the earth, causes grass to grow on the mountains, and gives bread to beasts and to birds who cry out. [9] He does not take joy in the

25 תְּהִלַּת יְיָ יְדַבֶּר-פִּי, וִיבָרֵךְ כָּל בָּשָׂר שֵׁם קָדְשׁוֹ לְעוֹלָם וָעֶד.

26 וַאֲנַחְנוּ נְבָרֵךְ יָהּ מֵעַתָּה וְעַד עוֹלָם. הַלְלוּיָהּ.

1 הַלְלוּיָהּ. הַלְלִי נַפְשִׁי אֶת יְיָ. 2 אֲהַלְלָה יְיָ בְּחַיָּי, אֲזַמְּרָה לֵאלֹהַי בְּעוֹדִי. 3 אַל תִּבְטְחוּ בִנְדִיבִים, בְּבֶן-אָדָם שֶׁאֵין לוֹ תְשׁוּעָה. תֵּצֵא רוּחוֹ יָשֻׁב לְאַדְמָתוֹ. 4 בַּיּוֹם הַהוּא אָבְדוּ עֶשְׁתֹּנֹתָיו. 5 אַשְׁרֵי שֶׁאֵל יַעֲקֹב בְּעֶזְרוֹ, שִׂבְרוֹ עַל יְיָ אֱלֹהָיו. עֹשֶׂה שָׁמַיִם וָאָרֶץ, אֶת הַיָּם, וְאֶת כָּל אֲשֶׁר בָּם, הַשֹּׁמֵר אֱמֶת לְעוֹלָם, עֹשֶׂה מִשְׁפָּט לָעֲשׁוּקִים, נֹתֵן לֶחֶם לָרְעֵבִים. 6 יְיָ מַתִּיר אֲסוּרִים. 7 יְיָ פֹּקֵחַ עִוְרִים. 8 יְיָ זֹקֵף כְּפוּפִים. 9 יְיָ אֹהֵב צַדִּיקִים. 10 יְיָ שֹׁמֵר אֶת גֵּרִים, יָתוֹם וְאַלְמָנָה יְעוֹדֵד, וְדֶרֶךְ רְשָׁעִים יְעַוֵּת. 11 יִמְלֹךְ יְיָ לְעוֹלָם, אֱלֹהַיִךְ צִיּוֹן לְדֹר וָדֹר. הַלְלוּיָהּ.

1 הַלְלוּיָהּ. כִּי טוֹב זַמְּרָה אֱלֹהֵינוּ, כִּי נָעִים, נָאוָה תְהִלָּה. 2 בֹּנֵה יְרוּשָׁלַיִם יְיָ, נִדְחֵי יִשְׂרָאֵל יְכַנֵּס. 3 הָרֹפֵא לִשְׁבוּרֵי לֵב, וּמְחַבֵּשׁ לְעַצְּבוֹתָם. 4 מוֹנֶה מִסְפָּר לַכּוֹכָבִים, לְכֻלָּם שֵׁמוֹת יִקְרָא. 5 גָּדוֹל אֲדוֹנֵינוּ וְרַב כֹּחַ, לִתְבוּנָתוֹ אֵין מִסְפָּר. 6 מְעוֹדֵד עֲנָוִים יְיָ, מַשְׁפִּיל רְשָׁעִים עֲדֵי אָרֶץ. 7 עֱנוּ לַיְיָ בְּתוֹדָה, זַמְּרוּ לֵאלֹהֵינוּ בְכִנּוֹר. 8 הַמְכַסֶּה שָׁמַיִם בְּעָבִים,

horse's strength, nor take pleasure in man's legs. [10] He takes pleasure in those who fear Him, in those who yearn for his kindness. [11] Exalt Adonai, Jerusalem; praise your God, Zion, for He has strengthened the bars of your gates, blessed your children in your midst. [12] He grants your borders peace, and sates you with choice wheat. [13] He sends his command earthward and his word runs quickly. [14] He grants snow like wool and scatters frost like ashes. [15] He casts out his ice like crumbs; who can stand before his cold? [16] He sends out his word and melts them. [17] By his wind He causes the water to flow. [18] He declares his word to Jacob, his laws and statutes to Israel. [19] He has not done so for every nation, who do not know his statutes. Halleluyah!

D. PSALM 148

[1] Praise God! Praise Adonai from the heavens; praise Him on high. [2] Praise Him, all his angels; praise Him, all his hosts. [3] Praise Him, sun and moon. [4] Praise Him, all stars of light. [5] Praise Him, heaven of heavens, and the water above the heavens. [6] Let them praise Adonai's name, because by his commandment they were created. [7] He fixed them for ever and ever; He gave a law that shall never pass. [8] Praise Adonai from the earth, sea monsters and all depths. [9] Fire and hail, snow and fog, stormy wind, all fulfill his word. [10] The mountains and all the hills, the fruit tree and all cedars, wild beasts and all animals, bugs and birds and fowl, kings of the earth and all nations, princes and all judges of the earth, young men and

הַמֵּכִין לָאָרֶץ מָטָר, הַמַּצְמִיחַ הָרִים חָצִיר, נוֹתֵן לִבְהֵמָה לַחְמָהּ, לִבְנֵי עֹרֵב אֲשֶׁר יִקְרָאוּ. [9] לֹא בִגְבוּרַת הַסּוּס יֶחְפָּץ, לֹא בְשׁוֹקֵי הָאִישׁ יִרְצֶה. [10] רוֹצֶה יְיָ אֶת יְרֵאָיו, אֶת הַמְיַחֲלִים לְחַסְדּוֹ. [11] שַׁבְּחִי, יְרוּשָׁלַיִם, אֶת יְיָ. הַלְלִי אֱלֹהַיִךְ צִיּוֹן. כִּי חִזַּק בְּרִיחֵי שְׁעָרָיִךְ, בֵּרַךְ בָּנַיִךְ בְּקִרְבֵּךְ. [12] הַשָּׂם גְּבוּלֵךְ שָׁלוֹם, חֵלֶב חִטִּים יַשְׂבִּיעֵךְ. [13] הַשֹּׁלֵחַ אִמְרָתוֹ אָרֶץ, עַד מְהֵרָה יָרוּץ דְּבָרוֹ. [14] הַנֹּתֵן שֶׁלֶג כַּצָּמֶר, כְּפוֹר כָּאֵפֶר יְפַזֵּר. [15] מַשְׁלִיךְ קַרְחוֹ כְפִתִּים, לִפְנֵי קָרָתוֹ מִי יַעֲמֹד. [16] יִשְׁלַח דְּבָרוֹ וְיַמְסֵם. [17] יַשֵּׁב רוּחוֹ, יִזְּלוּ מָיִם. [18] מַגִּיד דְּבָרָיו לְיַעֲקֹב, חֻקָּיו וּמִשְׁפָּטָיו לְיִשְׂרָאֵל. [19] לֹא עָשָׂה כֵן לְכָל גּוֹי, וּמִשְׁפָּטִים בַּל יְדָעוּם. הַלְלוּיָהּ.

[1] הַלְלוּיָהּ. הַלְלוּ אֶת יְיָ מִן הַשָּׁמַיִם, הַלְלוּהוּ בַּמְּרוֹמִים. [2] הַלְלוּהוּ כָל מַלְאָכָיו, הַלְלוּהוּ כָּל צְבָאָיו. [3] הַלְלוּהוּ שֶׁמֶשׁ וְיָרֵחַ. [4] הַלְלוּהוּ כָּל כּוֹכְבֵי אוֹר. [5] הַלְלוּהוּ שְׁמֵי הַשָּׁמַיִם, וְהַמַּיִם אֲשֶׁר מֵעַל הַשָּׁמָיִם. [6] יְהַלְלוּ אֶת שֵׁם יְיָ, כִּי הוּא צִוָּה וְנִבְרָאוּ. [7] וַיַּעֲמִידֵם לָעַד לְעוֹלָם, חָק נָתַן וְלֹא יַעֲבוֹר. [8] הַלְלוּ אֶת יְיָ מִן הָאָרֶץ, תַּנִּינִים וְכָל תְּהֹמוֹת. [9] אֵשׁ וּבָרָד, שֶׁלֶג וְקִיטוֹר, רוּחַ סְעָרָה עֹשָׂה דְבָרוֹ. [10] הֶהָרִים וְכָל גְּבָעוֹת, עֵץ פְּרִי וְכָל אֲרָזִים, הַחַיָּה וְכָל בְּהֵמָה, רֶמֶשׂ וְצִפּוֹר כָּנָף, מַלְכֵי אֶרֶץ וְכָל לְאֻמִּים, שָׂרִים וְכָל שֹׁפְטֵי אָרֶץ, בַּחוּרִים וְגַם בְּתוּלוֹת, זְקֵנִים עִם

women, the old with the young: Let them praise Adonai's name, for his name alone is exalted. [11] His majesty is on earth and in the heavens. [12] He is the strength of his nation, the praise of his faithful, of the children of Israel, the people near to Him. Halleluyah!

E. PSALM 149

[1] Halleluyah! Sing a new song to Adonai, who is praised in the congregation of the faithful. [2] Let Israel rejoice in their maker; let the children of Zion celebrate their king. [3] Let them praise his name in dance; let them play drums and harps for Him. [4] For Adonai takes pleasure in his people, and adorns the meek with triumph. [5] Let the faithful exult in honor; let them rejoice on their beds. [6] Let there be praises of God in their mouths, and a sword in their hand, for avenging the nations and punishing the peoples, for binding their kings with chains, and their nobles with iron fetters, for meting out judgment as written. [7] He is the glory of all his faithful. Halleluyah!

F. PSALM 150

[1] Halleluyah! Praise God in his sanctuary. [2] Praise Him in his heaven of power. [3] Praise Him in his might. [4] Praise Him for his abundant greatness. [5] Praise Him with the shofar's blast. [6] Praise Him with harp and lyre. [7] Praise Him with drum and dance. [8] Praise Him with strings and flute. [9] Praise Him with resounding cymbals. [10] Praise Him with blasting cymbals.

[The following verse is said twice.]

[11] Let every breath praise God! Halleluyah.

נְעָרִים, יְהַלְלוּ אֶת שֵׁם יְיָ, כִּי נִשְׂגָּב שְׁמוֹ לְבַדּוֹ. [11] הוֹדוֹ עַל אֶרֶץ וְשָׁמָיִם. [12] וַיָּרֶם קֶרֶן לְעַמּוֹ, תְּהִלָּה לְכָל חֲסִידָיו, לִבְנֵי יִשְׂרָאֵל עַם קְרֹבוֹ. הַלְלוּיָהּ.

[1] הַלְלוּיָהּ. שִׁירוּ לַיְיָ שִׁיר חָדָשׁ, תְּהִלָּתוֹ בִּקְהַל חֲסִידִים. [2] יִשְׂמַח יִשְׂרָאֵל בְּעֹשָׂיו, בְּנֵי צִיּוֹן יָגִילוּ בְמַלְכָּם. [3] יְהַלְלוּ שְׁמוֹ בְמָחוֹל, בְּתֹף וְכִנּוֹר יְזַמְּרוּ לוֹ. [4] כִּי רוֹצֶה יְיָ בְּעַמּוֹ, יְפָאֵר עֲנָוִים בִּישׁוּעָה. [5] יַעְלְזוּ חֲסִידִים בְּכָבוֹד, יְרַנְּנוּ עַל מִשְׁכְּבוֹתָם. [6] רוֹמְמוֹת אֵל בִּגְרוֹנָם, וְחֶרֶב פִּיפִיּוֹת בְּיָדָם, לַעֲשׂוֹת נְקָמָה בַּגּוֹיִם, תּוֹכֵחוֹת בַּלְאֻמִּים, לֶאְסֹר מַלְכֵיהֶם בְּזִקִּים, וְנִכְבְּדֵיהֶם בְּכַבְלֵי בַרְזֶל, לַעֲשׂוֹת בָּהֶם מִשְׁפָּט כָּתוּב. [7] הָדָר הוּא לְכָל חֲסִידָיו. הַלְלוּיָהּ.

[1] הַלְלוּיָהּ. הַלְלוּ אֵל בְּקָדְשׁוֹ. [2] הַלְלוּהוּ בִּרְקִיעַ עֻזּוֹ. [3] הַלְלוּהוּ בִגְבוּרֹתָיו. [4] הַלְלוּהוּ כְּרֹב גֻּדְלוֹ. [5] הַלְלוּהוּ בְּתֵקַע שׁוֹפָר. [6] הַלְלוּהוּ בְּנֵבֶל וְכִנּוֹר. [7] הַלְלוּהוּ בְּתֹף וּמָחוֹל. [8] הַלְלוּהוּ בְּמִנִּים וְעֻגָב. [9] הַלְלוּהוּ בְצִלְצְלֵי שָׁמַע. [10] הַלְלוּהוּ בְּצִלְצְלֵי תְרוּעָה.

[11] כֹּל הַנְּשָׁמָה תְּהַלֵּל יָהּ. הַלְלוּיָהּ.

BRETTLER (BIBLE)

4–5 *"David's Psalm: I will exalt You"* Psalm 145, but preceded by Pss. 84:5 and 144:15, and followed by all of Psalms 146–150, making this the longest biblical unit quoted in order in the daily prayer book. Linguistic evidence suggests that Psalm 145 is post-exilic, later than most of the other Psalms. Nevertheless, these six psalms, even in the Bible, compose a unit. Psalm 145 ends with the self-exhortation: "Let my mouth speak Adonai's praise, and all creatures praise his holy name for ever and ever"; the five following psalms do precisely that, each one opening with "Halleluyah" ("Praise God"). *(p. 116)*

FRANKEL (A WOMAN'S VOICE)

1 *"Happy are they who dwell in your house"* What does it mean to live in God's house? Where is it? How big is it? What is its architecture, its floor plan, its style? How many people can it accommodate? Who cleans it, and who repairs it? What goes on between its walls? Is it safe from fire and theft?

Clearly, the image of God's house is only a metaphor. But metaphors tell us much about the larger context of meaning in which they have been chosen to function. In this familiar psalm, God's house exists on several scales, like *matrushka* dolls nested within each other.

Imagine then that we are ancient pilgrims living when this psalm was composed and sung. The first *(p. 118)*

DORFF
(THEOLOGY)

1 *"Happy are they who dwell in your house"* Anyone who recites these opening verses together with Psalm 145 three times each day is, according to the Talmud, to be assured a place in the world-to-come (Ber. 4b). The psalm is therefore recited not only here, but twice more: after the morning *Amidah* and as the opening for the afternoon *(Minchah)* service: a total of three times daily. The Talmud's preference for Psalm 145 is the basis for advising the recitation of this psalm over others in the *P'sukei D'zimrah* if time does not allow the entire rubric to be said.

Why is this psalm so special as to require recitation three times a *(p. 118)*

A. PSALM 145 (ASHRE)

1 Happy are they who dwell in your house; they will ever praise You (Ps. 84:5).

2 Happy is the people like this. 3 Happy is the people whose God is Adonai (Ps. 144:15).

4 David's Psalm:

HAUPTMAN (TALMUD)

1 *"Happy are they who dwell in your house"* When the Gemara asks from where in the Bible do we learn about preparation for prayer, R. Joshua b. Levi answers (Ber. 32b) that it is from the verse, "Happy are they who dwell in your house" (Ps. 84:5). The Hebrew word for "dwell" is *yeshvu,* which also means "to sit." R. Joshua reads the verse midrashically to imply that those who take the time to sit in the synagogue prior to prayer are *me'usharim,* "happy" or "blessed." From another verse, the Gemara then derives the *(p. 118)*

KUSHNER & POLEN (CHASIDISM)

[18] *"Adonai supports all who fall"* Psalm 145:14. We have a tradition in the name of Rabbi Mordecai Yosef Liener of Izbica commenting on the meaning of "supporting those who fall." He teaches that not only does God support those who fall (*somekh noflim*), but so must lovers also. Izbica notes that according to Jewish law, all you need to get married is a coin. But then why does everyone use a wedding ring instead? This may be explained by considering the shape of a ring. It is round, just like the Hebrew letter *samekh*, the first letter of the phrase *somekh noflim*, "Adonai supports all who fall...." This reminds lovers that they must uphold one another when they stumble or fall. They say, "With this ring," if you fall I will (p. 120)

L. HOFFMAN (HISTORY)

THE ESSENCE OF THE P'SUKEI D'ZIMRAH IS THE LAST SIX PSALMS OF THE PSALTER, PSALMS 145–150, OF WHICH THE FIRST, PSALM 145, KNOWN POPULARLY AS ASHRE, IS THE MOST IMPORTANT.

[1-3] *"Happy [ashre] are they...Happy [ashre] is the people...Happy [ashre] is the people"* This introduction to Psalm 145, consisting of two additional verses from Psalms (84:5 and 144:15), is a play on words. By medieval days, Psalm 145 was being said three times daily. The Talmud had already remarked, "Those who says Psalm 145 daily are sure to receive a share in the world-to-come" (Ber. 4b). Eventually, (p. 122)

אַשְׁרֵי יוֹשְׁבֵי בֵיתֶךָ, עוֹד יְהַלְלוּךָ סֶּלָה.[1]

אַשְׁרֵי הָעָם שֶׁכָּכָה לוֹ. [3]אַשְׁרֵי הָעָם שֶׁיַי[2] אֱלֹהָיו.

תְּהִלָּה לְדָוִד.[4]

J. HOFFMAN (TRANSLATION)

[4] *"David's Psalm [T'hillah l'david]"*

Often translated, "a Psalm by David," but saying "David's Psalm" is preferable, because like the title in Hebrew, it leaves the exact connection between David and the psalm ambiguous. On the other hand, "a Psalm by David" makes it clear that this is but one of many, a fact clearly indicated by the Hebrew.

The whole of Psalm 145 is an alphabetic acrostic, each letter of the alphabet being used in order to start a line. We have no hope of capturing this in English. In addition to its acrostic nature, this Psalm (p. 123)

LANDES (HALAKHAH)

[1] *"Happy are they who dwell in your house"* The core section of *P'sukei D'zimrah* is Psalm 145, called by its opening two words, *T'hillah l'david* ("David's Psalm"), along with two other verses from Psalms that introduce it and that begin with the word *ashre*, "Happy." Worshipers are to say all the psalms of *P'sukei D'zimrah*, but if there is not enough time to do so, they may recite this one alone and be accounted as if they had recited them all. The logic behind this ruling is that (p. 120)

5I will exalt You, my God the king, and praise your name for ever and ever.

6Every day I will praise You, and extol your name for ever and ever.

7Great is Adonai and highly praised. Endless is his greatness.

8Generation upon generation will praise your deeds, and tell of your mighty acts.

9I will speak of your wondrous acts, and your glorious majesty in its splendor.

10People tell of your awe-inspiring might, and I proclaim your greatness.

11People spread your very great renown, and sing of your righteousness.

12Gracious and merciful is Adonai, endlessly patient and most kind.

13Adonai is good to all, showering all his creatures with mercy.

14All your creatures will thank You, Adonai, and your faithful will praise You.

15They will tell of the glory of your kingdom, and speak of your might.

16Announce his greatness to humankind, and the majestic glory of his kingdom.

17Your kingdom is a kingdom for all times, and your reign for every generation.

⁵אֲרוֹמִמְךָ אֱלֹהַי הַמֶּלֶךְ, וַאֲבָרְכָה שִׁמְךָ לְעוֹלָם וָעֶד.

⁶בְּכָל יוֹם אֲבָרְכֶךָ, וַאֲהַלְלָה שִׁמְךָ לְעוֹלָם וָעֶד.

⁷גָּדוֹל יְיָ וּמְהֻלָּל מְאֹד, וְלִגְדֻלָּתוֹ אֵין חֵקֶר.

⁸דּוֹר לְדוֹר יְשַׁבַּח מַעֲשֶׂיךָ, וּגְבוּרֹתֶיךָ יַגִּידוּ.

⁹הֲדַר כְּבוֹד הוֹדֶךָ, וְדִבְרֵי נִפְלְאֹתֶיךָ אָשִׂיחָה.

¹⁰וֶעֱזוּז נוֹרְאוֹתֶיךָ יֹאמֵרוּ, וּגְדֻלָּתְךָ אֲסַפְּרֶנָּה.

¹¹זֵכֶר רַב טוּבְךָ יַבִּיעוּ, וְצִדְקָתְךָ יְרַנֵּנוּ.

¹²חַנּוּן וְרַחוּם יְיָ, אֶרֶךְ אַפַּיִם וּגְדָל-חָסֶד.

¹³טוֹב יְיָ לַכֹּל, וְרַחֲמָיו עַל כָּל מַעֲשָׂיו.

¹⁴יוֹדוּךָ יְיָ כָּל מַעֲשֶׂיךָ, וַחֲסִידֶיךָ יְבָרְכוּכָה.

¹⁵כְּבוֹד מַלְכוּתְךָ יֹאמֵרוּ, וּגְבוּרָתְךָ יְדַבֵּרוּ.

¹⁸Adonai supports all who fall, and uprights all who are bent over.

¹⁹The eyes of all look to You, and You give them timely food.

²⁰You open your hand, and satisfy every living being.

²¹Adonai is righteous in all his ways, and gracious in all his acts.

²²Adonai is near to all who call upon Him, to all who call upon Him in truth.

²³He does the will of those who revere Him, and hears their cry and saves them.

²⁴Adonai guards all who love Him, and destroys all who are wicked.

²⁵Let my mouth speak Adonai's praise, and all creatures praise his holy name for ever and ever.

²⁶Let us praise Adonai from now and ever more. Halleluyah (Ps. 115:18).

לְהוֹדִיעַ לִבְנֵי הָאָדָם גְּבוּרֹתָיו, וּכְבוֹד הֲדַר מַלְכוּתוֹ.¹⁶

מַלְכוּתְךָ מַלְכוּת כָּל עֹלָמִים, וּמֶמְשַׁלְתְּךָ בְּכָל דּוֹר וָדֹר.¹⁷

סוֹמֵךְ יְיָ לְכָל הַנֹּפְלִים, וְזוֹקֵף לְכָל הַכְּפוּפִים.¹⁸

עֵינֵי כֹל אֵלֶיךָ יְשַׂבֵּרוּ, וְאַתָּה נוֹתֵן לָהֶם אֶת אָכְלָם בְּעִתּוֹ.¹⁹

פּוֹתֵחַ אֶת יָדֶךָ, וּמַשְׂבִּיעַ לְכָל חַי רָצוֹן.²⁰

צַדִּיק יְיָ בְּכָל דְּרָכָיו, וְחָסִיד בְּכָל מַעֲשָׂיו.²¹

קָרוֹב יְיָ לְכָל קֹרְאָיו, לְכֹל אֲשֶׁר יִקְרָאֻהוּ בֶאֱמֶת.²²

רְצוֹן יְרֵאָיו יַעֲשֶׂה, וְאֶת שַׁוְ-עָתָם יִשְׁמַע וְיוֹשִׁיעֵם.²³

שׁוֹמֵר יְיָ אֶת כָּל אֹהֲבָיו, וְאֵת כָּל הָרְשָׁעִים יַשְׁמִיד.²⁴

תְּהִלַּת יְיָ יְדַבֶּר-פִּי, וִיבָרֵךְ כָּל בָּשָׂר שֵׁם קָדְשׁוֹ לְעוֹלָם וָעֶד.²⁵

וַאֲנַחְנוּ נְבָרֵךְ יָהּ מֵעַתָּה וְעַד עוֹלָם. הַלְלוּיָהּ.²⁶

115

THE DAILY *HALLEL* (*HALLEL SHEB'KHOL YOM*)

BRETTLER (BIBLE)

This psalm is an alphabetic acrostic, where each verse follows the order of the Hebrew alphabet. (In the Hebrew, the *nun* verse is missing, although a [secondary?] *nun* verse [possibly added later?] is found in the Dead Sea Scrolls and in the Septuagint, the ancient Greek Bible translation.) The Bible knows many instances of acrostics, all following alphabetic order, but later Jewish liturgical poetry, like poems in old Babylonian Akkadian tradition, has acrostics that spell out the author's name. The purpose of writing alphabetic acrostic poetry is unclear. It may be a mnemonic aid to memory (by those who recited it or by scribes who wrote it), or perhaps it expresses a notion of completeness, in the case of this psalm, the complete greatness of God.

5 *"My God the king"* An expression again of God's kingship, but in this case, a psalm that describes the type of king God is: great, mighty, powerful, good, compassionate, righteous, and near. The centrality of kingship is evident from the fourfold repetition of *malkhut* ("kingdom") in lines 5, 11, 12, and 13.

7 *"Great is Adonai"* God is here spoken of in the third person, in distinction to the surrounding verses, which employ the second person "You." This variation, which continues throughout the psalm, expresses a type of schizophrenic indecision by the psalmist, who sometimes talks to and sometimes about God, balancing the need to be distant from such a great, domineering deity (third person) while praying to Him (second person).

10–11 *"People tell of your awe-inspiring might.... People spread your very great renown...righteousness"* Two successive verses with parallel structure, rather unusual in biblical poetry, where parallelism often occurs within a poetic line but rarely is extended from one line to another. On closer scrutiny, we see that the second verse is really a modification of the first: God is not only mighty and great, but righteous as well, a notion that leads naturally to the next two verses, which highlight God's mercy and goodness.

12 *"Gracious and merciful is Adonai"* A selective quotation and reworking of God's attributes found, among other places, in Exod. 34:6–7; however, the section of the Exodus text (v. 7) that mentions intergenerational punishment ("He visits the iniquities of the fathers upon children and children's children, upon the third and fourth generation") is omitted here (as in Jon. 4:2), because here the emphasis is on a purely good God.

14 *"All [kol] your creatures"* "All" or "every" *(kol)*, another theme of this psalm, is introduced early (v. 2, "Every day") and is used close to twenty times, to emphasize that all must praise the God of all.

14 *"And your faithful [chasidim]"* Meaning anyone who follows God; alternatively, *chasidim* may already have been a name given to a particular group of specially pietistic Jews, as in medieval Germany or today.

[17] *"Your kingdom is a kingdom for all times"* A combination of the psalm's two themes: God's kingdom and his eternality.

[18] *"Adonai supports all who fall"* As before, the theme of God's greatness is immediately followed by descriptions of his mercy and kindness.

[22–24] *"Adonai is near to all who call upon Him.... He does the will of those who revere Him...Adonai guards all who love Him, and destroys all who are wicked."* The theology of these verses is remarkably straightforward: call out to God in truth, and you will be saved, since God heeds the righteous and destroys the wicked. A similar theology may be seen in Psalm 1, which praises the righteous, noting that they will flourish, while comparing the wicked to chaff. The initial chapters of Daniel similarly illustrate how the righteous triumph, even under the most extreme circumstances.

There are, however, other retribution theologies in the Bible. Job depicts a very different world than the one described here, and several psalms as well suggest that God sometimes forgets or ignores the righteous sufferer. Psalm 13, for instance asks:

> How long, O Lord? Will You forget me forever?
> How long will You hide your face from me?
> How long must I bear pain in my soul
> And have sorrow in my heart all day long?

[25] *"Let my mouth speak Adonai's praise, and all creatures praise his holy name for ever and ever"* After describing a powerful and good God, the psalm arrives at the only possible conclusion: God must be praised by all *(kol)* forever. The conclusion reiterates the psalm's central themes, ending as it began, with a call for "praise" "for ever and ever." This structure, where the end returns to the beginning, is called an *inclusio,* or "envelope," structure and is very common in Bible. The Tower of Babel story, for instance, begins (Gen. 11:1), "All the earth [*kol ha'arets*] had one language..." and ends (11:9), "Adonai confounded the speech of all the earth...and scattered them over the face of all the earth [*kol ha'arets*]."

However, despite the return to the same language, the psalm is not static; it opened with the psalmist alone praising God for ever, but closes with a call for "all creatures" to do so.

[26] *"Let us praise Adonai...Halleluyah"* From the conclusion of Psalm 115 (v. 18), inserted here as a transition to the following five psalms, all of which open with "Halleluyah" ("Praise God!"). The verse is in the first-person plural, as if to suggest that the previous psalm (which called for "all" to praise God) has worked, since "all creatures" are now prepared to do so.

———◆———

The Daily Hallel (Hallel Sheb'khol Yom)

Dorff (Theology)

day? The reason given in the Talmud is that this psalm is an alphabetic acrostic and that it celebrates the providential sustenance of God: "You open your hand, and satisfy every living being" (Ps. 145:16). The alphabetic order would ensure that it would be easy to remember; the central verse expresses our hope that God at least provide for our basic needs, without which we could hardly have the luxury to anticipate that our spiritual needs be met as well — as expressed two verses later: "Adonai is near to all who call upon Him, to all who call upon Him in truth."

———◆———

Frankel (A Woman's Voice)

house we enter is probably God's house, the Temple in Jerusalem. It was here that the Levites would sing this psalm of David, accompanied by musical instruments and dance. Then we peer outside the windows of this house to take in "the majestic glory of his [God's] kingdom," a sweeping landscape of wonders, awe-inspiring might, and glory. And then, we find our way into the kitchen where the poor, the downtrodden, and the hungry gather, grateful for God's open hand. It is in this intimate chamber that we encounter "Adonai [who] is near to all who call upon Him."

———◆———

Hauptman (Talmud)

obligation to tarry at the conclusion of prayer as well, before returning to mundane pursuits. Knowing that Jews are obliged to pray three times daily (Shacharit, Minchah, and Ma'ariv), it considers, perhaps in jest, what will happen if pious people really follow this advice. They would have to spend at least an hour praying three times a day as well as a preparatory hour and a concluding hour each time: nine hours a day in total! How, then, will they study? How will they work? The answer the Gemara gives is that since such people would all be pious, these issues will work themselves out.

It is no coincidence that the very verse cited by R. Joshua b. Levi, "Happy are they who dwell in your house" (Ashre yoshvei veitekha), was chosen to introduce the beginning of Psalm 145, the first of the six psalms recited here as the essence of the P'sukei D'zimrah. So, too, is the last verse of the preceding psalm (144:15), which also begins with the word ashre.

Since every single time that Psalm 145 (T'hillah l'david) appears in the prayer book it is preceded by these two ashre verses (Ashre yoshvei veitekha [84:5] and Ashre ha'am shekakhah lo [144:15]), most people think that they are part of the psalm itself. But that is not so. The first of these two verses, which speaks of dwelling in God's house, is taken by the Rabbis to refer to a synagogue. A synagogue is sacred space. Entering it is assumed to evoke some acknowledgment by the person entering. This verse provides the opportunity for such an observation.

That function is still evident at *Minchah,* which opens with Psalm 145 and, therefore, with its first introductory *ashre* line, *Ashre yoshevei veitekha.* In the morning service, however, so many other prayers have been added through the years that we do not get to *Ashre yoshvei veitekhah* until a great deal of time has passed; its significance as a prayer of acknowledgment of sacred space has been lost. In its place, therefore, yet another prayer has become the norm. It begins with *Mah tovu ohalekha ya'akov mishk'notekha yisra'el, va'ani b'rov chasd'kha avo veitekha...* ("How lovely are your tents, O Jacob, your dwelling places O Israel. As for me, in your great loving-kindness I enter your house..." [see future volume in this series, *Birkhot Hashachar: The Morning Blessings*]).

⁴*"David's Psalm [T'hillah l'david]"* "Said Rabbi Elazar b. Abina: Anyone who recites *T'hillah l'david* (Psalm 145) three times every day is guaranteed to enter into the world-to-come. Why? It cannot be simply because it is an alphabet acrostic [although it is that], because [if we wanted to find the best possible acrostic], we would have cited another acrostic [Psalm 119] that is a better one because it repeats the alphabet eight times over. Rather, it must be because this psalm includes the line 'You open your hand, and satisfy every living being'" (Ber. 4b).

It is all too easy to think that the reason for seeing a psalm as ideal for praising God is that it praises God many times over using the alphabet arbitrarily to make sure that we heap up lines of praise. The implication of such a view would be that somehow, we are eventually able to give God praise that is comprehensive. Rabbi Elazar b. Abina implicitly denies the possibility of all-comprehensive praise of God. Psalm 145 is singled out instead because of a particular aspect of God that deserves being singled out for praise: God's merciful care of all living things, to make sure that the basic needs of every single creature are met. It is not so much that God is all-powerful as it is that God uses his power to benefit all. That is why we say Psalm 145 three times daily: God is concerned about and actively involved in the world that He created — a vital tenet of rabbinic thinking.

¹³*"Showering all his creatures with mercy"* The midrash to this verse (Bereshit Rabbah 33) tells the following story: In the days of R. Tanchuma, there was a drought. The people came to him and asked him to declare a fast, which he did. But still the rain did not come. So he called everyone together and began to preach: "My children, if you have compassion for each other, God will have compassion for you." As they were distributing funds to the poor, they noticed that one man was giving money to a woman he had divorced (which, to people at that time, suggested that the two were involved in a sexual relationship). They reported this to R. Tanchuma, who sent for the man and asked him, "What have you been doing?" "Giving money to my former wife," replied the man, "because she was in great need and I took pity on her." Upon hearing this, R. Tanchuma turned his face to heaven and said, "Lord of the universe, just as this man, who no longer had any obligation to support this woman, behaved

compassionately toward her, You, the all-compassionate One, should certainly take pity on us, your children, the descendants of Abraham, Isaac, and Jacob!"

The beauty of this anecdote is that it assumes that divine behavior is contingent upon human conduct. It is not enough that we direct our hearts to God and pray and declare fasts. He will not turn to us until we first turn to others. Worship of God is necessary but insufficient. In addition to acts of piety, Judaism requires acts of loving-kindness. Ironically, here, the person who is suspected of sinning turns out to be the most pious of all, the one who brings the rain. The subsidiary message seems to be that one should do what is right even if at the risk of having others assume impure motives when there are only pure ones.

[18] *"Adonai supports all who fall and uprights all who are bent over"* "Said Rabbah bar Chin'nah Saba in the name of Rav: One who prays should bend his knees and bow down when saying *barukh* [i.e., during the opening words of the *Amidah*] but stand straight when saying God's name. The reason for straightening up when uttering God's name is that the verse says, 'Adonai supports all who fall and uprights all who are bent over" (Ber. 12a). This rather playful interpretation of the verse tells us that although we bow down before God out of a sense of awe and thanksgiving and supplication, still, when saying his name, we must straighten up, which means we must sense our own importance as his creatures. We see here a complicated blend of subjection to someone greater than oneself and independent regard for oneself. If God created us and assigned us a job to do in this world, we should see ourselves as having been invested with importance. At the same time, we must never forget that we are dependent on God. This ongoing tension is characteristic of the religious person's outlook on life.

———◆———

KUSHNER & POLEN (CHASIDISM)

samakh you, I will support and uphold you. You are not giving a ring, you are giving a *samekh*. Indeed, when couples exchange rings, they pledge themselves to be present to support and uphold one another. And surely *that* is God's presence.

———◆———

LANDES (HALAKHAH)

P'sukei D'zimrah is constructed around Psalm 145 as its center. The Talmud advises, "Whoever recites *T'hillah l'david* [Psalm 145] three times daily is assured of gaining the world-to-come" (Ber. 4b).

The two anticipatory verses (from Psalm 84 and Psalm 144) are not accidental. By their common adjective, "happy," they indicate that the essence of the entire *P'sukei*

D'zimrah is an appreciation of wondrous joy. Psalm 145 (the main psalm of the rubric) is therefore joyous in its very essence.

It is possible that these two introductory verses highlight the alphabetical structure of Psalm 145 by reiterating for us the first letter, *alef,* since *ashre* (the first word of both verses) begins with that letter. Each *alef* is vocalized with a *patach* (the "ah" sound), formed by opening one's mouth. That sound is considered reminiscent of a form of "stuttering," as when we grope for a word and cannot find it, so say only, "Ah, ah, ah...." The sense of stuttering to find the right words to praise God leads dramatically to the full articulation of praise that Psalm 145 contains.

[20] *"You open your hand, and satisfy every living being"* Because this is the core verse of the psalm, a reason for its being chosen in the first place, according to the Talmud, it must be said with the *kavvanah* (the thought in one's mind) that God's providence extends over all living beings in order to sustain them. If it is not said with that *kavvanah,* it must be repeated, for without attending to God's beneficence at this point, one has not fulfilled the requirement of saying the *P'sukei D'zimrah.* Along with that kavvanah regarding God's goodness, I believe it is fitting to add the personal intention of imitating God's ways in this respect, for the Talmud tells us, "As God clothes the naked...so must you clothe the naked. As God visited the sick, so must you visit the sick..." (Sot. 14a). Similarly, therefore, as God sustains those who are hungry, so must we.

If one is wearing *t'fillin,* it is customary to touch the *bayit* (the box) of the hand phylactery and then that of the head phylactery with a strap and then to kiss the strap. This reverential act is meant to bind the left hand (representing the heart) and the head together into the common intent of pursuing moral action akin to God's.

[26] *"Let us praise A-donai from now and ever more. Halleluy-ah"* As the psalm began with additions (from Psalm 84 and Psalm 144), so now it ends with an extra verse, the last line of Psalm 115, in order to make this psalm consistent with those that follow, all of which end with the word "Halleluy-ah" [*Tur,* O. Ch. 51]. The fact that the other psalms also begin with "Halleluy-ah" results in our juxtaposing the final "Halleluy-ah" of one psalm with the opening "Halleluy-ah" of the next (*Arukh Hashulchan* 51:2). The halakhic import of this widespread (but not universal) custom is to tie the segments of *P'sukei D'Zimrah* together, much as the blessings of the *Sh'ma* or the *Amidah* are interconnected (see Volume 1, *The Sh'ma and Its Blessings,* and Volume 2, *The Amidah*).

This integral connection between psalms raises the importance of not pausing between them (in halakhic terms, not creating a *hefsek,* a "break," between them). One may not, for instance, pause between the psalms to greet someone who walks in late. Such an interruption would be an aesthetic problem anyway, but given the natural word flow from one "Halleluy-ah" to the next, it would constitute also a halakhic error.

———◆———

L. HOFFMAN (HISTORY)

in fact, the words "three times daily" were added to our talmudic text, reflecting the success of making Psalm 150 a thrice-daily staple. Whether purposefully or not, the "happy" prospect of receiving a share in the world-to-come, reinforced by a threefold recitation of the prayer that is supposed to guarantee that share, is alluded to in this introduction to the psalm, which contains the word "happy" three times. Classical Jewish literature usually refers to the psalm by its first words, "David's Psalm," but the introduction is so inextricably linked to the psalm liturgically that even the Talmud calls it *Ashre*, and it is almost universally called *Ashre* today. Medieval Halakhah ruled that someone who arrives at the synagogue late and has no time to say all the psalms in the Daily *Hallel* should at least say this one.

The addition of the two introductory verses was linked to another talmudic teaching (Ber. 32b) to the effect that before one begins to pray, one should "linger for an hour in the synagogue," the idea being that before the main statutory prayers (especially the *Amidah*), one should prepare oneself spiritually. The Talmud cites Ps. 84:5 as proof for that lesson. "Happy are they who dwell in your house; they will ever praise You" — that is, before we "praise You" in the *Amidah*, it is necessary to "dwell in your house," meaning "in the synagogue" for a while. Whether this lesson had anything to do with the choice of Ps. 84:5 as an introductory verse here is not clear, but the medieval authorities believed it did. Some of them added other introductory psalm verses also, all of them with the word *ashre* in them, in an attempt to drag out the preparation time as long as possible. It may be that Ashkenazi custom retained the practice of having only our two verses in order to retain the word play denoting "three."

Other medieval authorities could not believe that the Talmud really meant to promise the world-to-come to people who said this psalm daily but did not merit reward in other ways as well. Rabbi Samuel ben Meir, known as the Rashbam (1085–1174), explained, "Saying this prayer does not guarantee the world-to-come if your deeds are evil. The Talmud means to say that people who habitually take ethical stock of their affairs will naturally be careful in reciting this psalm as well. Knowing that they are God-fearing and that they turn away from evil, they may be certain that they merit the world-to-come."

[20] *"You open your hand, and satisfy every living being"* According to the Talmud, this is the most important line in the psalm because it celebrates God's gracious care for all creatures. Medieval Jews concentrated special attention on the line when they arrived at it.

[26] *"Let us praise Adonai from now and ever more. Halleluyah"* Psalm 115:18, which has been added to Psalm 145 to make the psalm end with "Halleluyah," the way Psalms 146–150, which follow, do.

———◆———

J. HOFFMAN (TRANSLATION)

has particularly lyrical Hebrew, whereas our English translation contains only hints of this beauty.

[6] *"Extol [ahal'lah]"* Translated immediately above as "praise," but here it follows *avar'kheka,* which we translate as "praise." In order to retain the two verbs with different meaning, we choose "extol" here.

[9] *"I will speak of your wondrous acts"* The Hebrew might also mean, "I will speak words of your wonders."

[14] *"All your creatures will thank"* In keeping with our translation elsewhere, "acknowledge You with thanks" might be more accurate, but the two parts of this line exhibit similar structure in the Hebrew, which we have tried to mimic in the English translation.

[16] *"Announce [l'hodi'a] his greatness"* The Hebrew is the infinitive "to announce" *(L'hodi'a),* but that choice was governed by the need for a word beginning with a *lamed,* so as to preserve the acrostic. The infinitive makes more sense in Hebrew than it would in English.

[16] *"The majestic glory [k'vod hadar]"* In Hebrew, too, this is a reversal of "glorious majesty" *(hadar k'vod)* a few lines up.

[20] *"Satisfy every living being"* It is not clear how the last word of this line (*ratson* literally "favor") relates to the rest of the line. Here we assume that it is part of a verbal idiom meaning "to satisfy." Another possibility is that it is an adverb, as in Birnbaum's "satisfy every living thing with favor."

◆ ◆ ◆

BRETTLER (BIBLE)

[1] *"Praise God!"* The introduction to Psalm 146, the first of five consecutive psalms that are structured as *inclusios,* beginning and concluding with "Halleluyah" ("Praise God!"). (See above, "Let my mouth speak Adonai's praise, and all creatures praise his name for ever and ever.") With the introduction of Psalm 145, which gives a detailed justification for why God should be praised, Psalms 146–150 may be considered *the* hymn collection of the Bible, a proper introduction to morning prayer.   *(p. 126)*

FRANKEL (A WOMAN'S VOICE)

[1] *"Praise God! Praise Adonai, my soul"* This psalm, together with the next one, affirms the popular saying, attributed to the architect Le Corbusier, that "God is in the details." We are here cautioned against trusting in earthly princes, whose "designs" will perish with them. Rather, we are called upon to give our allegiance only to the "Maker of heaven and earth, the sea, and all that they contain, keeper of truth forever," for God's perspective, unlike that of mortal rulers, transcends the utilitarian calculus of those in power. As sovereign of the universe, God can afford to take notice of even the lowliest subjects: the oppressed, the hungry, the captive, the blind, the bent over, the stranger, the orphan, and the widow. Only an unassailable ruler can attend to the endless minor details of governance while at the same time upholding his duty to "thwart the way of the wicked."

———◆———

B. PSALM 146

[1] Praise God! Praise Adonai, my soul. [2] I will praise Adonai so long as I live and sing to my God so long as I exist. [3] Do not trust in princes, in mortals who offer no salvation, whose spirit leaves them and who will return to the earth. [4] On that day his designs perish. [5] Happy are

DORFF (THEOLOGY)

[3-5] *"Do not trust in princes... whose spirit leaves them and who will return to the earth. On that day his designs perish"* The psalmist clearly does not expect people to live after death. That was a later Jewish belief, documented first in the biblical Book of Daniel (12:2), written in approximately 165 B.C.E., and later adopted by the Pharisees (the people we call "the Rabbis"), in sharp contrast to their rivals, the Sadducees.

While God is "maker of heaven and earth," God is not too big to be concerned about human affairs. On the contrary, God grants justice to the oppressed, provides bread to the hungry, frees the captive, opens the eyes of the blind, uprights the bent   *(p. 127)*

J. HOFFMAN (TRANSLATION)

[1] *"Praise God"* That is, *hall'luyah*.

[1] *"My soul"* Here the lack of a modern English vocative ("O my soul") is particularly unfortunate, leaving almost no way to reflect the beauty of the Hebrew, which addresses the soul directly.

[2] *"I will praise Adonai so long as I live…so long as I exist"* As in Birnbaum; another possibility is "with my life…with my very essence."

[6] *"Frees the captive"* Reminiscent of God's attributes as given in the *G'vurot*, the second blessing of the *Amidah*, and raising similar translation issues. (see Volume 2, *The Amidah*, pp. 73, 74, 82).

———◆———

¹הַלְלוּיָהּ. הַלְלִי נַפְשִׁי אֶת יְיָ. ²אֲהַלְלָה יְיָ בְּחַיָּי,
אֲזַמְּרָה לֵאלֹהַי בְּעוֹדִי. ³אַל תִּבְטְחוּ בִנְדִיבִים,
בְּבֶן־אָדָם שֶׁאֵין לוֹ תְשׁוּעָה.   תֵּצֵא רוּחוֹ
יָשֻׁב לְאַדְמָתוֹ. ⁴בַּיּוֹם הַהוּא אָבְדוּ עֶשְׁתֹּנֹתָיו.

those whose help is the God of Jacob, whose hope rests on Adonai their God, maker of heaven and earth, the sea, and all that they contain, keeper of truth forever, the grantor of justice to the oppressed, provider of bread to the hungry. [6] Adonai frees the captive. [7] Adonai opens the eyes of the blind. [8] Adonai uprights the bent over. [9] Adonai loves the righteous. [10] Adonai guards strangers, upholding the orphan and widow, but thwarting the way of the wicked. [11] Adonai will reign forever, your God, Zion, for all generations. Halleluyah.

5אַשְׁרֵי שֶׁאֵל יַעֲקֹב בְּעֶזְרוֹ, שִׂבְרוֹ עַל יְיָ אֱלֹהָיו. עֹשֶׂה שָׁמַיִם וָאָרֶץ, אֶת הַיָּם, וְאֶת כָּל אֲשֶׁר בָּם, הַשֹּׁמֵר אֱמֶת לְעוֹלָם, עֹשֶׂה מִשְׁפָּט לַעֲשׁוּקִים, נֹתֵן לֶחֶם לָרְעֵבִים. 6יְיָ מַתִּיר אֲסוּרִים. 7יְיָ פֹּקֵחַ עוְרִים. 8יְיָ זֹקֵף כְּפוּפִים. 9יְיָ אֹהֵב צַדִּיקִים. 10יְיָ שֹׁמֵר אֶת גֵּרִים, יָתוֹם וְאַלְמָנָה יְעוֹדֵד, וְדֶרֶךְ רְשָׁעִים יְעַוֵּת. 11יִמְלֹךְ יְיָ לְעוֹלָם, אֱלֹהַיִךְ צִיּוֹן לְדֹר וָדֹר. הַלְלוּיָהּ.

BRETTLER (BIBLE)

[2] *"I will praise Adonai so long as I live"* A reference to the common motif in psalms that the dead do not praise God (see, for instance, Ps. 115:17, "The dead do not praise the Lord, nor do any that go down into silence") and, therefore, an oblique request for long life. Additionally, it contrasts human mortality with God's greatness and immortality, themes that the psalm will later develop.

[3–4] *"Do not trust in princes...perish"* Humanity is set up as a foil for God; even princes who seem powerful ultimately die, taking all of their power and promises to the grave.

[5] *"Happy are those whose help is the God of Jacob"* The national God of Israel, as opposed to other national, but mortal rulers.

[5] *"Maker of heaven and earth...all that they contain"* From the biblical perspective, the greatest proof of God's power is his act of creation.

[5] *"Keeper of truth forever"* God's power is not just past. The covenant ("truth") extends forever, as demonstrated by the list of God's beneficent attributes that follow, especially God's care for the "oppressed," the "hungry," the "captive," the "blind," the "bent over," the "orphan and widow."

[10] *"But thwarting the way of the wicked"* A continuation of the attributes cited previously: by helping society's least fortunate, God "thwarts the way of the wicked," whose natural inclination is to prey upon the helpless poor and afflicted.

[11] *"Adonai will reign forever, your God, Zion, for all generations"* The psalm concludes with a well-balanced couplet, followed by "Halleluyah." We translate it here as a simple statement of fact: that this powerful and good God will indeed reign forever. But the Hebrew may also be a "jussive," that is, a wish, "May God reign."

———◆———

DORFF (THEOLOGY)

over, etc. This is one of my favorite psalms because in just a few short sentences it simultaneously bespeaks the awesomeness of God and the loving care of God in remarkably simple, but eloquent, language.

——————◆ ◆ ◆——————

BRETTLER (BIBLE)

[1] *"It is good to sing to our God, and it is pleasant; praise is beautiful"* One of the primary sentiments of biblical prayer, the notion that praise of God for its own sake, not for the sake of having petitions answered, is "good" — hence our hymns of praise in the first place (see "Prayer in the Bible and the use of the Bible in later Jewish Prayer," p. 16). The rest of the psalm lists attributes that make God so praiseworthy, including creation, building Jerusalem, helping the downtrodden, and giving Israel the law.

(p. 131)

C. PSALM 147

DORFF
(THEOLOGY)
9–10 *"He does not take joy in the horse's strength, nor take pleasure in man's legs.*

[1] Halleluyah. It is good to sing to our God and it is pleasant; praise is beautiful. [2] Adonai rebuilds Jerusalem; He will gather the dispersed among Israel. [3] The One who heals the broken-hearted will repair their sorrow. [4] The One who counts the stars will give each a name. [5] Great is our Lord and mighty; his wisdom is infinite. [6] Adonai raises the humble and casts the wicked down to

He takes pleasure in those who fear Him, in those who yearn for his kindness" This is reminiscent of the prophet Zechariah's famous words (4:6), "Not by might and not by power, but by my spirit, said the Lord of Hosts." Although we are tempted to value most that which gives us physical power, including strong bodies and effective instruments, these verses tell us to focus our lives on a proper relationship with God.

18–19 *"He declares his word to Jacob, his laws and statutes to Israel.* *(p. 132)*

FRANKEL (A WOMAN'S VOICE)

[1] *"Halleluyah. It is good to sing to our God"* Following the previous psalm's affirmation of God's protectiveness toward the most vulnerable members of the human community, we find here comparable praise for God's stewardship of the rest of the natural world. God counts and numbers the stars, regulates the weather, and sustains the animals. In counterpoint to the Darwinian imperative of survival, God prefers our faith to any show of power, taking no joy "in the horse's strength, nor…pleasure in man's legs." Blessings flow earthward because of our gratitude, not our pride. After all, what power do we really have over the forces of nature? What we interpret as impediments to our freedom and ease — snow, frost, and ice — are just the opposite in the divine household; they represent the wool, ashes, and crumbs of God's handiwork. When seen from God's vantage point, the earth is perfect.

———◆———

[1] *"It is good to sing to our God [ki tov zamrah eloheinu]"* This is the only likely interpretation of the Hebrew, but as we have it, the Hebrew is so strange as to appear totally ungrammatical.

[2] *"Adonai rebuilds Jerusalem"* Literally, "builds." For the translation of "rebuilds" as "builds," see Volume 2, *The Amidah*, pp. 140–41. The Hebrew has no word for *re*build, so regularly uses just "build," which must be understood as "build again" from the context. This verse is the first of several that share a similar structure in Hebrew and that are therefore provided with the same structure in English also.

הַלְלוּיָהּ. כִּי טוֹב זַמְּרָה אֱלֹהֵינוּ, כִּי נָעִים, נָאוָה תְהִלָּה. [2]בֹּנֵה יְרוּשָׁלַיִם יְיָ, נִדְחֵי יִשְׂרָאֵל יְכַנֵּס. [3]הָרוֹפֵא לִשְׁבוּרֵי לֵב, וּמְחַבֵּשׁ לְעַצְּבוֹתָם. [4]מוֹנֶה מִסְפָּר לַכּוֹכָבִים, לְכֻלָּם שֵׁמוֹת יִקְרָא. [5]גָּדוֹל אֲדוֹנֵינוּ וְרַב כֹּחַ, לִתְבוּנָתוֹ אֵין מִסְפָּר. [6]מְעוֹדֵד עֲנָוִים יְיָ, מַשְׁפִּיל רְשָׁעִים עֲדֵי

[3] *"Heals...will repair"* In the Hebrew, as in our English, the verbs ("heals...repair") refer to physical healing, but the objects ("the brokenhearted" and "their sorrow") are spiritual in nature, as if to indicate that God's healing moves beyond the physical to the spiritual.

[4] *"Counts the stars"* Literally (as in Birnbaum), "counts the number of the stars."

[7] *"The harp"* The exact musical instrument intended here cannot be known for sure, though modern translations seem to agree on "harp."

[8] *"To birds [v'nei orev]"* Literally, "young raven" (or something like it); the exact type of bird is unknown.

[12] *"Choice wheat [cheilev chitim]"* The Hebrew idiom uses *cheilev*, the word for "milk," suggesting the translation "cream of the crop." Many languages (e.g., French, Russian, modern Hebrew, English) have similar idioms involving cream or rich milk, suggesting that this imagery might be quite universal. We would have used "cream of the crop," but it seemed too colloquial.

[13] *"His word runs quickly [ad m'herah yaruts d'varo]"* So reads the Hebrew, but it is not clear what the Hebrew idiom intends.

◆

earth. ⁷Answer Adonai with grateful acknowledgment; play music for God with the harp. ⁸He covers the sky with clouds, provides rain for the earth, causes grass to grow on the mountains, and gives bread to beasts and to birds who cry out. ⁹He does not take joy in the horse's strength, nor take pleasure in man's legs. ¹⁰He takes pleasure in those who fear Him, in those who yearn for his kindness. ¹¹Exalt Adonai, Jerusalem; praise your God, Zion, for He has strengthened the bars of your gates, blessed your children in your midst. ¹²He grants your borders peace, and sates you with choice wheat. ¹³He sends his command earthward and his word runs quickly. ¹⁴He grants snow like wool and scatters frost like ashes. ¹⁵He casts out his ice like crumbs; who can stand before his cold? ¹⁶He sends out his word and melts them. ¹⁷By his wind He causes the water to flow. ¹⁸He declares his word to Jacob, his laws and statutes to Israel. ¹⁹He has not done so for every nation, who do not know his statutes. Halleluyah!

אָרֶץ. ⁷עֱנוּ לַיִי בְּתוֹדָה, זַמְּרוּ לֵאלֹהֵינוּ בְכִנּוֹר. ⁸הַמְכַסֶּה שָׁמַיִם בְּעָבִים, הַמֵּכִין לָאָרֶץ מָטָר, הַמַּצְמִיחַ הָרִים חָצִיר, נוֹתֵן לִבְהֵמָה לַחְמָהּ, לִבְנֵי עֹרֵב אֲשֶׁר יִקְרָאוּ. ⁹לֹא בִגְבוּרַת הַסּוּס יֶחְפָּץ, לֹא בְשׁוֹקֵי הָאִישׁ יִרְצֶה. ¹⁰רוֹצֶה יְיָ אֶת יְרֵאָיו, אֶת הַמְיַחֲלִים לְחַסְדּוֹ. ¹¹שַׁבְּחִי, יְרוּשָׁלַיִם, אֶת יְיָ. הַלְלִי אֱלֹהַיִךְ צִיּוֹן. כִּי חִזַּק בְּרִיחֵי שְׁעָרָיִךְ, בֵּרַךְ בָּנַיִךְ בְּקִרְבֵּךְ. ¹²הַשָּׂם גְּבוּלֵךְ שָׁלוֹם, חֵלֶב חִטִּים יַשְׂבִּיעֵךְ. ¹³הַשֹּׁלֵחַ אִמְ-רָתוֹ אָרֶץ, עַד מְהֵרָה יָרוּץ דְּבָרוֹ. ¹⁴הַנֹּתֵן שֶׁלֶג כַּצָּמֶר, כְּפוֹר כָּאֵפֶר יְפַזֵּר. ¹⁵מַשְׁלִיךְ קַרְחוֹ כְפִתִּים, לִפְנֵי קָרָתוֹ מִי יַעֲמֹד. ¹⁶יִשְׁלַח דְּבָרוֹ וְיַמְסֵם. ¹⁷יַשֵּׁב רוּחוֹ, יִזְּלוּ מָיִם. ¹⁸מַגִּיד דְּבָרָיו לְיַעֲקֹב, חֻקָּיו וּמִשְׁפָּטָיו לְיִשְׂרָאֵל. ¹⁹לֹא עָשָׂה כֵן לְכָל גּוֹי, וּמִשְׁפָּטִים בַּל יְדָעוּם. הַלְלוּיָהּ.

BRETTLER (BIBLE)

This variety is precisely the point: God's greatness in so many spheres of life evokes our praise.

² *"Adonai rebuilds Jerusalem: He will gather the dispersed among Israel"* A sign that this psalm is post-exilic. "The broken-hearted" (in the next line) likely refers to those who are distressed at the weakened condition of Judea observable upon the return from Babylonian exile.

⁴ *"The One who counts the stars"* An allusion to a tradition about creation that has not survived in the initial chapters of Genesis. Elsewhere, the Bible emphasizes that the stars cannot be counted (Gen. 15:5)! If we may combine these two traditions, the idea seems to be that only God, as God, can truly compute creation's mysteries. Hence (next verse), "his wisdom is infinite."

⁶ *"Adonai raises the humble and casts the wicked down to earth"* An idea thematically more central to the previous psalm, but mentioned here specifically to emphasize that God, though a creator deity, is not distant.

⁷ *"Answer Adonai with grateful acknowledgment"* The psalm is structured so that such cries for congregational involvement are interspersed with descriptions of God's greatness.

⁸ *"He covers the sky with clouds…birds who cry out"* A list of God's activities in nature, from the most significant, rain, to the least significant, the needs of hungry birds.

⁹⁻¹⁰ *"He does not take joy in the horse's strength…. He takes pleasure in those who fear Him, in those who yearn for his kindness"* The logic of this couplet is not entirely clear, but it seems to suggest that God, as creator of all, takes no pleasure in the strength of what He has created, for that strength ultimately derives from Him. Rather, God takes pleasure in those who are pious, who (acknowledging God's power) yearn for his *chesed* (his "kindness" — see Brettler, "For Adonai is good, his mercy [*chesed*] is everlasting," p. 98). This couplet makes particular sense in the early post-exilic period, when God's chesed was particularly necessary to rebuild Jerusalem.

¹¹ *"Exalt Adonai, Jerusalem"* Another cry for congregational involvement, this time focused on the inhabitants of Jerusalem-Zion, who should be thankful for God's political beneficence.

¹³ *"He sends his command earthward"* This and the following verses are similar to the idea of Genesis 1, where God creates by speech. Here, it is not the world's creation but its maintenance that God's speech accomplishes. Hence (v. 60), "He sends out his word and melts" the frost.

¹⁸⁻¹⁹ *"He declares his word to Jacob…. He has not done so for every nation, who do not know his statutes"* The psalmist effects a beautiful transition from the "word" that sustains the universe to the "word" given to Israel: the Torah. Torah is viewed as a gift,

given only to Israel, God's treasured possession. It might seem quite remarkable to us that the climactic conclusion of God's beneficence is the gift of Torah, but within the ancient world, kings, not gods, promulgated laws, so Israel could see itself as specially blessed by having the only *divine* law.

———◆———

DORFF (THEOLOGY)

He has not done so for every nation, who do not know his statutes. Halleluyah!" Like Deut. 4:5–8, this passage reminds us that Jews should not take the Torah for granted or see it as only a set of commands imposed on us by God; it is a blessing that God has not shared with other peoples and that we should therefore treasure as a great gift.

————————◆ ◆ ◆————————

BRETTLER (BIBLE)

[1] *"Praise God! Praise Adonai from the heavens"* In contrast to the previous psalm, which emphasized many different aspects of God's greatness, Psalm 148 concentrates on God as creator, suggesting that all of creation owes God praise — even the heavenly bodies, like angels and luminaries. Other biblical texts (especially Isaiah 6, whence we get the angelic choir singing, "Holy, holy, holy") feature angels praising God, an idea that is further developed in the Dead Sea Scrolls and that serves as the basis for the *K'dushah* section of the *Amidah* (see Volume 2, *The Amidah*, p. 84).

[5] *"And the water above the heavens"* According to one biblical cosmogony, these celestial waters were created on the second day (Gen. 1:6–8). They are responsible for rain, which could fall when the windows of heaven would open, as we see from the story of Noah (Gen. 7:11), "The floodgates of the sky burst open."

[6] *"Because by his commandment they were created"* In agreement with the first creation story of Genesis 1. In general, this psalm shows many thematic and vocabulary agreements with that chapter, though (as we shall see) other traditions influenced it also.   (p. 136)

D. PSALM 148

[1] Praise God! Praise Adonai from the heavens; praise Him on high. [2] Praise Him, all his angels; praise Him, all his hosts. [3] Praise Him, sun and moon. [4] Praise Him, all stars of light. [5] Praise Him, heaven of heavens, and the water above the heavens. [6] Let them praise Adonai's name, because by his commandment they were created. [7] He fixed them for ever and ever; He

FRANKEL (A WOMAN'S VOICE)

[1] *"Praise God! Praise Adonai from the heavens"* This psalm celebrates the interconnectedness of all creation, which is unified through its subordination to God's sovereign will. From the heavenly heights and the waters above those heights, including our own young, who crawl upon the earth, God's grandeur invites universal praise. Ranging in scale from the cosmic to the human, the vividly concrete imagery of this psalm, portraying a God both remote and intimate, lyrically reconciles these opposites. So, for instance, we are assured that God's name is *nisgav*, literally "inaccessible," like a wall too high to scale, yet we are also assured that we are *am k'rovo*, the people near to God, a word that derives from the same Hebrew root as for "kinsman" and the innermost organs of the body. Thus, even as we praise God's transcendent name, we draw near to God's intimate presence. And so, paradoxically, when we surrender our individual voices to the universal symphony, God singles us out to hear the call of God's *keren*, the "horn of plenty" that sustains faithful Israel.

——◆——

KUSHNER & POLEN (CHASIDISM)

[11] *"His majesty is on earth and in the heavens"* Levi Yitzhak of Berditchev (1740–1810) in his *Kedushas Levi* (Jerusalem, 1958) draws a teaching from Gen. 2:4, "These are the generations of the heavens and the earth when they were created — on the day the Lord, God, made earth and heaven." He notes that when God created the universe, God made the heavens first but, as we learn from the reversed order of the end of the verse, this is not our goal. This same order of earth followed by heaven in Psalm 148 teaches us that the earth must come first. Our responsibility is to realize, that is, *make real*, the divine potential in the ordinary, physical reality of this world. Any beginning student of religion can easily see how to find God's majesty in the heavens and make them holy, but can we do the same for our everyday, mundane reality?

———◆———

L. HOFFMAN (HISTORY)

[1] *"Praise God! Praise Adonai from the heavens"* The beginning of Psalm 148. Psalm 148 and the following Psalm 149 may have enjoyed special favor in the Middle Ages. The Talmud (Shab. 118b) mentions the *P'sukei D'zimrah,* and Rashi (France, eleventh century) expressly identifies it only as Psalms 148 and 149. We know that he said the other psalms as well, but he apparently had special regard for these.

———◆———

הַלְלוּיָה. הַלְלוּ אֶת יְיָ מִן הַשָּׁמַיִם, הַלְלוּהוּ בַּמְּרוֹמִים. ²הַלְלוּהוּ כָל מַלְאָכָיו, הַלְלוּהוּ כָּל צְבָאָיו. ³הַלְלוּהוּ שֶׁמֶשׁ וְיָרֵחַ. ⁴הַלְלוּהוּ כָּל כּוֹכְבֵי אוֹר. ⁵הַלְלוּהוּ שְׁמֵי הַשָּׁמָיִם, וְהַמַּיִם אֲשֶׁר מֵעַל הַשָּׁמָיִם. ⁶יְהַלְלוּ אֶת שֵׁם יְיָ, כִּי הוּא צִוָּה וְנִבְרָאוּ. ⁷וַיַּעֲמִידֵם לָעַד לְעוֹלָם,

J. HOFFMAN (TRANSLATION)

[3] *"Praise Him, sun and moon"* Once again, the lack of a modern English vocative makes the English awkward here.

[7] *"A law that shall never pass [chok natan v'lo ya'avor]"* Or "that none shall transgress," as in Birnbaum. The phrase finds its way into the blessing following the *Sh'ma* (see Volume 1, *The Sh'ma and Its Blessings,* p. 117).

[10] *"Bugs"* See parallel comment by Brettler ("Animals and all wild beasts, bugs and birds and fowl") on how the Bible classified the animal kingdom.

[12] *"The strength of his nation [vayarem keren l'amo]"* A dubious translation, trying to (p. 137)

gave a law that shall never pass. [8] Praise Adonai from the earth, sea monsters and all depths. [9] Fire and hail, snow and fog, stormy wind, all fulfill his word. [10] The mountains and all the hills, the fruit tree and all cedars, wild beasts and all animals, bugs and birds and fowl, kings of the earth and all nations, princes and all judges of the earth, young men and women, the old with the young: Let them praise Adonai's name, for his name alone is exalted. [11] His majesty is on earth and in the heavens. [12] He is the strength of his nation, the praise of his faithful, of the children of Israel, the people near to Him. Halleluyah!

חָק־נָתַן וְלֹא יַעֲבוֹר. [8] הַלְלוּ אֶת יְיָ מִן הָאָרֶץ, תַּנִּינִים וְכָל תְּהֹמוֹת. [9] אֵשׁ וּבָרָד, שֶׁלֶג וְקִיטוֹר, רוּחַ סְעָרָה עֹשָׂה דְבָרוֹ. [10] הֶהָרִים וְכָל גְּבָעוֹת, עֵץ פְּרִי וְכָל אֲרָזִים, הַחַיָּה וְכָל בְּהֵמָה, רֶמֶשׂ וְצִפּוֹר כָּנָף, מַלְכֵי אֶרֶץ וְכָל לְאֻמִּים, שָׂרִים וְכָל שֹׁפְטֵי אָרֶץ, בַּחוּרִים וְגַם בְּתוּלוֹת, זְקֵנִים עִם נְעָרִים, יְהַלְלוּ אֶת שֵׁם יְיָ, כִּי נִשְׂגָּב שְׁמוֹ לְבַדּוֹ. [11] הוֹדוֹ עַל אֶרֶץ וְשָׁמָיִם. [12] וַיָּרֶם קֶרֶן לְעַמּוֹ, תְּהִלָּה לְכָל חֲסִידָיו, לִבְנֵי יִשְׂרָאֵל עַם קְרֹבוֹ. הַלְלוּיָהּ.

BRETTLER (BIBLE)

[7] *"He gave a law that shall never pass"* Probably referring to a myth, not preserved in Genesis, that the waters attempted to rebel against God, who quelled them by establishing a boundary that they may not pass. The myth is reflected in a wide variety of biblical sources and rabbinic literature and is probably influenced by earlier Canaanite traditions that are also found in the literature of Ugarit, a Syrian city on the Mediterranean coast that has yielded a large number of texts from a civilization that preceded Israel.

[10] *"All cedars"* Throughout the Bible, the cedar is an image of strength. The psalmist thus emphasizes that even the strongest building material is not autonomous, but grows according to God's will.

[10] *"Wild beasts and all animals, bugs and birds and fowl"* This is the way that the biblical world viewed the animal kingdom: it classified large animals as either wild or domesticated, leaving over creepy crawly and swarming things (*remes* — here "bugs") and birds. Oddly, here, as in the flood account, fish are absent.

[10] *"Kings of the earth"* As in Genesis 1, people are mentioned last, beginning with the upper echelons of society, then continuing with the ordinary.

[12] *"He is the strength of his nation"* A highly nationalistic reference to Israel, with unclear meaning, but clearly meant to encourage Israel to praise God following the example of the angels, various meteoric phenomena, and foreign kings. The previous psalms evoked God's praise as a natural consequence of recognizing his wondrous deeds. This psalm resorts to imperatives, asking Israel to praise God as the rest of the natural order does.

———◆———

J. HOFFMAN (TRANSLATION)

understand the idiom "to lift up a horn." Perhaps a particular sort of strength is intended, either sexual (see Volume 2, *The Amidah,* p. 143) or military or both. The syntax "strength of his nation" parallels "the phrase of his faithful," which constitutes the completion of this sentence where both expressions seem to be in apposition.

———◆ ◆ ◆———

BRETTLER (BIBLE)

[1] *"Sing a new song to Adonai"* (Psalm 149) This sentiment of singing a "new song" to God is found elsewhere, too (Isa. 42:10; Pss. 33:3; 40:4; 96:1; 98:1; 144:9). Though we typically think of ancient Israel as a highly traditional society, this call for a new song suggests that some believed then, as now, that newer was better.

[1] *"The faithful"* The *chasidim* (see Brettler, "And your faithful [*chasidim*]," p. 116).

[2] *"Let Israel rejoice in their maker"* Previous psalms mentioned Israel but had *(p. 140)*

FRANKEL (A WOMAN'S VOICE)

[1] *"Halleluyah! Sing a new song to Adonai"* How profoundly this psalm challenges our modern sensibilities! After praising God's goodness in birthing and sustaining creation, how can we now delight in wreaking vengeance *bagoyim,* on "the nations," those who are not God's *chasidim,* God's select "pious ones"? How can we set out, our swords drawn, to "bind their kings with chains, and their nobles with iron fetters"? Do we, in fact, still pray to this wrathful God? Do we still wish to number ourselves among this bloodthirsty tribe?

So uncomfortable have liberal Jews been with this particular psalm that many contemporary liberal prayer books — the Reform *Gates of Prayer,* the Reconstructionist *Kol Haneshamah,* Marcia Falk's *Book of Blessings* — have deleted either the entire psalm or just the four offending verses near its conclusion. Havurat Shalom's *Siddur Birkat Shalom* has substituted two verses from Isaiah — "Let them praise God with their voices, and the noise of violence will be heard no more in their land" (60:18) and "For the God of holiness is sanctified by acts of justice" (5:16) — in place of verses 6–9 in the psalm. As a people all too familiar with the vengeance of other nations, we Jews have *(p. 141)*

E. PSALM 149

DORFF (THEOLOGY)

[3] *"Let them praise his name in dance; let them play drums and harps for Him."* Worship with musical instruments and dance is an ancient Jewish practice, evidenced by this psalm and the next. Since fixing things is prohibited on the Sabbath, Festivals, and High Holy Days, instruments that can easily be fixed by the player should not be used then, but on all other days instruments are certainly permissible. Dance, too, is an ancient Jewish mode of worship. In the nineteenth and early twentieth centuries, Jews eschewed dance and most instruments in their worship, but these forms are *(p. 141)*

[1] Halleluyah! Sing a new song to Adonai, who is praised in the congregation of the faithful. [2] Let Israel rejoice in their maker; let the children of Zion celebrate their king. [3] Let them praise his name in dance; let them play drums and harps for Him. [4] For Adonai takes pleasure in his people, and adorns the meek with triumph. [5] Let the faithful exult in honor; let them rejoice on

J. HOFFMAN (TRANSLATION)

[4]*"Adonai takes pleasure in [rotseh b']"*
The Hebrew, which literally means
"wants in," is commonly used to express
how God feels about the people Israel.
Translated here as "takes pleasure in," it
might also mean "loves."

Spanish recognizes two words for
love: *amar* represents primarily love
between husband and wife, while
querer, which literally means "to want,"
represents platonic love. (Unlike "like"
in English, the platonic *querer* in
Spanish is used between children and
parents as well as between friends.) The
semantic connection between "want"
and "like/love" is attested in English as
well: "if you like" means the same thing
as "if you want." Perhaps in Hebrew, as
in Spanish, *rotseh,* which literally means
"wants," represents a specific type of
affection.

[6]*"A sword"* Others, "double-edged
sword," but that is an idiom in English
lacking in the Hebrew.

———◆———

הַלְלוּיָהּ. שִׁירוּ לַייָ שִׁיר חָדָשׁ, תְּהִלָּתוֹ בִּקְהַל[1]
חֲסִידִים. יִשְׂמַח יִשְׂרָאֵל בְּעֹשָׂיו, בְּנֵי צִיּוֹן[2]
יָגִילוּ בְמַלְכָּם. יְהַלְלוּ שְׁמוֹ בְמָחוֹל, בְּתֹף[3]
וְכִנּוֹר יְזַמְּרוּ לוֹ. כִּי רוֹצֶה יְיָ בְּעַמּוֹ, יְפָאֵר[4]
עֲנָוִים בִּישׁוּעָה. יַעְלְזוּ חֲסִידִים בְּכָבוֹד, יְרַנְּנוּ[5]

their beds. [6] Let there be praises of God in their mouths, and a sword in their hand, for avenging the nations and punishing the peoples, for binding their kings with chains, and their nobles with iron fetters, for meting out judgment as written. [7] He is the glory of all his faithful. Halleluyah!

עַל מִשְׁכְּבוֹתָם. [6] רוֹמְמוֹת אֵל בִּגְרוֹנָם, וְחֶרֶב פִּיפִיּוֹת בְּיָדָם, לַעֲשׂוֹת נְקָמָה בַּגּוֹיִם, תּוֹכֵחוֹת בַּלְאֻמִּים, לֶאְסֹר מַלְכֵיהֶם בְּזִקִּים, וְנִכְבְּדֵיהֶם בְּכַבְלֵי בַרְזֶל, לַעֲשׂוֹת בָּהֶם מִשְׁפָּט כָּתוּב. [7] הָדָר הוּא לְכָל חֲסִידָיו. הַלְלוּ־יָהּ.

BRETTLER (BIBLE)

a broader focus, while this psalm focuses exclusively on Israel. The previous psalm extolled God as universal creator; here, God is Israel's maker.

[3] *"Let them praise his name in dance"* The previous verse had called God "king"; kings regularly were praised with dance, not just music, as we see from 1 Sam. 18:6, "The women came out singing and dancing to greet King Saul." The continuation of this psalm ("a sword...for avenging the nations") locates this praise and dance within a military context.

[4] *"And adorns the meek with triumph"* The meaning of the people called *anavim* "meek," is uncertain. Some link them to the *chasidim,* understood as being a particular class or group (see Brettler, "And your faithful [*chasidim*]," p. 116). What exacerbates the problem is the fact that the Hebrew *anavim* (the "meek" or "humble") is often confused with *aniyim* ("the poor"). In any case, the point seems to be that even the most downtrodden will be saved by God — unlike typical military victories, which benefit the rich with booty, but not the poor.

[6] *"Let there be praises of God in their mouths, and a sword in their hand"* The referent is to the *chasidim* (the "faithful") of the previous verse. The ideal presented here is not quietistic piety, but faith combined with military action. God will avenge the nations, but only by coming to the aid of the pious as together they vanquish their common enemy.

[7] *"He is the glory of all his faithful"* Hadar ("glory") is sometimes used in a specifically military context — as in Ps. 45:4, for instance, "Gird your sword upon your thigh, O mighty One, in your glory and your majesty." That is clearly the context intended here. Although structured as a hymn of praise, the psalm has a covert purpose of encouraging

people to be *chasidim*, the true victors (see Brettler, "And your faithful [*chasidim*]," p. 116).

———◆———

Dorff (Theology)

increasingly reappearing. As Rabbi Abraham Isaac Kook, Chief Rabbi of the Jewish community in Palestine in the first third of the twentieth century, said in another context, "The old is becoming new, and the new is becoming sacred."

———◆———

Frankel (A Woman's Voice)

become hypervigilant about the consequences of violence. History has taught us that, more often than not, swords are indeed *pifiyot*, literally, "double-edged," frequently turning back upon those who brandish them.

So should we continue to recite this vindictive psalm as part of our morning prayers? Can it be redeemed, or should it be retired? Perhaps we can borrow a page from German Jewish folklore: Centuries ago, when it had become common practice for pregnant Jewish women to place an iron object under their pillows to protect themselves and their babies against demons, their rabbis cleverly co-opted this pagan ritual by "Judaizing" it. Through ingenious word play, they reinterpreted the Hebrew word for iron, *barzel*, as an acronym for Jacob's four wives — Bilhah, Rachel, Zilpah, and Leah — whose merits were being called upon to protect the woman and her unborn child.

So, too, can we transform these once angry words into our prayer that the leaders of other nations might one day be embraced by the wisdom of our foremothers so that we all, Jew and gentile, might together sing a new song.

———◆ ◆ ◆———

BRETTLER (BIBLE)

[1] *"Halleluyah! Praise God in his sanctuary"* This final psalm of the Psalter (Psalm 150) has a quite simple but elegant structure: with the exception of the last verse, each verse may be divided in half, where the second half is the synonymous parallel of the first. In addition, each successive verse in verses 1–5 is slightly longer than the previous one. Given that the theme of the psalm is the praise of God, this suggests a continuing, ever-growing groundswell of praise that will never end. It is hard to imagine a more success-ful ending to the group of Psalms 145–150, and to the Psalter itself.

[1-2] *"Sanctuary ... heaven of power"* "Sanctuary" probably refers to God's earthly abode, the Temple in Jerusalem; the verse's parallelism then suggests that the earthly praise of God mirrors that of the heavenly temple, the exact sentiment of the opening of the *K'dushah* in the *Amidah* (see Volume 2, *The Amidah*, p. 59): "Let us sanctify your name on earth as it is sanctified in the heavens on high."

[3-4] *"Praise him in his might... abundant greatness"* The reference to God's "might" and (p. 144)

FRANKEL (A WOMAN'S VOICE)

[1] *"Halleluyah! Praise God in his sanctuary"* Contemporary feminist scholars have documented a widespread practice among women in ancient Mediterranean cultures, including Israel, of greeting their people's triumphant armies with song, dance, and drumming. In certain traditional communities in this region, such practices continue to this day. Scholars have also found evidence that Israelite women once participated in levitical choirs in the Temple, which included performances with musical instruments and dance. Thus this psalm may afford us a glimpse of lost cultural norms that are now being rein-tegrated into Jewish tra-dition.

————◆————

F. PSALM 150

[1]Halleluyah! Praise God in his sanctuary. [2]Praise Him in his heaven of power. [3]Praise Him in his might. [4]Praise Him for his abundant greatness. [5]Praise Him with the shofar's blast. [6]Praise Him with harp and lyre. [7]Praise Him with drum and dance. [8]Praise Him with strings and flute. [9]Praise Him with resounding cymbals. [10]Praise Him with blasting cymbals.

[The following verse is said twice.]

[11]Let every breath praise God! Halleluyah.

HAUPTMAN (TALMUD)

[11] *"Let every breath [n'shamah] praise God"* This final verse in the Book of Psalms receives two diverse, but equally intriguing, interpretations in Jewish tradition, since its Hebrew subject, *n'shamah,* can mean either "breath" or "soul." Assuming that *n'shamah* means soul, the Gemara cites Mar Zutra bar Tuviah in the name of Rav: "From where do we learn that we must thank God even for fragrant smells? From the verse that says, 'Let every (p. 144)

KUSHNER & POLEN (CHASIDISM)

[11] *"Let every breath praise God! Halleluyah"* The Hebrew word for "breath," *n'shamah*, can also mean "soul." Levi Yitzhak of Berditchev, in his *Kedushas Levi* (Rosh Hashanah [after *devarim*], p. 277), understands "soul" as if it were a breath, a vapor whose natural state is floating upward. He reminds us, therefore, that at every moment our souls effectively want to leave us. Or to put it in a more sobering but accurate way, being alive is *not* the default position. The natural state of life is death. Without some intervening force, our souls would leave us all. It's almost as if what keeps us alive is that God, as it were, is pressing down on the lid and keeping our soul from escaping *(p. 145)*

L. HOFFMAN (HISTORY)

[11] *"Let every breath praise God. Halleluyah"* The last verse of Psalm 150 and, therefore, the last verse of the Book of Psalms. Traditionally, it is recited twice at this point in the service. It is a doxology (see p. 153, "Blessed be Adonai forever.... May his glory fill the entire earth. Amen and Amen"). The custom in medieval Spain was to recite the last verse of every psalm twice.

◆

¹הַלְלוּיָהּ. הַלְלוּ אֵל בְּקָדְשׁוֹ. ²הַלְלוּהוּ בִּרְקִיעַ
עֻזּוֹ. ³הַלְלוּהוּ בִגְבוּרֹתָיו. ⁴הַלְלוּהוּ כְּרֹב גֻּדְלוֹ.
⁵הַלְלוּהוּ בְּתֵקַע שׁוֹפָר. ⁶הַלְלוּהוּ בְּנֵבֶל וְכִנּוֹר.
⁷הַלְלוּהוּ בְּתֹף וּמָחוֹל. ⁸הַלְלוּהוּ בְּמִנִּים וְעֻגָב.
⁹הַלְלוּהוּ בְצִלְצְלֵי שָׁמַע. ¹⁰הַלְלוּהוּ בְּצִלְצְלֵי
תְרוּעָה.

¹¹כֹּל הַנְּשָׁמָה תְּהַלֵּל יָהּ. הַלְלוּיָהּ.

J. HOFFMAN (TRANSLATION)

9–10 *"Resounding cymbals [tsilts'lei shama]... blasting cymbals [tsilts'lei t'ruah]"*

Literally, *tsilts'lei shama* means "cymbals of sound," possibly a technical term for a type of cymbal, as opposed to "blasting cymbals," another specific percussion instrument of antiquity.

◆

LANDES (HALAKHAH)

[11] *"Let every breath praise God! Halleluyah"* This final verse of Psalm 150 is repeated because it is the last psalm verse in the Book of Psalms and, appropriately, the last psalm verse in the *P'sukei D'Zimrah*, too. Other material follows in this rubric, but none of it psalms (R'ma to *Shulchan Arukh*, O. Ch. 51:7 and *Sefer Hapardes*, a collection of law stemming from the school of Rashi [France, eleventh century]).

◆

BRETTLER (BIBLE)

"greatness" follows directly from the previous verse's reference to "his heaven of *power*." Together, these lines sum up the previous psalms, all of which emphasize, in different ways, God's abundant power as justification for praising Him.

6–10 *"Praise him with harp and lyre"* What follows is a veritable catalogue of musical instruments that must have been used in the Temple. In the Second Temple period, the Levites are recorded as using such instruments in connection with Temple worship. 1 Chron. 15:16 and 2 Chron. 5:12, for instance, list cymbals, harps, lyre, and trumpets.

9–10 *"Resounding cymbals…blasting cymbals"* Probably two types of cymbals, the loudest of the instruments. The list here ends with the music reaching an ever-louder crescendo.

11 *"Let every breath praise God! Halleluyah"* The poetic pattern of the rest of the psalm is broken by having a single line without parallelism, a typical rhetorical device to end a biblical poem. In content, the last half of the final verse of Psalm 145 (see Brettler, p. 117) ends with a similar line ("…and all creatures praise his holy name for ever and ever") and brings Psalms 145–150 together as a group, with the theme of all must praise God. This final psalm neatly provides the details of this praise, noting why God should be praised (He is powerful), where He must be praised (in the heavenly and earthly temples), how He must be praised (with various instruments), and who must praise Him (all that breathe). It is difficult to imagine a more suitable conclusion to Psalms.

HAUPTMAN (TALMUD)

n'shamah ["soul"] praise the Lord.' What is it that gives the soul, not the body pleasure? Fragrant smells" (Ber. 43b). Assuming that it means "breath," however, the Midrash cites Rabbi Levi in the name of Rabbi Chaninah: "For every single breath that we take we must praise God, for it says, 'Let every *n'shamah* ["breath"] praise God,'" (Bereshit Rabbah 14).

These two interpretations emphasize two equally important aspects of human experience. The notion that we are to thank God even for things that have no material substance, but that, nevertheless, give us pleasure, is deeply religious. We are to extend our gratitude even for phenomena that are so transitory as to have no physical substance. Not a moment goes by when we are not beneficiaries of God's generosity, since absolutely nothing in this world is our own creation — everything can be traced back to God. Anyone who benefits from anything at all in the world, even the smell of a blossoming flower, without thanking God is guilty of misappropriating holy property.

The second interpretation emphasizes an equally chimerical entity, but in our own bodies rather than in the outside world that our bodies experience. The only reason we can experience anything at all is that we are gifted with complex biological systems that operate automatically. We normally pay no attention at all to the internal organs that constitute our circulatory or pulmonary systems. Only if they stop functioning smoothly do we even know we have them, at which time we frantically pray for help to make them work effectively once again. Symbolic of these bodily processes, says Rabbi Levi, is every single breath we utter — the tiniest but most necessary of things that sustain us as interactive agents in God's universe. Each breath should be recognized as deriving from God.

———◆———

KUSHNER & POLEN (CHASIDISM)

from our bodies into the void! Here we have an expression of core spirituality. Every moment is now worthy of the simple ecstasy of and gratitude for simply being alive. "Oh, I'm alive *again!* Yet another moment of life!"

To this insight, Rabbi Israel Friedmann of Rizhyn (1797–1850) adds another teaching. If each moment God literally restores our life anew, then, in addition to joy and gratitude, we should also draw courage when we pray. For often when we try to raise ourselves in worship, our *yetzer,* our self-destructive side, our own personal internal enemy, seeks to undermine our resolve by asking, Who are we to pray? How dare such a sinner open his or her mouth!

We must realize, says the Rizhyner, that each and every moment we are new creatures. Just this instant, again, we have been born anew. And therefore we are without sin!

———————◆ ◆ ◆———————

4 | *Biblical Interlude II: Medieval Additions*

A. MIXTURE OF PSALM VERSES

1 Blessed be Adonai forever. Amen and Amen! (Ps. 89:53).

2 Blessed be Adonai from Zion, the One who dwells in Jerusalem. Halleluyah (Ps. 135:21).

3 Blessed be God, Adonai, the God of Israel, sole worker of wonders. 4 And blessed be his glorious name forever. 5 May his glory fill the entire earth. Amen and Amen (Ps. 72:18–19).

B. 1 CHRONICLES 29:10–13

1 So David blessed Adonai with the entire assembly watching. 2 David said: Blessed are You, Adonai, the God of Israel our father, from the beginning of time to the ends of time. 3 Greatness and power and glory and victory and majesty are yours, Adonai, with everything in the heavens and on earth. 4 The Kingdom is yours, Adonai, rising above everyone. 5 Riches and honor are arrayed before You, as You rule over all. 6 Your hand controls strength and power, and your hand makes everyone great and strong.

1 בָּרוּךְ יְיָ לְעוֹלָם. אָמֵן וְאָמֵן.

2 בָּרוּךְ יְיָ מִצִּיּוֹן, שֹׁכֵן יְרוּשָׁלָיִם. הַלְלוּיָה.

3 בָּרוּךְ יְיָ אֱלֹהִים, אֱלֹהֵי יִשְׂרָאֵל, עֹשֵׂה נִפְלָאוֹת לְבַדּוֹ. 4 וּבָרוּךְ שֵׁם כְּבוֹדוֹ לְעוֹלָם. 5 וְיִמָּלֵא כְבוֹדוֹ אֶת כָּל הָאָרֶץ. אָמֵן וְאָמֵן.

1 וַיְבָרֶךְ דָּוִיד אֶת יְיָ לְעֵינֵי כָּל הַקָּהָל. 2 וַיֹּאמֶר דָּוִיד, בָּרוּךְ אַתָּה יְיָ, אֱלֹהֵי יִשְׂרָאֵל אָבִינוּ, מֵעוֹלָם וְעַד עוֹלָם. 3 לְךָ יְיָ הַגְּדֻלָּה וְהַגְּבוּרָה וְהַתִּפְאֶרֶת וְהַנֵּצַח וְהַהוֹד, כִּי כֹל בַּשָּׁמַיִם וּבָאָרֶץ. 4 לְךָ יְיָ הַמַּמְלָכָה וְהַמִּתְנַשֵּׂא לְכֹל לְרֹאשׁ. 5 וְהָעֹשֶׁר וְהַכָּבוֹד מִלְּפָנֶיךָ, וְאַתָּה מוֹשֵׁל בַּכֹּל. 6 וּבְיָדְךָ כֹּחַ וּגְבוּרָה, וּבְיָדְךָ לְגַדֵּל וּלְחַזֵּק לַכֹּל.

7 And now, our God, we gratefully acknowledge You, and praise your glorious name.

⁷וְעַתָּה אֱלֹהֵינוּ, מוֹדִים אֲנַחְנוּ לָךְ, וּמְהַלְלִים לְשֵׁם תִּפְאַרְתֶּךָ.

C. Nehemiah 9:6–11

¹ You alone are Adonai. ² You made the heavens, the heavens of the heavens and all their hosts, the earth and all that is upon it, the seas and all that is in them, and You give life to all of them, and the heavenly hosts bow down to You. ³ You are Adonai our God, who chose Abram; ⁴ You brought him out of Chaldean Ur; ⁵ You made his name Abraham; ⁶ You found his heart true before You; ⁷ You made a covenant with him to give the land of the Canaanite, the Hittite, the Amorite, the Perizzite, the Jebusite, and the Girgashite, to give this to his descendants; ⁸ You fulfilled your word, for You are righteous; ⁹ You saw the poverty of our ancestors in Egypt; ¹⁰ You heard their cry by the Red Sea; ¹¹ You brought signs and wonders before Pharaoh and all his servants and all the people of his land, for You knew they were cruel to them; ¹² You made a name for yourself until this day; ¹³ You parted the sea before them so that they passed through the sea on dry land; ¹⁴ and You cast their pursuers into the depths, like a stone into mighty waters.

¹אַתָּה הוּא יְיָ לְבַדֶּךָ. ²אַתָּה עָשִׂיתָ אֶת הַשָּׁמַיִם, שְׁמֵי הַשָּׁמַיִם וְכָל צְבָאָם, הָאָרֶץ וְכָל אֲשֶׁר עָלֶיהָ, הַיַּמִּים וְכָל אֲשֶׁר בָּהֶם, וְאַתָּה מְחַיֶּה אֶת כֻּלָּם, וּצְבָא הַשָּׁמַיִם לְךָ מִשְׁתַּחֲוִים. ³אַתָּה הוּא יְיָ הָאֱלֹהִים, אֲשֶׁר בָּחַרְתָּ בְּאַבְרָם ⁴וְהוֹצֵאתוֹ מֵאוּר כַּשְׂדִּים ⁵וְשַׂמְתָּ שְׁמוֹ אַבְרָהָם. ⁶וּמָצָאתָ אֶת לְבָבוֹ נֶאֱמָן לְפָנֶיךָ. ⁷וְכָרוֹת עִמּוֹ הַבְּרִית לָתֵת אֶת אֶרֶץ הַכְּנַעֲנִי, הַחִתִּי, הָאֱמֹרִי, וְהַפְּרִזִּי וְהַיְבוּסִי וְהַגִּרְגָּשִׁי, לָתֵת לְזַרְעוֹ. ⁸וַתָּקֶם אֶת דְּבָרֶיךָ, כִּי צַדִּיק אָתָּה. ⁹וַתֵּרֶא אֶת עֳנִי אֲבוֹתֵינוּ בְּמִצְרָיִם. ¹⁰וְאֶת זַעֲקָתָם שָׁמַעְתָּ עַל יַם סוּף. ¹¹וַתִּתֵּן אֹתֹת וּמֹפְתִים בְּפַרְעֹה וּבְכָל עֲבָדָיו וּבְכָל עַם אַרְצוֹ, כִּי יָדַעְתָּ כִּי הֵזִידוּ עֲלֵיהֶם. ¹²וַתַּעַשׂ לְךָ שֵׁם כְּהַיּוֹם הַזֶּה. ¹³וְהַיָּם בָּקַעְתָּ לִפְנֵיהֶם, וַיַּעַבְרוּ בְתוֹךְ הַיָּם בַּיַּבָּשָׁה. ¹⁴וְאֶת רֹדְפֵיהֶם הִשְׁלַכְתָּ בִמְצוֹלֹת, כְּמוֹ אֶבֶן בְּמַיִם עַזִּים.

D. Shirat Hayam ("Song of the Sea" [Exodus 14:30–15:18])

¹ So on that day Adonai saved Israel from the power of the Egyptians, and Israel saw the Egyptians dead on the

¹וַיּוֹשַׁע יְיָ בַּיּוֹם הַהוּא אֶת יִשְׂרָאֵל מִיַּד מִצְרָיִם. וַיַּרְא יִשְׂרָאֵל אֶת מִצְרַיִם מֵת עַל שְׂפַת הַיָּם. ²וַיַּרְא

148

seashore. 2 Israel saw the great power that Adonai displayed before the Egyptians. 3 The nations feared Adonai, and believed in Adonai and in Moses his servant.

4 Moses and the children of Israel then sang unto Adonai this song:

5 I shall sing unto Adonai, who hath emerged victorious; He hurled horse and rider into the sea.

6 My strength and my might are God, who is my salvation.

7 This is my God whom I shall glorify; my father's God, whom I shall exalt.

8 Adonai is a warrior, Adonai is his name.

9 He cast Pharaoh's chariots and army into the sea, his choicest of officers drowning in the Red Sea.

10 The deep waters covered them; they plummeted into the depths like a stone.

11 Thy right hand, O Adonai, glorious in power; thy right hand, O Adonai, crushes the foe.

12 In thy triumph Thou destroyest thine enemies.

13 Thou sendest forth thy fury, to consume them as straw.

14 Thou didst blow the wind that piled up the waters, which stood like a liquid wall.

15 The depths froze in the heart of the sea.

16 Said the enemy: I will pursue and overtake, I will divide the spoil, that my appetite be sated by them. 17 I will bare my sword, that my hand subdue them.

יִשְׂרָאֵל אֶת הַיָּד הַגְּדֹלָה אֲשֶׁר עָשָׂה יְיָ בְּמִצְרַיִם, ²וַיִּירְאוּ הָעָם אֶת יְיָ, וַיַּאֲמִינוּ בַּייָ וּבְמשֶׁה עַבְדּוֹ.

⁴אָז יָשִׁיר משֶׁה וּבְנֵי יִשְׂרָאֵל אֶת הַשִּׁירָה הַזֹּאת לַייָ, וַיֹּאמְרוּ לֵאמֹר.

⁵אָשִׁירָה לַייָ כִּי גָאֹה גָּאָה. סוּס וְרֹכְבוֹ רָמָה בַיָּם.

⁶עָזִּי וְזִמְרָת יָהּ וַיְהִי לִי לִישׁוּעָה.

⁷זֶה אֵלִי וְאַנְוֵהוּ, אֱלֹהֵי אָבִי וַאֲרֹמְמֶנְהוּ.

⁸יְיָ אִישׁ מִלְחָמָה. יְיָ שְׁמוֹ.

⁹מַרְכְּבֹת פַּרְעֹה וְחֵילוֹ יָרָה בַיָּם, וּמִבְחַר שָׁלִשָׁיו טֻבְּעוּ בְיַם סוּף.

¹⁰תְּהֹמֹת יְכַסְיֻמוּ. יָרְדוּ בִמְצוֹלֹת כְּמוֹ אָבֶן.

¹¹יְמִינְךָ יְיָ נֶאְדָּרִי בַּכֹּחַ, יְמִינְךָ יְיָ תִּרְעַץ אוֹיֵב.

¹²וּבְרֹב גְּאוֹנְךָ תַּהֲרֹס קָמֶיךָ.

¹³תְּשַׁלַּח חֲרֹנְךָ, יֹאכְלֵמוֹ כַּקַּשׁ.

¹⁴וּבְרוּחַ אַפֶּיךָ נֶעֶרְמוּ מַיִם, נִצְּבוּ כְמוֹ נֵד נֹזְלִים.

¹⁵קָפְאוּ תְהֹמֹת בְּלֶב-יָם.

¹⁶אָמַר אוֹיֵב, אֶרְדֹּף אַשִּׂיג, אֲחַלֵּק שָׁלָל, תִּמְלָאֵמוֹ נַפְשִׁי. ¹⁷אָרִיק חַרְבִּי, תּוֹרִישֵׁמוֹ יָדִי.

18 Thou didst blow thy wind, that the sea cover them. 19 They sank like lead in the majestic waters.

20 Who is like Thee among the gods, Adonai!

21 Who is like Thee, adorned in holiness, revered in praise, worker of wonders.

22 Thou didst stretch out thy right hand, that the earth swallow them up.

23 In love didst Thou lead this people Thou redeemed.

24 In thy strength Thou hast led them to thine abode of holiness.

25 The peoples heard this, and they trembled.

26 Agony gripped the inhabitants of Philistia.

27 The clans of Edom dismayed.

28 The mighty of Moab by fear were gripped.

29 All the inhabitants of Canaan melted away.

30 Fear and trembling did befall them.

31 Thy mighty arm silences them like a stone, till thy people cross over, Adonai, till this people Thou hast redeemed crosses over.

32 Bring them and plant them on thy very mountain, the place Thou made for dwelling,

33 O Adonai, the sanctuary which thy hands established, O Adonai.

34 Adonai will reign for ever and ever.

35 Adonai will reign for ever and ever.

18 נָשַׁפְתָּ בְרוּחֲךָ, כִּסָּמוֹ יָם. 19 צָלְלוּ כַּעוֹפֶרֶת בְּמַיִם אַדִּירִים.

20 מִי כָמֹכָה בָּאֵלִם, יְיָ.

21 מִי כָּמֹכָה נֶאְדָּר בַּקֹּדֶשׁ, נוֹרָא תְהִלֹּת, עֹשֵׂה פֶלֶא.

22 נָטִיתָ יְמִינְךָ, תִּבְלָעֵמוֹ אָרֶץ.

23 נָחִיתָ בְחַסְדְּךָ עַם-זוּ גָּאָלְתָּ.

24 נֵהַלְתָּ בְעָזְּךָ אֶל נְוֵה קָדְשֶׁךָ.

25 שָׁמְעוּ עַמִּים, יִרְגָּזוּן.

26 חִיל אָחַז יֹשְׁבֵי פְּלָשֶׁת.

27 אָז נִבְהֲלוּ אַלּוּפֵי אֱדוֹם.

28 אֵילֵי מוֹאָב יֹאחֲזֵמוֹ רָעַד.

29 נָמֹגוּ כֹּל יֹשְׁבֵי כְנָעַן.

30 תִּפֹּל עֲלֵיהֶם אֵימָתָה וָפַחַד.

31 בִּגְדֹל זְרוֹעֲךָ יִדְּמוּ כָּאָבֶן עַד יַעֲבֹר עַמְּךָ, יְיָ, עַד יַעֲבֹר עַם-זוּ קָנִיתָ.

32 תְּבִאֵמוֹ וְתִטָּעֵמוֹ בְּהַר נַחֲלָתְךָ, מָכוֹן לְשִׁבְתְּךָ פָּעַלְתָּ.

33 יְיָ, מִקְּדָשׁ, אֲדֹנָי, כּוֹנְנוּ יָדֶיךָ.

34 יְיָ יִמְלֹךְ לְעֹלָם וָעֶד.

35 יְיָ יִמְלֹךְ לְעֹלָם וָעֶד.

36 For dominion is Adonai's, who rules over the nations.

37 Deliverers shall go up to Mount Zion to rule Esau's mountain, and dominion shall be Adonai's. 38 And Adonai shall be king over the entire earth.

39 On that day Adonai shall be one and his name shall be one.

³⁶כִּי לַיְיָ הַמְּלוּכָה, וּמוֹשֵׁל בַּגּוֹיִם.

³⁷וְעָלוּ מוֹשִׁיעִים בְּהַר צִיּוֹן לִשְׁפֹּט אֶת הַר עֵשָׂו, וְהָיְתָה לַיְיָ הַמְּלוּכָה. ³⁸וְהָיָה יְיָ לְמֶלֶךְ עַל כָּל הָאָרֶץ.

³⁹בַּיּוֹם הַהוּא יִהְיֶה יְיָ אֶחָד וּשְׁמוֹ אֶחָד.

BRETTLER (BIBLE)

[1] *"Blessed be Adonai forever. Amen and Amen!"* The previous section of P'sukei D'zimrah focused on the Hebrew root *h.l.l,* "to acknowledge" or "praise"(whence we get the liturgical term *Hallel* as psalms of praise). The Bible links prayer to other terms also, however, especially *b.r.kh,* "to bless" (from which we get *b'rakhah* ["blessing"] and the formal liturgical call to prayer, *Bar'khu et Adonai ham'vorakh* ["Bless Adonai who is to be blessed" — see Volume 1, *The Sh'ma and Its Blessings*, p. 27]) and the concluding formula *amen.* As if to balance the preponderance of *h.l.l* in the previous section, this short prayer begins immediately with the other two terms. It comprises three verses from Psalms (89:53; 135:21; 72:18–19), all of which begin, "Blessed be Adonai." Both the opening and closing lines contain "Amen and Amen." This structuring, where each verse begins the same way and the end of the last verse mirrors the end of the first, is typical of the Bible, so that the poetic juxtaposition of three diverse biblical verses, which occurs only here, is made to seem authentically biblical.

——◆——

A. MIXTURE OF PSALM VERSES

[1] Blessed be Adonai forever. Amen and Amen! (Ps. 89:53).

[2] Blessed be Adonai from Zion, the One who dwells in Jerusalem. Halleluyah (Ps. 135:21).

[3] Blessed be God, Adonai, the God of Israel, sole worker of wonders. [4] And blessed be his glorious name forever. [5] May his glory fill the entire earth. Amen and Amen (Ps. 72:18–19).

L. HOFFMAN (HISTORY)

ORIGINALLY, THE DAILY HALLEL LED DIRECTLY TO THE CONCLUDING BLESSING, KNOWN AS "THE BLESSING OF SONG" (BIRKAT HASHIR). MEDIEVAL JEWS, HOWEVER, INSERTED BIBLICAL QUOTATIONS: COLLECTION OF PSALM VERSES, 1 CHRON. 29:10–13, NEH. 9:6–11, AND EXOD. 14:30–15:18 ("THE SONG OF THE SEA" [SHIRAT HAYAM]).

1–5 *"Blessed be Adonai forever.... May his glory fill the entire earth. Amen and Amen"* Psalms 89:53, 135:21, and 72:18–19, which have been added after Psalm 150, the last psalm of the Psalter. We do not know for sure why these psalm verses are added here, but the choice of what to add is significant. The Book of Psalms is divided into five parts, each of which is called a book unto itself (Book 1 — Psalms 1–41; Book 2 — Psalms 42–72; Book 3 — Psalms 73–89; Book 4 — Psalms 90–106; Book 5 — Psalms 107–150). Each book ends with a verse offering God praise forever, followed by "Amen and Amen." These concluding verses are called doxologies. It cannot be accidental that two of the three additions here (Ps. 89:53, 72:18–19) are doxologies, the ends of Book 3 and then Book 2. In addition, it is traditional to repeat the last line of Psalm 150 (the end of

Book 5), which precedes these verses, so we really have three doxologies recited in all. We are, however, for reasons unknown, missing two: the ends of Book 1 (Ps. 41:14) and Book 4 (Ps. 106:48). Also the final verse of Psalm 135, which we do have, is not a doxology at all.

It is probable that various customs were once in use. Communities that added verses to the morning *Hallel* sometimes chose doxologies and sometimes did not; some of them used one or two verses only, and some chose three, four, or more. The final selection as we have it may be more accidental than anything else. However, once they were chosen, people tried to explain them, especially given the anomaly of one verse (Ps. 135:21) that seems to have been selected at random. Fourteenth-century David Abudarham, living in Spain, says that it too is a doxology that ends a Psalms book, and if he is right, then the books of Psalms were once divided differently. David ben Solomon ibn Yachya, a rabbi in Portugal who was exiled to Italy when the Spanish exile extended to Portugal also, offers the most interesting interpretation, perhaps, by looking carefully at the message of the verse in question: "Blessed be Adonai from Zion, the One who dwells in Jerusalem." In his day, that *(p. 154)*

¹בָּרוּךְ יְיָ לְעוֹלָם. אָמֵן וְאָמֵן.

²בָּרוּךְ יְיָ מִצִּיּוֹן, שֹׁכֵן יְרוּשָׁלָיִם. הַלְלוּיָהּ.

³בָּרוּךְ יְיָ אֱלֹהִים, אֱלֹהֵי יִשְׂרָאֵל, עֹשֵׂה נִפְלָאוֹת לְבַדּוֹ. ⁴וּבָרוּךְ שֵׁם כְּבוֹדוֹ לְעוֹלָם. ⁵וְיִמָּלֵא כְבוֹדוֹ אֶת כָּל הָאָרֶץ. אָמֵן וְאָמֵן.

L. HOFFMAN (History)

verse was clearly seen as messianic, looking ahead to the rebuilding of Jerusalem and the restoration of God's presence to the Temple. Ibn Yachya says that when God reenters Jerusalem, the messiah will be crowned and verse 135:21 will serve as a blessing that the people pronounce for the messiah's coronation.

◆ ◆ ◆

BRETTLER (BIBLE)

[1] *"So David blessed [vay'varekh] Adonai"* 1 Chronicles 29:10–13, a prayer by David after he laid the groundwork for the Temple that his son Solomon would build. In style, it mirrors the previous prayer here (see prior comment) by opening with a form of the root *b.r.kh* ("to bless"). Other parallel terms follow, however, thus recalling and tying together the various themes of Psalms 145–150, above.

[2] *"Blessed are You Adonai"* As noted in "Prayer in the Bible and the Use of the Bible in Later Jewish Prayer" (see p. 20), this is a late biblical formula, which becomes standard in rabbinic prayer. The Bible typically blesses God in the third rather than the second person.

[3-6] *"Greatness and power and glory...great and strong"* What follows is a list of (mostly) abstract attributes for God, joined together with the conjunction "and." Although many of these attributes were seen in Psalms 145–150, the structure here lacks the poetic parallelism of those psalms. Instead, it relies on accumulations of largely synonymous nouns, which we find again and again in post-biblical liturgical compositions, such as "Let your name be forever praised," the concluding section of *P'sukei D'zimrah* (see p. 178). *(p. 158)*

ELLENSON (MODERN LITURGIES)

[1] *"So David blessed Adonai with the entire assembly watching"* It is noteworthy that liberal liturgists such as Abraham Geiger in his 1854 Siddur and Isaac Mayer Wise in his *Minhag America* have included passages such as this as well as the Song of the Sea *(Shirat Hayam)*, which recalls the great epic of Israel's redemption at the Red Sea. *(p. 158)*

FRANKEL (A WOMAN'S VOICE)

[1] *"So David blessed Adonai"* Just as Psalm 148 harmonizes the images of God as both transcendent and immanent, as both remote and intimate, so here we find the seamless integration of myth and history in this chronicle of the world's unfolding. According to this account, God first made the natural cosmos; then chose Abraham, made a covenant with him, and deeded him a land inhabited by other nations. In time, God redeemed Abraham's descendants from Egyptian bondage to bring them to their promised land.

Not only for the Israelites but for all ancient cultures, this leap from primordial to national history was an altogether legitimate move: each people regarded itself as chosen to fulfill a sacred destiny — until a stronger nation's destiny trumped theirs. But unlike these other vanished *(p. 159)*

B. 1 CHRONICLES 29:10–13

[1] So David blessed Adonai with the entire assembly watching. [2] David said: Blessed are You, Adonai, the God of Israel our father, from the beginning of time to the ends of time. [3] Greatness and power and glory and victory and majesty are yours, Adonai, with everything in the

LANDES (Halakhah)

[1] *"So David blessed A-donai"* Even those who sit during the *P'sukei D'zimrah* (see Landes, "Blessed is the One by whose speech," p. 65) customarily stand from this point until the rubric's end, even though, technically, sitting is permitted during the beginning of the paragraph, "You alone are A-donai" *(atah hu A-donai l'vedekha)*, as this is only the introductory section to the Song of the Sea *(Shirat Hayam)*, which is of such importance that it is considered, by its nature, to be a section of prayer where standing is demanded.

———◆———

L. HOFFMAN (History)

[1] *"So David blessed Adonai"* The main section of the *P'sukei D'zimrah* is the psalms known as the Daily *Hallel* (see Introduction to the Liturgy, p. 7), but over time other material was inserted. "So David blessed Adonai" begins the second large insertion, a set of three biblical readings: 1 Chron. 29:10–13; Neh. 9:6–11; and Exod. 14:30–15:18, the Song of the Sea *(Shirat Hayam)*. Our first known prayer book, *Seder Rav Amram* (c. 860; see Volume 1, *The Sh'ma and Its Blessings*, p. 8), contains only the section from Chronicles, although elsewhere people were saying the Song of the Sea, and *(p. 159)*

¹וַיְבָרֶךְ דָּוִיד אֶת יְיָ לְעֵינֵי כָּל הַקָּהָל. ²וַיֹּאמֶר דָּוִיד, בָּרוּךְ אַתָּה יְיָ, אֱלֹהֵי יִשְׂרָאֵל אָבִינוּ, מֵעוֹלָם וְעַד עוֹלָם. ³לְךָ יְיָ הַגְּדֻלָּה וְהַגְּבוּרָה וְהַתִּפְאֶרֶת וְהַנֵּצַח וְהַהוֹד, כִּי כֹל

J. HOFFMAN (Translation)

[2] *"From the beginning of time to the ends of time [me'olam v'ad olam]"* The Hebrew is more succinct, but expresses the same point. Hebrew has (among others) two parallel words for "forever." *Me'olam* expresses "forever in the past up to now," and *l'olam* expresses "forever more" in the sense of from now on to the end of time.

[5] *"Are arrayed"* Literally, "are before you." But the addition of "You [God]" in English helps capture the flavor of the Hebrew.

———◆———

heavens and on earth. [4] The Kingdom is yours, Adonai, rising above everyone. [5] Riches and honor are arrayed before You, as You rule over all. [6] Your hand controls strength and power, and your hand makes everyone great and strong. [7] And now, our God, we gratefully acknowledge You, and praise your glorious name.

בַּשָּׁמַיִם וּבָאָרֶץ. [4] לְךָ יְיָ הַמַּמְ־לָכָה וְהַמִּתְנַשֵּׂא לְכֹל לְרֹאשׁ. [5] וְהָעֹשֶׁר וְהַכָּבוֹד מִלְּפָנֶיךָ, וְאַ־תָּה מוֹשֵׁל בַּכֹּל. [6] וּבְיָדְךָ כֹּחַ וּגְבוּרָה, וּבְיָדְךָ לְגַדֵּל וּלְחַזֵּק לַכֹּל. [7] וְעַתָּה אֱלֹהֵינוּ, מוֹדִים אֲנַחְנוּ לָךְ, וּמְהַלְלִים לְשֵׁם תִּפְאַרְתֶּךָ.

BRETTLER (BIBLE)

[7] *"And now, our God, we gratefully acknowledge You"* The logical conclusion of seeing God's vast power: acknowledging God through words of praise. In Chronicles, whence it is taken, the verse actually introduces a long prayer of praise, but that prayer refers expressly to the building of the Temple. Since that would not fit the general prayer context here, the excerpt from Chronicles concludes here.

———◆———

ELLENSON (MODERN LITURGIES)

Reconstructionist policy is interesting here. Its *Daily Prayer Book* of 1965, still echoing Mordecai Kaplan's theology and liturgical policy, had truncated the *P'sukei D'zimrah* to the point where it included only a single psalm, Psalm 67, which was entitled, "Let All the Peoples Acclaim God." Kaplan's emphatic universalism is evident in the choice.

The Reconstructionist *Kol Haneshamah* (1994), however, faithfully reproduces almost all the Hebrew of the Ashkenazi rite. But it omits the two passages that Wise included. This contemporary Reconstructionist prayer book may have two reasons in mind. First, these passages are accretions to this service and are needlessly repetitious of the themes found in the psalms already. Secondly, Reconstructionist editors may have had ethical problems with the way these prayers emphasize how God gave Abraham a land that belonged to others and how Israel celebrated God's furious destruction of the Egyptians. In both instances, we find a chauvinism and particularism that runs counter to the movement's traditional universalism. Reconstructionist authors may well have found that troubling.

———◆———

FRANKEL (A WOMAN'S VOICE)

peoples, the Jewish people — stubborn, stiff-necked, ever-hopeful Israel — has continued to point to its long-ago liberation from Egypt as irrefutable proof of its ultimate redemption, despite all historical experience to the contrary. Perhaps the key to such unshakable faith can be found in the paragraph preceding the historical narrative, where David affirms: "The Kingdom is yours, Adonai, rising above everyone…And now, our God, we gratefully acknowledge You, and praise your glorious name." David reminds us that gratitude, not pride, is the raw material of faith.

———◆———

L. HOFFMAN (HISTORY)

Amram's predecessor, Natronai Gaon (c. 855) writes explicitly to explain why he does *not* say it. By the eleventh century, it was becoming common in Europe to say the Song of the Sea, at least on Shabbat, probably because of a talmudic tradition (R.H. 31a) that it had been sung then in the Temple. Eventually, it became a daily staple as well, but there was still no agreement on where to say it. Maimonides, for instance, put it after the *P'sukei D'zimrah* was completed. French Jews said it here, however, as did some Jews in the Balkans, and in time, the custom of including it within the *P'sukei D'zimrah* spread throughout Europe.

But the juxtaposition of the two passages (1 Chronicles 29 and Exodus 14–15) was arbitrary, and the transition from one to the other was abrupt. So at some point (we do not know when) the passage from Nehemiah was added to link the two. The Chronicles paragraph ends with, "And now, our God, we gratefully acknowledge You and praise your glorious name." Nehemiah begins with that acknowledgment: "You alone are Adonai. You made the heavens…." The same Nehemiah passage ends with two verses that describe the safe passage of the Israelites through the Red Sea — exactly the event that prompted the Song of the Sea in Exodus 14–15!

————————◆ ◆ ◆————————

BRETTLER (BIBLE)

1-2 *"You alone are Adonai...and the heavenly hosts bow down to You"* Neh. 9:6–11, which was recited after Sukkot in the post-exilic community. Although we think of Nehemiah as a peripheral book, it is closer in time to the individual who inserted it here and thus reflects his ideology more closely than many of the earlier, "classical" sections of the Bible. It follows nicely from the prior prayer because in context (according to Neh. 9:5) the Levites recited this prayer, using the root *b.r.k*, "to bless." It also introduces the next prayers nicely (Nehemiah's recollection of Israel's sacred history and the Song of the Sea), since it introduces God's acts in history, a theme that is largely absent from Psalms 145–150.

From here to the end of the Song of the Sea (pp. 164–168), we get a balance to the psalms by emphasizing not just God's general greatness and his creative majesty but his salvation of Israel specifically.

The idea of God as the sole God, whom all must worship, becomes particularly predominant in late biblical texts, such as this one. By contrast, Deut. 4:19, for instance, mentions astral deities that God gave other nations to worship ("When you look up to the sky and behold the sun and the moon and the stars, the whole heavenly host, you must not be lured into bowing down to them or serving them. These the Lord your God allotted to other peoples"). Nevertheless, the heavenly hosts remain as angels of sorts. In contrast to later (especially Maimonidean) Judaism, such "beings" are not understood as interfering with monotheism.

3-8 *"You are Adonai...who chose Abram...You fulfilled your word, for You are righteous"* The depiction of Abraham largely follows the narrative of Genesis, with one significant exception: here, the covenant occurs only after God found Abraham's heart to be true, whereas in Genesis, it is "a covenant of grace," that is, an act of unexplained grace. Like the rabbinic tradition that follows, Nehemiah wonders why Abraham was chosen and provides a text with an appropriate answer.

9-14 *"You saw the poverty...into mighty waters"* A summary of the Exodus, following traditions from the Book of Exodus and from various psalms. The depiction of Abraham and the Exodus are placed in the context of a hymn. However, these events are not mentioned here merely as a matter of historical recollection; *(p. 162)*

C. NEHEMIAH 9:6–11

1 You alone are Adonai. 2 You made the heavens, the heavens of the heavens and all their hosts, the earth and all that is upon it, the seas and all that is in them, and You give life to all of them, and the heavenly hosts bow down to You. 3 You are Adonai our God, who chose Abram; 4 You brought him out of Chaldean Ur; 5 You made his name Abraham; 6 You found his heart true before

J. HOFFMAN (TRANSLATION)

[9] *"Poverty [oni]"* Birnbaum, "distress."

[12] *"Until this day"* Or, perhaps, "on that day." The question is whether God is being praised for what occurred on that specific day or for the echo of that day that has reverberated through history even unto now.

———◆———

¹אַתָּה הוּא יְיָ לְבַדֶּךָ. ²אַתָּה עָשִׂיתָ אֶת הַשָּׁמַיִם, שְׁמֵי הַשָּׁמַיִם וְכָל צְבָאָם, הָאָרֶץ וְכָל אֲשֶׁר עָלֶיהָ, הַיַּמִּים וְכָל אֲשֶׁר בָּהֶם, וְאַתָּה מְחַיֶּה אֶת כֻּלָּם, וּצְבָא הַשָּׁמַיִם לְךָ מִשְׁתַּחֲוִים. ³אַתָּה הוּא יְיָ הָאֱלֹהִים, אֲשֶׁר בָּחַרְתָּ בְּאַבְרָם ⁴וְהוֹצֵאתוֹ מֵאוּר כַּשְׂדִּים ⁵וְשַׂמְתָּ שְּׁמוֹ אַבְרָהָם. ⁶וּמָצֵאתָ אֶת לְבָבוֹ נֶאֱמָן

You; [7] You made a covenant with him to give the land of the Canaanite, the Hittite, the Amorite, the Perizzite, the Jebusite, and the Girgashite, to give this to his descendants; [8] You fulfilled your word, for You are righteous; [9] You saw the poverty of our ancestors in Egypt; [10] You heard their cry by the Red Sea; [11] You brought signs and wonders before Pharaoh and all his servants and all the people of his land, for You knew they were cruel to them; [12] You made a name for yourself until this day; [13] You parted the sea before them so that they passed through the sea on dry land; [14] and You cast their pursuers into the depths, like a stone into mighty waters.

לְפָנֶיךָ. [7] וְכָרוֹת עִמּוֹ הַבְּרִית לָתֵת אֶת אֶרֶץ הַכְּנַעֲנִי, הַחִתִּי, הָאֱמֹרִי, וְהַפְּרִזִּי וְהַיְבוּסִי וְהַגִּרְגָּשִׁי, לָתֵת לְזַרְעוֹ. [8] וַתָּקֶם אֶת דְּבָרֶיךָ, כִּי צַדִּיק אָתָּה. [9] וַתֵּרֶא אֶת עֳנִי אֲבֹתֵינוּ בְּמִצְרָיִם. [10] וְאֶת זַעֲקָתָם שָׁמַעְתָּ עַל יַם סוּף. [11] וַתִּתֵּן אֹתֹת וּמֹפְתִים בְּפַרְעֹה וּבְכָל עֲבָדָיו וּבְכָל עַם אַרְצוֹ, כִּי יָדַעְתָּ כִּי הֵזִידוּ עֲלֵיהֶם. [12] וַתַּעַשׂ לְךָ שֵׁם כְּהַיּוֹם הַזֶּה. [13] וְהַיָּם בָּקַעְתָּ לִפְנֵיהֶם, וַיַּעַבְרוּ בְתוֹךְ הַיָּם בַּיַּבָּשָׁה. [14] וְאֶת רֹדְפֵיהֶם הִשְׁלַכְתָּ בִמְצוֹלֹת, כְּמוֹ אֶבֶן בְּמַיִם עַזִּים.

BRETTLER (BIBLE)

they have an implicit element of petition as well, as God is asked to repeat these salvific activities.

◆ ◆ ◆

BRETTLER (Bible)

1–3 *"So on that day Adonai saved Israel...and believed in Adonai and in Moses his servant"* The conclusion of the prose account of the drowning of the Egyptians from Exod. 14:30–31 and used here to introduce the poetic account in chapter 15.

4 *"Moses and the children of Israel then sang unto Adonai this song"* The Song of the Sea (Exod. 15:1–18) is one of the most difficult and most beautiful biblical poems. Its poetic imagery and rare words make it exceedingly difficult to understand. The story that it offers differs

(p. 168)

ELLENSON (Modern Liturgies)

34–35 *"Adonai will reign for ever and ever. Adonai will reign for ever and ever"* In accordance with Sefardi custom, the prayer book of the Israeli Masorti (Conservative) Movement, includes, as optional, the Hebrew of Exod. 15:20–21 here. (As an Israeli book, no English is required.) The English version of the 1962 JPS Bible *(p. 171)*

FRANKEL (A Woman's Voice)

8 *"Adonai is a warrior"* Beginning with Psalm 149, which calls for vengeance against Israel's enemies, and concluding with this victory song celebrating Egypt's defeat at the Red Sea, we are swept along *(p. 171)*

D. *SHIRAT HAYAM* ("SONG OF THE SEA" [EXODUS 14:30–15:18])

DORFF
(Theology)
5–8 *"I shall sing unto Adonai, who hath emerged victorious... Adonai is a warrior;*

1 So on that day Adonai saved Israel from the power of the Egyptians, and Israel saw the Egyptians dead on the seashore. 2 Israel saw the great power that Adonai displayed before the Egyptians. 3 The nations feared Adonai, and believed in Adonai and in Moses his servant.

Adonai is his name" This song that Moses and the children of Israel sang after crossing the Red Sea is understandably a song of triumph. It aptly speaks of the great might God manifested in his victory over the Egyptians, arguably the most powerful nation of the time. The poem is filled with exuberant joy, as one might expect from those being surprisingly liberated from slavery in a most unanticipated way! Under such circumstances, one can readily understand, and perhaps even excuse, the militancy of the song. *(p. 170)*

HAUPTMAN (Talmud)

4 *"Moses and the children of Israel then sang"* According to the Talmud (R. H. 31a), this Song of the Sea (as it is called) was once recited only once a week, on Shabbat afternoons at *Minchah*, not every morning as part of *P'sukei D'zimrah*. Only in the Middle Ages did it become a standard part of the daily prayer service. The question is, Why was this song expanded to a daily occurrence? What was its appeal?

The answer may lie in its origins: it was first sung at the precise moment that the fleeing Israelites first *(p. 173)*

KUSHNER & POLEN (CHASIDISM)

[4] *"Moses and the children of Israel then sang unto Adonai this song"* The splitting of the sea happened twice! We have a second tradition of a "miraculous splitting of waters" and Israel passing through on dry ground, but few people think of it when asked to envision the splitting of the waters. The scene is recounted in Josh. 3:16–17, where we read that "the waters coming down from upstream piled up in a single heap a great way off.... So the people crossed near Jericho. The priests who bore the Ark of the Lord's covenant stood on dry land exactly in the middle of the Jordan, while all Israel crossed over on dry land, until the entire nation had finished crossing the Jordan."

(p. 173)

L. HOFFMAN (HISTORY)

[4] *"This song"* The Song of the Sea, known in Hebrew as *Shirat Hayam,* but so central to Jewish imagination that it is often called simply *Hashirah,* "The Song," as if there are no others to compare to it.

———

וַיּוֹשַׁע יְיָ בַּיּוֹם הַהוּא אֶת יִשְׂרָאֵל מִיַּד מִצְרָיִם. וַיַּרְא יִשְׂרָאֵל אֶת מִצְרַיִם מֵת עַל שְׂפַת הַיָּם. ²וַיַּרְא יִשְׂרָאֵל אֶת הַיָּד הַגְּדֹלָה אֲשֶׁר עָשָׂה יְיָ בְּמִצְרַיִם, ³וַיִּירְאוּ הָעָם אֶת יְיָ, וַיַּאֲמִינוּ בַּיְיָ וּבְמֹשֶׁה עַבְדּוֹ.

J. HOFFMAN (TRANSLATION)

[1] *"The power of the Egyptians"* Literally, "hand of the Egyptians," which would work well in English too, but below the word is repeated and there we need to see it as "power." We therefore use "power" here too, for consistency.

[4] *"This song"* The following text, taken from Exodus 15:1–18, is known as *Shirat Hayam,* the Song of the Sea. It contains what is perhaps the oldest Hebrew in the entire Bible and uses several Hebrew constructions that would have been archaic even when the Bible was written. In order to mimic this archaic flavor, and so that the English might stand out as the Hebrew did, we have used archaic English here in the translation. *(p. 174)*

LANDES (HALAKHAH)

[4] *"Moses and the children of Israel then sang"* This, the Song of the Sea *(Shirat Hayam)* is to be said with joy, as if one were presently crossing the Red Sea. This joy is sufficient to bring about atonement, causing forgiveness for sin *(Mishnah B'rurah* 51:17, following the Zohar). The verse that culminates the song section sums up its religious significance: "Adonai will rein for ever and ever" *(A-donai yimlokh l'olam va'ed).* Because it is such an important statement of faith, it is to be repeated before moving on (R'ma 51:7).

———

⁴Moses and the children of Israel then sang unto Adonai this song:

⁵I shall sing unto Adonai, who hath emerged victorious; He hurled horse and rider into the sea.

⁶My strength and my might are God, who is my salvation.

⁷This is my God whom I shall glorify; my father's God, whom I shall exalt.

⁸Adonai is a warrior; Adonai is his name.

⁹He cast Pharaoh's chariots and army into the sea, his choicest of officers drowning in the Red Sea.

¹⁰The deep waters covered them; they plummeted into the depths like a stone.

¹¹Thy right hand, O Adonai, glorious in power, thy right hand, O Adonai, crushes the foe.

¹²In thy triumph Thou destroyest thine enemies.

¹³Thou sendest forth thy fury, to consume them as straw.

¹⁴Thou didst blow the wind that piled up the waters, which stood like a liquid wall.

¹⁵The depths froze in the heart of the sea.

¹⁶Said the enemy: I will pursue and overtake, I will divide the spoil, that my appetite be sated by them. ¹⁷I

⁴אָז יָשִׁיר מֹשֶׁה וּבְנֵי יִשְׂרָאֵל אֶת הַשִּׁירָה הַזֹּאת לַיָי, וַיֹּאמְרוּ לֵאמֹר.

⁵אָשִׁירָה לַיָי כִּי גָאֹה גָּאָה. סוּס וְרֹכְבוֹ רָמָה בַיָּם.

⁶עָזִּי וְזִמְרָת יָהּ וַיְהִי לִי לִישׁוּעָה.

⁷זֶה אֵלִי וְאַנְוֵהוּ, אֱלֹהֵי אָבִי וַאֲרֹמְמֶנְהוּ.

⁸יָי אִישׁ מִלְחָמָה. יָי שְׁמוֹ.

⁹מַרְכְּבֹת פַּרְעֹה וְחֵילוֹ יָרָה בַיָּם, וּמִבְחַר שָׁלִשָׁיו טֻבְּעוּ בְיַם סוּף.

¹⁰תְּהֹמֹת יְכַסְיֻמוּ. יָרְדוּ בִמְצוֹלֹת כְּמוֹ אָבֶן.

¹¹יְמִינְךָ יָי נֶאְדָּרִי בַּכֹּחַ, יְמִינְךָ יָי תִּרְעַץ אוֹיֵב.

¹²וּבְרֹב גְּאוֹנְךָ תַּהֲרֹס קָמֶיךָ.

¹³תְּשַׁלַּח חֲרֹנְךָ, יֹאכְלֵמוֹ כַּקַּשׁ.

¹⁴וּבְרוּחַ אַפֶּיךָ נֶעֶרְמוּ מַיִם, נִצְּבוּ כְמוֹ נֵד נֹזְלִים.

¹⁵קָפְאוּ תְהֹמֹת בְּלֶב-יָם.

will bare my sword, that my hand subdue them.

18 Thou didst blow thy wind, that the sea cover them. 19 They sank like lead in the majestic waters.

20 Who is like Thee among the gods, Adonai!

21 Who is like Thee, adorned in holiness, revered in praise, worker of wonders.

22 Thou didst stretch out thy right hand, that the earth swallow them up.

23 In love didst Thou lead this people Thou redeemed.

24 In thy strength Thou hast led them to thine abode of holiness.

25 The peoples heard this, and they trembled.

26 Agony gripped the inhabitants of Philistia.

27 The clans of Edom dismayed.

28 The mighty of Moab by fear were gripped.

29 All the inhabitants of Canaan melted away.

30 Fear and trembling did befall them.

31 Thy mighty arm silences them like a stone, till thy people cross over, Adonai, till this people Thou hast redeemed crosses over.

16 אָמַר אוֹיֵב, אֶרְדֹּף אַשִּׂיג, אֲחַלֵּק שָׁלָל, תִּמְלָאֵמוֹ נַפְשִׁי. 17 אָרִיק חַרְבִּי, תּוֹרִישֵׁמוֹ יָדִי.

18 נָשַׁפְתָּ בְרוּחֲךָ, כִּסָּמוֹ יָם. 19 צָלְלוּ כַּעוֹפֶרֶת בְּמַיִם אַדִּירִים.

20 מִי כָמֹכָה בָּאֵלִם, יְיָ.

21 מִי כָּמֹכָה נֶאְדָּר בַּקֹּדֶשׁ, נוֹרָא תְהִלֹּת, עֹשֵׂה פֶלֶא.

22 נָטִיתָ יְמִינְךָ, תִּבְלָעֵמוֹ אָרֶץ.

23 נָחִיתָ בְחַסְדְּךָ עַם-זוּ גָּאָלְתָּ.

24 נֵהַלְתָּ בְעָזְּךָ אֶל נְוֵה קָדְשֶׁךָ.

25 שָׁמְעוּ עַמִּים, יִרְגָּזוּן.

26 חִיל אָחַז יֹשְׁבֵי פְּלָשֶׁת.

27 אָז נִבְהֲלוּ אַלּוּפֵי אֱדוֹם.

28 אֵילֵי מוֹאָב יֹאחֲזֵמוֹ רָעַד.

29 נָמֹגוּ כֹּל יֹשְׁבֵי כְנָעַן.

30 תִּפֹּל עֲלֵיהֶם אֵימָתָה וָפַחַד.

31 בִּגְדֹל זְרוֹעֲךָ יִדְּמוּ כָּאָבֶן עַד יַעֲבֹר עַמְּךָ, יְיָ, עַד יַעֲבֹר עַם-זוּ קָנִיתָ.

³²Bring them and plant them on thy very mountain, the place Thou made for dwelling,

³³O Adonai, the sanctuary which thy hands established, O Adonai.

³⁴Adonai will reign for ever and ever.

³⁵Adonai will reign for ever and ever.

³⁶For dominion is Adonai's, who rules over the nations.

³⁷Deliverers shall go up to Mount Zion to rule Esau's mountain, and dominion shall be Adonai's. ³⁸And Adonai shall be king over the entire earth.

³⁹On that day Adonai shall be one and his name shall be one.

³²תְּבִאֵמוֹ וְתִטָּעֵמוֹ בְּהַר נַחֲלָתְךָ, מָכוֹן לְשִׁבְתְּךָ פָּעַלְתָּ, יי.

³³מִקְדָּשׁ, אֲדֹנָי, כּוֹנְנוּ יָדֶיךָ.

³⁴יי יִמְלֹךְ לְעֹלָם וָעֶד.

³⁵יי יִמְלֹךְ לְעֹלָם וָעֶד.

³⁶כִּי לַיי הַמְּלוּכָה, וּמוֹשֵׁל בַּגּוֹיִם.

³⁷וְעָלוּ מוֹשִׁיעִים בְּהַר צִיּוֹן לִשְׁפֹּט אֶת הַר עֵשָׂו, וְהָיְתָה לַיי הַמְּלוּכָה. ³⁸וְהָיָה יי לְמֶלֶךְ עַל כָּל הָאָרֶץ.

³⁹בַּיּוֹם הַהוּא יִהְיֶה יי אֶחָד וּשְׁמוֹ אֶחָד.

BRETTLER (BIBLE)

slightly from the prose parallel of Exodus 14, and it "narrates" the Exodus in an expressionistic, nonchronological fashion, which makes it difficult to reconstruct the events as the poet understood them.

⁵ *"I shall sing unto Adonai, who hath emerged victorious; He hurled horse and rider into the sea"* As poetry, rather than historical narrative, the chapter starts at the end of the events — the drowning of the Egyptians.

⁶⁻⁷ *"My strength…whom I shall exalt"* As is typical of some hymns, praise of God is interspersed with the deeds that describe why God is so praiseworthy. God is called a "warrior," but the rest of the psalm establishes him as a king also. The central message is that God is a divine warrior-king who vanquished Pharaoh, a mere human warrior-king.

9–10 *"He cast Pharaoh's chariots and army into the sea...they plummeted into the depths like a stone"* The imagery here hardly fits the previous chapter's account of the sea splitting, allowing Israel to go through, and then suddenly closing in on the Egyptians.

11 *"Thy right hand"* Another general hymnic praise of God, interspersed with the narration of the events.

14–15 *"Thou didst blow the wind...like a liquid wall...heart of the sea"* Again, the imagery seems not to fit the prose version's account of a split sea with two columns of water. Instead, it suggests a type of tidal wave.

16 *"Said the enemy"* In this nonchronological telling of the tale, this is probably the earliest event.

20 *"Who is like Thee among the gods, Adonai!"* In this early poem, God is described as greater than any other God, but the existence of other deities is implicitly allowed. This early sentiment should be contrasted to Neh. 9:6, "You alone are Adonai" (see Brettler, "You alone are Adonai...and the heavenly hosts bow down to you," p. 160).

22 *"Thou didst stretch out thy right hand, that the earth swallow them up"* If this is not fancifully poetic, it suggests an earthquake, which is nowhere mentioned in the prose account of Exodus 14.

23–24 *"In love didst Thou lead this people...to thine abode of holiness"* The emphasis is on God's great power, so the various traditions about murmuring and rebellion in the desert are glossed over in this selective retelling.

25–30 *"The peoples heard this, and they trembled...Fear and trembling did befall them"* Not all biblical sources agree that the nations were afraid of Israel, though a similar tradition is attributed to Rahab the prostitute, who tells the spies how she has heard of God's great power and how she now fears God as the only God (Josh. 2:9–11).

31 *"Thy mighty arm silences them like a stone"* This image harks back to the depiction of God's powerful right hand and to the depiction of the Egyptians sinking like a stone.

32–33 *"On thy very mountain, the place Thou made for dwelling, O Adonai, the sanctuary which thy hands established"* Most likely, a reference to the Temple in Jerusalem, suggesting that this poem reached its current form in the tenth century or later, after the period of Solomon. The Temple is called "the place You made for your dwelling," in contrast to the later Deuteronomic conception, where only God's name dwells in Jerusalem, or the Priestly conception, where God's presence, *kavod*, dwells there.

34–35 *"Adonai will reign for ever and ever. Adonai will reign for ever and ever"* "Adonai will reign for ever and ever" is the short but climactic conclusion of the poem. For heightened effect it is repeated here liturgically. It underscores the song's main image: God's eternal kingship. This is most likely the earliest reference to God's kingship in the

Bible, and the archaic nature of the poem suggests how early and prevalent this theological idea was. Given the description of the surrounding deities as kings within their cultures, the early attribution of kingship to God should not be surprising.

36–39 *"For dominion is Adonai's...and his name shall be one."* The Song of the Sea concluded with a declaration of God's kingship, but tacked on here we get three additional biblical verses (Ps. 22:29; Obad. 1:21; Zech. 14:9 — "For dominion is Adonai's...his name shall be one") that also proclaim God's sovereignty. In context, they imply that God's kingship involves Israel's domination over the nations as well. They thereby explicitly develop an eschatological wish for the future — something absent in Exodus 15, which is concerned with the past.

—◆—

DORFF (THEOLOGY)

And yet, there is something disturbing and even embarrassing about this song. Yes, we rejoice in God's saving power, and yes, we understand that the Jewish people came into being as a nation through the events celebrated in it. But the image of God as a warrior is probably not what most of us have in mind when we think of God or what we have in heart when we pray to Him. We certainly want God to judge the arrogant and wicked; we understand that such judgment may require that they be killed; and we agree with the Bible when it says, "When the wicked perish, there is joy" (Prov. 11:10). But we still find ourselves disturbed by the image of God as a warrior and by the loss of Egyptian lives that was entailed in God's act of liberation and salvation.

We are not alone in this ambivalence. The Rabbis, too, felt it. Thus on Passover night we are told to diminish the cup of joy for our Exodus, and we shorten the *Hallel* during the last six days of Passover because some of God's children (the Egyptians) had to be killed in order for the Exodus to happen. God requires this diminished joy, say the Rabbis, for when the ministering angels began singing God's praise after the victory over the Egyptians, God rebuked them, saying, "My children are drowning in the sea, and you are singing songs?" (Meg. 10b).

The compiler of the Siddur, though, wanted to mute that ambivalence here. By putting the Song of the Sea at the end of *P'sukei D'zim'rah,* he concluded our preparation for prayer by having us ride the exuberant waves of our victory over our enemies and our celebration of the birth of our existence as a nation. We, as it were, march along with our ancestors from the slavery of our lethargy and our worldly concerns to Mount Sinai and the Promised Land, where we come to know the God of the *Sh'ma* and the *Amidah.* Moreover, in the last lines before the last paragraph, we look forward to the messianic times when Israel, Egypt, and all other nations will recognize God's sovereignty, when "Adonai shall be king over the entire earth. On that day Adonai shall be one and his name shall be one" — a verse written by the prophet Zechariah (14:9), articulating a hope important enough to be chosen as the final affirmation of the *Alenu* prayer, with which we ultimately end the service. If we were at all tentative and unsure of ourselves when we began the morning prayers, by the time we reach this point in the service we are to feel very much part of the community of Israel, eager to cross into an intense relationship with God.

———◆———

ELLENSON (MODERN LITURGIES)

reads, "Then Miriam the prophetess, Aaron's sister, took a timbrel in her hand, and all the women went out after her in dance with timbrels. And Miriam chanted for them, 'Sing to the Lord, for He has triumphed gloriously. Horse and driver He has hurled into the sea.'" By offering the Sefardi option here, *Va'ani T'filati* self-consciously selects a Jewish precedent that is consonant with its self-proclaimed goal of creating a gender-inclusive prayer book.

[39] *"On that day Adonai shall be one and his name shall be one"* Abraham Geiger did not conclude this prayer with this passage. Instead, following the Polish custom that informed the liturgy of Jews in Northern Germany, he added the line, "And in your Torah it is written, saying, 'Hear O Israel, Adonai is your God, Adonai is one.'" Indeed, this line is included in all German prayer books of the nineteenth century, including those of traditionalists such as Samson Raphael Hirsch (foremost ideologue and leader of nineteenth-century German Orthodoxy), Michael Sachs (of Berlin, whose translation of the traditional Siddur in 1855 influenced countless liturgies, both Orthodox and liberal), and Manuel Joel (prayer book author who succeeded Abraham Geiger in the 1860s as spiritual leader in Breslau, serving there also as professor of religious philosophy at the Jewish Theological Seminary).

———◆———

FRANKEL (A WOMAN'S VOICE)

by a triumphalist current. The imagery of this section of the morning prayers is graphic and violent: God is depicted as "a man of war," who sinks his enemy like a stone in the sea. So swift and total is God's victory that all the other nations are paralyzed by fear. Perhaps we too, as the survivors, are meant to tremble before this display of divine wrath, mindful of our own shortcomings and tendencies to backslide.

As with most militaristic imagery within the traditional liturgy, many contemporary liberal congregations have struggled to rehabilitate this scriptural passage. Some prayer books have simply omitted it. Some congregations skip over it when they come upon it in their prayer books. Others recite it quickly without translation. The fact is that, although the ancient Egyptians are long dead, we are still uncomfortable gloating over their defeat. In keeping with the spirit of our Seders, during which we pour out drops of wine to recall the sufferings of the Egyptians, we would rather not purchase our victory at another people's expense.

And in more recent times, many of us have identified another source of discomfort associated with this passage. As we recall here the ancient drama at the Red Sea, we realize that the compilers of the prayer book silenced Miriam's song when excerpting these biblical verses. Even though she speaks only one line in Exodus (15:21), and that line is a direct quotation from her brother's song, at least the Bible records her participation in the victory celebration. Why not the prayer book? Why do we hear only the voice of Moses? If our liturgists insist on including the Song of the Sea in our morning prayers, should we not include Miriam's brief song as well?

Some feminist scholars even claim that what we have preserved in the biblical account represents only a fragment of Miriam's original song. They maintain that over the centuries her much longer poem was either censured or lost, so that now we have only a trace of the original battle hymn, now irrecoverable. The least we can do, they argue, is to include what remains of her song within the holy space of our prayers.

But now we are caught on the horns of a dilemma: Should we *delete* the Song of the Sea because of its militarism, or should we *affirm and broaden* that militarism by including Miriam's victory chant: "Sing to Adonai, for God has triumphed gloriously; horse and driver God has hurled into the sea" (Exod. 15:21)? Which is the better course: to give voice to a second battle cry, or to silence them both?

Traditional liturgists attempted to address the issue of triumphalism by adding several verses after the conclusion of the Song of the Sea, culminating with the familiar phrases also found at the end of the *Alenu* prayer: "And Adonai shall be king over the entire earth. On that day Adonai shall be one and his name shall be one." When the messianic era dawns, there will no longer be a need for battles such as the one fought between Egypt and Israel at the Red Sea. At that time, we will no longer need to recite the Song of the Sea, "for nation shall no longer lift up sword against nation, neither shall they learn war any more."

But their solution is not adequate. We also need to address the issue of Miriam's song. Must she remain silent until that far-off day when all injustices will be righted? Have we not all, Jewish men and women, struggled together to survive as one people? As Miriam herself declares when she and Aaron later challenge their brother Moses (Num. 12:2), "Has Adonai spoken only through Moses? Has God not spoken through us as well?" What fighting words!

Alternatively, we might include here a second victory song, comparable in length and literary force to that of Moses: the Song of Deborah, which celebrates Israel's defeat of Sisera's army (Judges 5). Long ago, the Rabbis paired this poem with the Song of the Sea by making it the *Haftarah* for *Parashat B'shalach*. Why not carry forward their ancient insight?

——◆——

HAUPTMAN (TALMUD)

felt saved and safe, when they reached the far shore of the waters that they thought would drown them, with the Egyptian army miraculously gone before their very eyes. Not only were they no longer slaves — reason enough to break forth in song — but, in addition, there was the means by which salvation had occurred: God had just parted the sea on their behalf, a magnificent reversal of the laws of nature.

The Torah tells us (Exod. 15:1) that Moses and the Israelites sang this song to God, but the Talmud expands on the idea of collective recital, saying that children sitting on their mother's lap paused to sing the song. Even the infants feeding at their mother's breasts saw the *Sh'khinah* (the presence of God) and let go of the nipple to join the chorus. R. Meir adds: even the fetus inside the womb, who is said to have sensed God's presence and joined the festive singing (Sot. 30b). This delightful elaboration of the biblical verse illustrates the deeply spiritual and anti-elitist stance of the Rabbis. According to them, everyone, even the tiniest baby, experiences the awe that is inherent in God's presence. There is no limitation by age, gender, or level of sophistication. When God suspends the laws of nature, social barriers that are constructed by human beings, not by nature, disappear.

Rabbi Akiba and Rabbi Nehemiah (Sot. 30b) debate the details of how the people sang together with Moses: Did he call out the first line, after which they repeated part of the line after him, as was the practice for the recitation of *Hallel* in the synagogue? Or did they repeat everything that Moses said, the way they said the *Sh'ma?* To be sure, neither the *Hallel* nor the *Sh'ma* was around as a liturgical entity at the time of the Exodus, but the Rabbis, living much later, sought to understand the Song of the Sea through the filter of their own ritual experience. Neither they nor we can know the answer to questions like these, but the very fact that the Rabbis cared to ask them indicates their fascination with the Song of the Sea as, perhaps, *the* central instance of a Jewish response to the presence of God in history. No wonder this biblical poem was added to precisely the part of the morning service that is dedicated to praising God.

——◆——

KUSHNER & POLEN (CHASIDISM)

Yet only the miracle of the splitting of the Red Sea endures in the memory of the people. It is because of this song they sang there. The miracle of the splitting of the Jordan has not survived because there was no song (*Itturay Torah,* vol. III, p. 124).

——◆——

J. HOFFMAN (TRANSLATION)

⁶ *"My strength [ozi] and my might [zimrat] are God [yah]"* Rashi notes that if *ozi* is to mean "my strength," it ought to appear with different vowels *(uzi not ozi),* and so, perhaps, it is just a variant of the word "strength" *(oz)* Hebrew often adds the ending *-i* for poetic reasons. But it seems difficult to reconcile this otherwise reasonable suggestion with the rest of the line. *Zimrat* is even harder to understand. It is usually translated as "song," from the Hebrew *zemer,* but it is in parallelism with *ozi* and so ought to be something similar to "my strength." The probability of their intended parallelism is increased by the fact that *zimrat* reads *zimrati* in alternative manuscripts. The word means both "song" and "might," presenting a double entendre we cannot translate into English. But we choose "my might" here so as to parallel "my power."

¹⁴ *"Thou didst blow thy wind"* Literally, "by the wind of your [thy] nostrils," which was probably an idiom, and so best not translated word for word.

¹⁴ *"A liquid wall [ned nozlim]"* The Hebrew *ned* means "wall" but seems to be used exclusively with water.

¹⁶ *"That my appetite be sated"* This begins a series of parallel phrases in Hebrew, each employing the archaic Hebrew verbal ending *-eimo* ("them"). We translate each not archaically, since we have no parallel form, but we do make sure that the parallelism stands out by employing the subjunctive (and by now formal) English clause beginning with "that" (as in "that my appetite be sated").

²⁰ *"Who is like Thee"* Because we have chosen archaic language, our rendering here differs slightly from our translation of *Mi kamokha,* in the *Sh'ma* and Its Blessings (see Volume 1, *The Sh'ma and Its Blessings,* p. 130). Here, complete as in the original biblical context, it sounded archaic; taken over in part as a line in the blessing that follows the *Sh'ma,* it did not. Our translations in both places attempt to mirror the original intent.

²⁴ *"Thine abode of holiness"* Literally, just "holiness."

²²–²⁹ *"Philistia…Edom…Moab…Canaan"* Biblical enemies of Israel, a connotation lost, obviously, on today's reader.

²⁸ *"The mighty"* Or "elders."

²⁸ *"By fear were gripped"* This is the same *-eimo* ending mentioned above (see "That my appetite be sated"), no longer in a parallel string of several words using that ending, but still archaic. The expression in Hebrew is literally "gripped by trembling."

³⁰ *"Trembling"* Literally, something like "fear and dread," for which we have used the English idiom "fear and trembling."

³¹ *"Silences them like a stone"* That is, they (the people) are silent like a stone. This appears to be a metaphor whose meaning has been lost.

[31] *"The people Thou hast redeemed [am zu kanita]"* The Hebrew root *k.n.h* usually implies ownership and is translated as "bought, purchased." But that meaning is secondary to its larger meaning of "being master of." Humans achieve the right and power of mastery through purchase. God normally does so by creation (see discussion in Volume 1, *The Sh'ma and Its Blessings,* "Your creatures," p. 49). Here, God takes mastery of Israel by redeeming them. Hence, our translation, "The people Thou hast redeemed."

[34–35] *"Adonai will reign for ever and ever"* This line appears twice in Hebrew also.

[37] *"Esau's mountain"* Birnbaum, "hill country of Esau."

◆ ◆ ◆

5 | *Closing Blessing*

Yishtabach ("The Blessing of Song" *[Birkat Hashir]*)

¹Let your name be forever praised, our king, great and holy king and God, in the heavens and on earth. ²For song and praise, veneration and melody, strength and power, eternity, greatness and might, exaltation and glory, holiness and dominion, blessings and thanks befit You, Adonai our God and our ancestors' God, from now and ever more! ³Blessed are You, Adonai, God, greatly lauded king and God, God of grateful acknowledgment, Lord of wonders, who chooses melodious songs, our king, our God, eternal life.

¹שִׁשְׁתַּבַּח שִׁמְךָ לָעַד, מַלְכֵּנוּ, הָאֵל הַמֶּלֶךְ הַגָּדוֹל וְהַקָּדוֹשׁ, בַּשָּׁמַיִם וּבָאָרֶץ. ²כִּי לְךָ נָאֶה, יְיָ אֱלֹהֵינוּ וֵאלֹהֵי אֲבוֹתֵינוּ, שִׁיר וּשְׁבָחָה, הַלֵּל וְזִמְרָה, עֹז וּמֶמְשָׁלָה, נֶצַח, גְּדֻלָּה וּגְבוּרָה, תְּהִלָּה וְתִפְאֶרֶת, קְדֻשָּׁה וּמַלְכוּת, בְּרָכוֹת וְהוֹדָאוֹת, מֵעַתָּה וְעַד עוֹלָם. ³בָּרוּךְ אַתָּה, יְיָ, אֵל מֶלֶךְ גָּדוֹל בַּתִּשְׁבָּחוֹת, אֵל הַהוֹדָאוֹת, אֲדוֹן הַנִּפְלָאוֹת, הַבּוֹחֵר בְּשִׁירֵי זִמְרָה, מֶלֶךְ, אֵל, חֵי הָעוֹלָמִים.

BRETTLER (BIBLE)

[1] *"Let your name be forever praised"* The concluding prayer of *P'sukei D'zimrah*, and a post-biblical composition. With the rubric's introduction, "Blessed is the One," it forms an *inclusio* (a rhetorical style whereby the end reiterates the beginning; see Brettler, "Let my mouth speak Adonai's praise, and all creatures praise his holy name for ever and ever," p. 117).

[1] *"Our king, great and holy king"* As a summary prayer, it continues the central image of the *P'sukei D'zimrah*, God's kingship, which was stressed in the prayers leading up to it and in Psalms 145–150 before that.

[1] *"In the heavens and on earth"* Returning to the introductory verse of Psalm 150 (see Brettler, "Sanctuary… heaven of power," p. 142)

[2] *"For song and praise…blessings and thanks"* A string of largely synonymous nouns. This style begins in the late biblical period and develops later (see Brettler, "Greatness and power and glory…great and strong," p. 156).

[3] *"God, greatly lauded king…God of grateful acknowledgment"* A continuation of the style of the previous section, in this case, using short phrases that are very similar in meaning.

(p. 180)

FRANKEL (A WOMAN'S VOICE)

[1] *"Let your name be forever praised"* The *P'sukei D'zimrah* section of the morning prayers begins and ends with a call to praise God. We begin with a personal *kavvanah* (a prayer of intention): "With this do prepare my mouth to thank, praise, and glorify my creator" (see p. 49). Then, after having recited many psalms and hymns of praise, we round out this section with a concluding blessing, thanking God for accepting our songs of praise. After all, how dare we assume that our words will be adequate to the task of praising God? For even here, as we pile up a mountain of accolades — "song and praise, veneration and melody, strength and power, eternity, greatness and might, exaltation and *(p. 180)*

---

[1] Let your name be forever praised, our king, great and holy king and God, in the heavens and on earth. [2] For song and praise, veneration and melody, strength and power, eternity, greatness and might, exaltation and glory, holiness and dominion, blessings and thanks befit You, Adonai our God and our ancestors' God, from now and ever more! [3] Blessed are You, Adonai, God, greatly lauded king and God, God of grateful

---

HAUPTMAN (TALMUD)

[1] *"Let your name be forever praised"* The opening word of this concluding blessing *(Yishtabach)* comes from the Hebrew root *sh.b.ch*, meaning "praise." It is a very wordy, even repetitive prayer of praise that suggests how hopeless it is for finite human beings to relate God's infinite greatness with any degree of adequacy. To compensate for this insufficiency, we repeat God's praises again and again, thereby suggesting that his qualities are unmeasurable and hence untellable.

KUSHNER & POLEN (Chasidism)

[3] *"Who chooses melodious songs"* Zev Wolf of Zhitomir, in his *Or HaMeir* (*Yesod HaAvodah*, p. 28), is struck by the pleonasm of "melodious" and "songs" used together. Either word would have sufficed. He solves the problem by suggesting that the consonants that make up *shir,* the word for song *(shin, yod, resh),* might also be pronounced as *sh'yar,* meaning "leftover" (plural, *sh'yarim,* or, popularly, *shirayim).* Among Chasidim, *shirayim,* or "leftovers," refer to the crumbs remaining from a rebbe's meal. Though it strikes the modern reader as strange, to partake of these remnants — after they had been on the plate of such a holy person — was a great honor, even a gift. Disciples were *(p. 180)*

L. HOFFMAN (History)

AS THE P'SUKEI D'ZIMRAH *BEGAN WITH A BLESSING, SO NOW IT ENDS WITH ONE, CALLED, APPROPRIATELY, "THE BLESSING OF SONG"* (BIRKAT HASHIR). *SEVERAL ALTERNATIVE BLESSINGS WERE AVAILABLE WHEN THE RUBRIC BEGAN, BUT NOWADAYS, THE ONE WE USE IS* YISHTABACH *("LET YOUR NAME BE FOREVER PRAISED").*

[1] *"Let your name be forever praised"* The beginning of the closing blessing. We have several instances of a *Hallel* in the liturgy (see "The Daily *Hallel:* The Core of the *P'sukei D'zimrah,"* p. 7), all of which begin and end with a blessing. Bracketing biblical *(p. 181)*

¹יִשְׁתַּבַּח שִׁמְךָ לָעַד, מַלְכֵּנוּ, הָאֵל הַמֶּלֶךְ הַגָּדוֹל וְהַקָּדוֹשׁ, בַּשָּׁמַיִם וּבָאָרֶץ. ²כִּי לְךָ נָאֶה, יְיָ אֱלֹהֵינוּ וֵאלֹהֵי אֲבוֹתֵינוּ, שִׁיר וּשְׁבָחָה, הַלֵּל וְזִמְרָה, עֹז וּמֶמְשָׁלָה, נֶצַח, גְּדֻלָּה וּגְבוּרָה, תְּהִלָּה וְתִפְאֶרֶת, קְדֻשָּׁה וּמַלְכוּת, בְּרָכוֹת וְהוֹדָאוֹת, מֵעַתָּה וְעַד עוֹלָם. ³בָּרוּךְ אַתָּה, יְיָ, אֵל מֶלֶךְ גָּדוֹל בַּתִּשְׁבָּחוֹת, אֵל

J. HOFFMAN (Translation)

[3] *"Eternal life"* That is, the One who lives forever. ("Eternal liver" is obviously wrong.)

———◆———

LANDES (Halakhah)

[1] *"Let your name be forever praised"* Some blessings begin and end with *Barukh,* while others just end that way. The general rule is that the first of a series of blessings one after the other starts with the familiar *Barukh* formula, but blessings that follow it do not. Individual blessings that are not part of a string normally have the *Barukh* opening also. We would expect, then, that this, the culminating blessing of the *P'sukei D'zimrah,* would begin with *Barukh,* for it seems to *(p. 181)*

acknowledgment, Lord of wonders, who chooses melodious songs, our king, our God, eternal life.

הַהוֹדָאוֹת, אֲדוֹן הַנִּפְלָאוֹת, הַבּוֹחֵר בְּשִׁירֵי זִמְרָה, מֶלֶךְ, אֵל, חֵי הָעוֹלָמִים.

BRETTLER (BIBLE)

[3] *"Who chooses melodious songs"* "Choose" in the sense of "desire." The entire section concludes by justifying itself. The *P'sukei D'zimrah* will work because God likes melodious songs.

[3] *"Our king, our God, eternal life"* An effective summary of many of the attributes of God recited in the earlier hymns; indeed, the final phrase, *chei olamim,* here translated "eternal life," reiterates the extent of God's great power, the main theme of Psalms 145–150.

FRANKEL (A WOMAN'S VOICE)

glory, holiness and dominion, blessings and thanks are yours" — we fall far short of rendering sufficient homage to the infinite and eternal One. In the end, we can only *aspire* to praise, and hope that *el hahoda'ot,* "the God of grateful acknowledgment," will accept our yearning as its own fulfillment.

KUSHNER & POLEN (CHASIDISM)

known to fight with one another over the *shirayim:* the crumbs (or the songs!) from the master's table. It was not uncommon, furthermore, for each rebbe to have his (or her) own, either self-composed or favorite, melody. In this context, "melodious songs" now means "melodious leftovers" or "the remnants of a melody."

What remains when the music stops? Surely there must be more than dumb silence. The silence of the walk to the car after a symphony concert is now silent in a new way. The air is redolent with the remnants of the music. Some things simply cannot be uttered. And this is what God chooses — these remnants of song.

LANDES (HALAKHAH)

stand alone as the final bracket, so to speak, of the rubric as a whole. However, it is treated halakhically as if it is integrally connected to the opening blessing, "Blessed is the One by whose speech" *(Barukh she'amar),* with which the rubric began (see p. 49). A worshiper therefore never makes this blessing without the opening one and, since they are intended as brackets for biblical praise, at least the *Ashre* must be recited (Psalm 145, see p. 112). If one says it alone, it is treated as a "blessing said in vain" *(b'rakhah l'vatalah),* an instance of taking God's name in vain *(Shulchan Arukh,* O. Ch. 536; *Mishnah B'rurah* 3:4).

Because it is a blessing over the singing of praise to God, by which we mean all the psalms and songs that precede it and that constitute the *P'sukei D'zimrah,* it should be sung sweetly *(Kaf Hachayim* 48).

[2]*"Song and praise...blessings and thanks"* Fifteen terms of praise, all in all. It is customary to sing all the way through them without any interruption.

———◆———

L. HOFFMAN (HISTORY)

material with rabbinic blessings was the norm. We have it in the *Sh'ma* too, for instance, and also in the reading of Torah.

The blessing that follows a *Hallel* is called *Birkat Hashir,* "The Blessing of Song," an apt title for the conclusion of a section dedicated to singing God's praise. The Mishnah (Pes. 10:7) already knows about a Blessing of Song said after the *Hallel* that is recited as part of the Passover Seder, but it does not tell us what the prayer actually was. The Talmud's attempt to identify it evokes the citation of two prayers that must have functioned as Blessings of Song, and the one we have here is yet a third.

There is no way to know who wrote it or when, but that has not stopped people from trying to deduce its authorship. The fourteenth-century Spanish commentator, David Abudarham, for instance, noted that the five words in the middle of the prayer *shimkha la'ad malkenu ha'el* begin with *shin, lamed, mem,* and *heh*—the consonants that spell the Hebrew name Shlomo, from which he concluded, "Perhaps the sage who wrote this was named Solomon, and he composed it in honor of King Solomon."

The person who is the prayer leader usually changes at this point in the service. Until now, the liturgy has been a "warm-up" to the main prayers, the *Sh'ma* and Its Blessings and the *Amidah.* Traditionally, the role of leading the congregation in prayer becomes more important once the introductory warm-up is completed. The person who acts officially as the cantor, therefore, usually takes over the service only at this point.

Technically, the change should wait until the Blessing of Song is over, since the blessing is still part of the *P'sukei D'zimrah.* But it was considered unlucky to stop for conversation between the end of the *P'sukei D'zimrah* and the beginning of the *Sh'ma* and Its Blessings. Medieval authorities cite the Palestinian Talmud as saying that anyone who talks then commits a sin. Our versions of the Palestinian Talmud lack that line, but we do have a midrash that tells a relevant story in the name of Rabbi Elazar ben Rabbi Yose: "I was out for a walk once, when I ran into Elijah the prophet, may he be remembered for good, and with him were 4,000 camels, all loaded with a heavy burden. 'What are the camels carrying?' I asked. He answered, 'They are carrying fury and anger, to pay back people who talk between the end of *P'sukei D'zimrah* and the beginning of the *Sh'ma* and Its Blessings.'"

Now we know why the prayer leader for the main prayers does not wait to begin until after the *P'sukei D'zimrah* really concludes. In order to go directly from one rubric to the other without a pause in which people might converse, the prayer leader for the main sections of the service begins here.

Interestingly enough, Amram, the author of our first prayer book, reports the ban on talking, but he modifies it. He permits discussion regarding the needs of the community or on behalf of someone poor who is being fed from the communal *tzedakah* fund and who stops by to receive help.

In their discussion of this prayer, medieval law codes usually include requirements for a prayer leader. These go back to the Mishnah (c. 200) but received considerable interpretation in the years that followed. They are matters of knowledge and of character. According to Joseph Caro (sixteenth century), prayer leaders must be free of sin, with a good reputation, humble, and acceptable to the congregation. They must also be gifted with a "sweet voice that penetrates the heart of those who hear it," and they have to be practiced in reading any passage in the Bible. If no one is available with all these traits, we are to choose "the best person available in terms of wisdom and good deeds."

◆ ◆ ◆

About the Commentators

MARC BRETTLER

Marc Brettler, PhD, is Dora Golding Professor of Biblical Studies in the Department of Near Eastern and Judaic Studies at Brandeis University. His major areas of research are biblical historical texts, religious metaphors, and gender issues in the Bible. Brettler is author of *God Is King: Understanding an Israelite Metaphor* (Sheffield Academic Press), *The Creation of History in Ancient Israel* (Routledge), *The Book of Judges* (Routledge), *How to Read the Bible* (Jewish Publication Society), and *How to Read the Jewish Bible* (Oxford University Press), as well as a variety of articles on the Bible, and he has contributed to *Who by Fire, Who by Water* —Un'taneh Tokef; *All These Vows* —Kol Nidre; *We Have Sinned: Sin and Confession in Judaism* —Ashamnu *and* Al Chet; *May God Remember: Memory and Memorializing in Judaism* —Yizkor; *Naming God:* Avinu Malkeinu— *Our Father, Our King*; and *Encountering God:* El Rachum V'chanun— *God Merciful and Gracious*, all in the *Prayers of Awe* series (Jewish Lights). He is also associate editor of the new edition of the *Oxford Annotated Bible* and coeditor of the *Jewish Study Bible* (Oxford University Press).

ELLIOT N. DORFF

Elliot N. Dorff, PhD, is rector and Sol and Anne Dorff Distinguished Professor of Philosophy at American Jewish University (formerly the University of Judaism) in Los Angeles. His book *Knowing God: Jewish Journeys to the Unknowable* (Rowman and Littlefield) includes an extensive analysis of the nature of prayer. Ordained a rabbi at The Jewish Theological Seminary of America, Dorff is vice-chair of the Conservative Movement's Committee on Jewish Law and Standards, and he contributed to the Conservative Movement's Torah commentary, *Etz Hayim*. He has chaired the Jewish Law Association, the Society of Jewish Ethics, and the Academy of Jewish Philosophy, and he is immediate past president of Jewish Family Service of Los Angeles. He has served on several federal and California government commissions on issues in bioethics. Winner of the National Jewish Book Award for *To Do the Right and the Good: A Jewish Approach to Modern Social Ethics*, he has written numerous books and more than 150 articles on Jewish thought, law, and ethics. His latest books are *The Way Into Tikkun Olam (Repairing the World)*, a finalist for the National Jewish Book Award; *The Jewish Approach to Repairing the World (Tikkun Olam): A Brief Introduction for Christians* (both Jewish Lights); and *The Unfolding Tradition: Jewish Law After Sinai* (Aviv Press of the Rabbinical Assembly).

DAVID ELLENSON

David Ellenson, PhD, is chancellor of Hebrew Union College–Jewish Institute of Religion. He holds the Gus Waterman Herrman Presidential Chair and is the I. H. and Anna Grancell Professor of Jewish Religious Thought. Ordained a rabbi by Hebrew Union College–Jewish Institute of Religion, he has served as a visiting professor at Hebrew University in Jerusalem, at The Jewish Theological Seminary in New York, and at the University of California at Los Angeles. Ellenson has also taught at the Pardes Institute of Jewish Studies and at the Shalom Hartman Institute, both in Jerusalem. Ellenson has published and lectured extensively on diverse topics in modern Jewish thought, history, and ethics. His book *After Emancipation* (HUC Press) won the National Jewish Book Award in the category of Modern Jewish Thought and Experience. He is also a contributor to *Encountering God:* El Rachum V'chanun— *God Merciful and Gracious* (Jewish Lights).

ELLEN FRANKEL

Dr. Ellen Frankel is editor emerita of and a consultant to the Jewish Publication Society. A scholar of Jewish folklore, Frankel has published several books, including *The Classic Tales; The Encyclopedia of Jewish Symbols,* coauthored with artist Betsy Teutsch; *The Five Books of Miriam: A Woman's Commentary on the Torah; The Jewish Spirit;* and *The Illustrated Hebrew Bible.* Frankel travels widely as a storyteller and lecturer, speaking at synagogues, summer study institutes, Hillels, Jewish women's groups, Jewish community centers, museums, schools, retirement communities, and nursing homes, and to radio audiences.

JUDITH HAUPTMAN

Judith Hauptman, PhD, is the E. Billi Ivry Professor of Talmud at the Jewish Theological Seminary in New York City. Her many publications focus on Talmud, Jewish feminism, and their points of intersection. The author of *Rereading the Mishnah: A New Approach to Ancient Jewish Texts* (Paul Mohr Verlag); *Development of the Talmudic Sugya: Relationship between Tannaitic and Amoraic Sources* (University Press of America); and *Rereading the Rabbis: A Woman's Voice* (Westview/HarperCollins), she is currently researching religious pluralism in the Talmud.

JOEL M. HOFFMAN

Dr. Joel M. Hoffman lectures around the globe on popular and scholarly topics spanning history, Hebrew, prayer, and Jewish continuity. He has served on the faculties of Brandeis University, the Academy for Jewish Religion, and Hebrew Union College–Jewish Institute of Religion in New York. Hoffman writes about Hebrew for the international *Jerusalem Post,* and is the author of *In the Beginning: A Short History of the Hebrew Language* and *And God Said: How Translations Conceal the Bible's Original Meaning.* He contributed to *My People's Passover Haggadah: Traditional Texts, Modern Commentaries*; and *Who by Fire, Who by Water* —Un'taneh Tokef; *We Have Sinned: Sin and Confession in Judaism* —Ashamnu *and* Al Chet; *May God Remember: Memory and Memorializing in Judaism* —Yizkor; *All the World: Universalism, Particularism and the High Holy Days; Naming God:* Avinu Malkeinu—*Our Father, Our King*; and *Encountering God:* El Rachum V'chanun— *God Merciful and Gracious,* all in the *Prayers of Awe* series (Jewish Lights). He lives in Katonah, New York.

LAWRENCE A. HOFFMAN

Lawrence A. Hoffman, PhD, was ordained by and received his doctorate from Hebrew Union College–Jewish Institute of Religion. He has served in its New York campus for more than three decades, most recently as the Barbara and Stephen Friedman Professor of Liturgy, Worship and Ritual. Widely recognized for his scholarship and classroom teaching, Hoffman has combined research with a passion for the spiritual renewal of contemporary Judaism. He has written and edited over thirty books, including *Who by Fire, Who by Water*—Un'taneh Tokef; *All These Vows*—Kol Nidre; *We Have Sinned: Sin and Confession in Judaism*—Ashamnu *and* Al Chet; *May God Remember: Memory and Memorializing in Judaism*—Yizkor; *All the World: Universalism, Particularism and the High Holy Days*; *Naming God:* Avinu Malkeinu—*Our Father, Our King*; and *Encountering God:* El Rachum V'chanun—*God Merciful and Gracious*, all in the *Prayers of Awe* series; *My People's Passover Haggadah: Traditional Texts, Modern Commentaries*, in two volumes (all Jewish Lights), a finalist for the National Jewish Book Award; *The Art of Public Prayer: Not for Clergy Only* (SkyLight Paths, Jewish Lights' sister imprint), now used nationally by Jews and Christians as a handbook for liturgical planners in church and synagogue; as well as a revision of *What Is a Jew?*, the best-selling classic that remains the most widely read introduction to Judaism ever written in any language. He is also the author of *Israel—A Spiritual Travel Guide: A Companion for the Modern Jewish Pilgrim* and *The Way Into Jewish Prayer* (both Jewish Lights). Hoffman is a founder of Synagogue 3000, a transdenominational project designed to transform synagogues into the moral and spiritual centers of the twenty-first century. His book *Rethinking Synagogues: A New Vocabulary for Congregational Life* (Jewish Lights), an outgrowth of that project, was a finalist for the National Jewish Book Award.

REUVEN KIMELMAN

Reuven Kimelman, PhD, is professor of Near Eastern and Judaic studies at Brandeis University. He has written extensively on the liturgy, ethics, and history of the Talmudic period with a special focus on Jewish-Christian relations in late antiquity. He has written two books on the liturgy, *The Rhetoric of Jewish Prayer: A Historical and Literary Commentary on the Prayerbook* (The Littman Library of Jewish Civilization) and *The Mystical Meaning of* Lekha Dodi *and* Kabbalat Shabbat (Magnes Press, The Hebrew University), and is a contributor to *Who by Fire, Who by Water*—Un'taneh Tokef; *All These Vows*—Kol Nidre; *We Have Sinned: Sin and Confession in Judaism*—Ashamnu *and* Al Chet; *All the World: Universalism, Particularism and the High Holy Days*; and *Naming God:* Avinu Malkeinu—*Our Father, Our King*, all in the *Prayers of Awe* series; and the *Modern Men's Torah Commentary* (all Jewish Lights).

LAWRENCE KUSHNER

Lawrence Kushner is the Emanu-El scholar at Congregation Emanu-El in San Francisco, an adjunct faculty member at Hebrew Union College–Jewish Institute of Religion, and a visiting professor of Jewish spirituality at the Graduate Theological Union in Berkeley, California. He served as spiritual leader of Congregation Beth El in Sudbury, Massachusetts, for twenty-eight years and is widely regarded as one of the most creative religious writers in America. Ordained a rabbi by Hebrew Union College–Jewish Institute of Religion, Kushner led his congregants in publishing their own prayer book, *V'taher Libenu* (Purify Our Hearts), the first gender-neutral liturgy ever written. Through his lectures and many books, including *Filling Words with Light: Hasidic and Mystical Reflections on Jewish Prayer* (with Nehemia Polen); *The Way Into Jewish Mystical Tradition; Invisible Lines of Connection: Sacred Stories of the Ordinary; The Book of Letters: A Mystical Hebrew Alphabet; Honey from the Rock: An Introduction to Jewish Mysticism; God Was in This Place and I, i Did Not Know: Finding Self, Spirituality, and Ultimate Meaning; Eyes Remade for Wonder: A Lawrence Kushner Reader; Jewish Spirituality: A Brief Introduction for Christians;* and *I'm God; You're Not: Observations on Organized Religion and other Disguises of the Ego*, all published by Jewish Lights, he has helped shape the Jewish community's present focus on personal and institutional spiritual renewal. He has also published a novel, *Kabbalah: A Love Story.*

DANIEL LANDES

Daniel Landes is director and Rosh HaYeshivah of the Pardes Institute of Jewish Studies in Jerusalem and was an adjunct professor of Jewish law at Loyola University Law School in Los Angeles. Ordained a rabbi by Rabbi Isaac Elchanan Theological Seminary, Landes was a founding faculty member of the Simon Wiesenthal Center and the Yeshiva of Los Angeles. He has lectured and written various popular and scholarly articles on the subjects of Jewish thought, social ethics, and spirituality. He is also a contributor to *Who by Fire, Who by Water—* Un'taneh Tokef; *All These Vows*—Kol Nidre; *We Have Sinned: Sin and Confession in Judaism—* Ashamnu *and* Al Chet; *May God Remember: Memory and Memorializing in Judaism*—Yizkor; and *All the World: Universalism, Particularism and the High Holy Days*, all in the *Prayers of Awe* series (Jewish Lights).

NEHEMIA POLEN

Nehemia Polen is professor of Jewish thought and director of the Hasidic Text Institute at Boston's Hebrew College. He is the author of *The Holy Fire: The Teachings of Rabbi Kalonymus Shapira, the Rebbe of the Warsaw Ghetto* (Jason Aronson) as well as many academic and popular articles on Chasidism and Jewish spirituality, and coauthor of *Filling Words with Light: Hasidic and Mystical Reflections on Jewish Prayer* (Jewish Lights). He received his PhD from Boston University, where he studied with and served as teaching fellow for Nobel laureate Elie Wiesel. In 1994 he was Daniel Jeremy Silver Fellow at Harvard University, and he has also been a visiting scholar at the Hebrew University in Jerusalem. He was ordained a rabbi at the Ner Israel Rabbinical College in Baltimore, Maryland, and served as a congregational rabbi for twenty-three years. In 1998–1999 he was a National Endowment for the Humanities Fellow, working on the writings of Malkah Shapiro (1894–1971), the daughter of a noted Chasidic master, whose Hebrew memoirs focus on the spiritual lives of women in the context of prewar Chasidism in Poland. This work is documented in his book *The Rebbe's Daughter* (Jewish Publication Society), winner of the National Jewish Book Award.

List of Abbreviations

Artscroll	*Siddur Kol Ya'akov,* 1984.
Birnbaum	*Daily Prayer Book: Hasiddur Hashalem,* 1949.
FOP	*Forms of Prayer,* 1997.
Fox	Everett Fox, *The Five Books of Moses* (New York: Schocken Books, 1995).
GOP	*Gates of Prayer,* 1975.
SSS	*Siddur Sim Shalom,* 1985.
KH	*Kol Haneshamah,* 1994.
JPS	*Jewish Publication Society Bible* (Philadelphia: Jewish Publication Society, 1962).
NRSV	*New Revised Standard Bible,* 1989.
SLC	*Siddur Lev Chadash,* 1995.
SOH	*Service of the Heart,* 1967.
UPB	*Union Prayer Book,* 1894–1895.

Glossary

The following glossary defines Hebrew words used regularly throughout this volume, and provides the way the words are pronounced. Sometimes two pronunciations are common, in which case the first is the way the word is sounded in proper Hebrew, and the second is the way it is sometimes heard in common speech, under the influence of Yiddish, the folk language of Jews in northern and eastern Europe (it is a combination, mostly, of Hebrew and German). Our goal is to provide the way that many Jews actually use these words, not just the technically correct version.

- The pronunciations are divided into syllables by dashes.
- The accented syllable is written in capital letters.
- "Kh" represents a guttural sound, similar to the German (as in "sprach").
- The most common vowel is "a" as in "father," which appears here as "ah."
- The short "e" (as in "get") is written either "e" (when it is in the middle of a syllable) or "eh" (when it ends a syllable).
- Similarly, the short "i" (as in "tin") is written either "i" (when it is in the middle of a syllable) or "ih" (when it ends a syllable).
- A long "o" (as in "Moses") is written "oe" (as in the English word "toe") or "oh" (as in the English word "Oh!").

Acharonim (pronounced ah-khah-roe-NEEM, or, commonly, ah-chah-ROE-nim): The name given to Jewish legal authorities from roughly the sixteenth century on. The word means, literally, "later ones," as opposed to the "earlier ones," authorities prior to that time who are held in higher regard and are called *rishonim* (pronounced ree-shoe-NEEM, or, commonly, ree-SHOE-nim). Singular: *acharon* (pronounced ah-chah-RONE) and *rishon* (pronounced ree-SHONE).

Adon Olam (pronounced ah-DOHN oh-LAHM): An early morning prayer of unknown authorship, but dating from medieval times, and possibly originally intended as a nighttime prayer, because it praises God for watching over our souls when we sleep. Nowadays, it is used also as a concluding song for which composers have provided a staggering variety of tunes.

Alenu (pronounced ah-LAY-noo): The first word and, therefore, the title of a major prayer compiled in the second or third century as part of the New Year *(Rosh Hashanah)* service, but from about the fourteenth century on, used also as part of the concluding section of every daily service. *Alenu* means "it is incumbent upon us…" and introduces the prayer's theme: our duty to praise God.

Amidah (pronounced either ah-mee-DAH or ah-MEE-dah): One of three commonly used titles for the second of two central units in the worship service, the first being The *Sh'ma* and Its Blessings. It is composed of a series of blessings, many of which are petitionary, except on Sabbaths and holidays, when the petitions are removed out of deference to the holiness of the day. Also called *T'fillah* and *Sh'moneh Esreh*. *Amidah* means "standing," and refers to the fact that the prayer is said standing up.

Amora (pronounced ah-MOE-rah): A title for talmudic authorities and, therefore, living roughly from the third to the sixth centuries. Plural: *amoraim* (pronounced ah-moe-rah-EEM, or, commonly, ah-moe-RAH-yim). Often used in contrast to a *tanna* (pronounced TAH-nah), the title of authorities in the time of the Mishnah, that is, prior to the third century. Plural: *tannaim* (pronounced tah-nah-EEM, or, commonly, tah-NAH-yim).

Arvit (pronounced ahr-VEET, or, commonly, AHR-veet): From the Hebrew word *erev* (pronounced EH-rev) meaning "evening." One of two titles used for the evening worship service (also called *Ma'ariv*).

Ashkenazi (pronounced ahsh-k'-nah-ZEE, or, commonly, ahsh-k'-NAH-zee): From the Hebrew word *Ashkenaz,* meaning the geographic area of northern and eastern Europe; *Ashkenazi* is the adjective, describing the liturgical rituals and customs practiced there, as opposed to *Sefardi,* meaning the liturgical rituals and customs that are derived from *Sefarad,* Spain (see *Sefardi*).

Ashre (pronounced ahsh-RAY, or, commonly, AHSH-ray): The first word and, therefore, the title of a prayer said three times each day, composed primarily of Psalm 145. *Ashre* means "happy" and introduces the phrase "Happy are they who dwell in your [God's] house."

Avodah (pronounced ah-voe-DAH): Literally, "sacrificial service," a reference to the sacrificial cult practiced in the ancient Temple until its destruction by the Romans in the year 70 C.E.; also the title of the third to last blessing in the *Amidah,* a petition for the restoration of the Temple in messianic times. Many liberal liturgies either omit the blessing or reframe it as a petition for divine acceptance of worship in general.

Avot (pronounced ah-VOTE): Literally, "fathers" or "ancestors," and the title of the first blessing in the *Amidah.* The traditional wording of the blessing recollects the covenantal relationship between God and the patriarchs: Abraham, Isaac, and Jacob. Most liberal liturgies include also explicit reference to the matriarchs: Sarah, Rebekah, Rachel, and Leah.

[The] Bach (pronounced BAHKH): An acronym for Rabbi Joel Sirkes (Poland, 1561–1640), formed by juxtaposing the two Hebrew initials of his major legal work, *Bayit Chadash* (BaCH).

Bar'khu (pronounced bah-r'-KHOO, or, commonly, BAH-r'khoo): The first word and, therefore, the title of the formal call to prayer with which the section called The *Sh'ma* and Its Blessings begins. *Bar'khu* means "praise," and introduces the invitation to the assembled congregation to praise God.

Barukh k'vod (pronounced bah-RUKH k'-VOD): The first two words of a response in the third blessing of the *Amidah* taken from Ezekiel 3:12, meaning "the glory of Adonai is blessed from his place."

Barukh she'amar (pronounced bah-ROOKH sheh-ah-MAHR): Literally, "Blessed is the One by whose speech [the world came to be]," the first words, and, therefore, the title of the blessing that opens the *P'sukei D'zimrah,* the "warm-up" section to the morning service composed mainly of biblical material (chiefly psalms) that were intended to be sung as praise of God.

Benediction (also called **Blessing**): One of two terms used for the Rabbis' favorite prose formula for composing prayers. The worship service is composed of many different literary genres, but most of it is benedictions. Long benedictions end with a summary line that begins *Barukh atah Adonai...* "Blessed are You, Adonai..." Short blessings have only the summary line alone.

Ben Sirah (pronounced behn SIH-rah): Author of a book of wisdom similar in style to Proverbs, probably dating to 180 or 280 B.C.E., and containing, among other things, a moving description of the High Priest in the Jerusalem Temple. Though not included in the Jewish Bible, it is known because it became part of Catholic scripture. The book carries the author's name, but is called, by Catholics, Ecclesiasticus. A recently discovered Hebrew edition of Ben Sirah contains a prayer that some identify (probably incorrectly) as an early version of the *Amidah* (see *Amidah*).

Binah (pronounced bee-NAH, or, commonly, BEE-nah): Literally, "knowledge" or "understanding," and the title of the fourth blessing in the daily *Amidah*. It is a petition for human knowledge, particularly insight into the human condition, leading to repentance.

Birkat (pronounced beer-KAHT): Literally, "Blessing of..." The titles of many blessings are known as "Blessing of...," for example, "Blessing of Torah" and "Blessing of Jerusalem." Some titles are commonly shortened so that only the qualifying last

MY PEOPLE'S PRAYER BOOK

words are used (such as "Jerusalem" instead of "Blessing of Jerusalem"), and they are listed in the glossary by the last words, e.g., *Y'rushalayim* instead of *Birkat Y'rushalayim* ("Jerusalem" instead of "Blessing of Jerusalem"). Those blessings that are more generally cited with the full title appear under *Birkat.*

Birkat Hashir (pronounced beer-KAHT hah-SHEER): Literally, "Blessing of song," and the title, therefore, of the final blessing to the *P'sukei D'zimrah,* the "warm-up" section to the morning service composed mainly of biblical material (chiefly psalms) that were intended to be sung as praise of God. Technically, a *Birkat Hashir* concludes any *Hallel* (see **Hallel**), in this case, the Daily Hallel, which is the central component of the *P'sukei D'zimrah.*

Birkat Hatorah (pronounced beer-KAHT hah-toe-RAH): Literally, "Blessing of Torah," the title for the second blessing in the liturgical section called The *Sh'ma* and Its Blessings; its theme is the revelation of the Torah to Israel on Mount Sinai.

Birkat Kohanim (pronounced beer-KAHT koe-hah-NEEM): Literally, "blessing of the priests," but usually referred to as "the priestly benediction," a reference to Numbers 6:24–25. Also the title of the final blessing of the *Amidah.* See also **Kohanim.**

Birkhot Hashachar (pronounced beer-KHOT hah-SHAH-khar): Literally, "Morning Blessings," the title of the first large section in the morning prayer regimen of Judaism; originally said privately upon arising in the morning, but now customarily recited immediately upon arriving at the synagogue. It is composed primarily of benedictions thanking God for the everyday gifts of health and wholeness, as well as study sections taken from the Bible and rabbinic literature.

B'rakhah (pronounced b'-rah-KHAH): The Hebrew word for "benediction" or "blessing." See **Benediction.** Plural ("benedictions") is *b'rakhot* (pronounced b-'rah-KHOT).

Chanukah (pronounced KHAH-noo-kah): An eight-day festival beginning on the twenty-fifth day of the Hebrew month of Kislev, corresponding, usually, to some time in December. Chanukah celebrates the miraculous deliverance of the Jews as described in the books known as *Maccabees* (pronounced MA-ka-bees). Although not canonized in the Jewish Bible, Maccabees is carried in Catholic scripture and describes the heroic acts of a priestly family, known also as the Maccabees, or the Hasmoneans (pronounced has-moe-NEE-'ns), in 167 B.C.E.

Chasidism (pronounced KHAH-sih-dism or khah-SEE-dism): The doctrine generally traced to an eighteenth-century Polish Jewish mystic and spiritual leader known as the Ba'al Shem Tov (called also the BeSHT, an acronym composed of the initials of his name B, SH, and T.) Followers are called *Chasidim* (pronounced khah-see-DEEM or khah-SIH-dim; singular, *Chasid* pronounced khah-SEED, or, commonly, KHA-sid) from the Hebrew word *chesed* (pronounced KHEH-sed), meaning "loving-kindness" or "piety."

Chatimah (pronounced chah-tee-MAH): The final summary line of a benediction (see *Benediction*).

Cheshvan (pronounced KHESH-vahn): A Hebrew month corresponding to late October or November.

Daily Hallel (pronounced hah-LAYL, or, commonly, HAH-layl): English for *Hallel sheb'khol yom*. See *Hallel*.

David (pronounced dah-VEED): Literally, "David," a reference to the biblical King David, and the title of the fifteenth blessing of the daily *Amidah*, a petition for the appearance of the messianic ruler said by tradition to be a descendent of King David. Some liberal liturgies omit the blessing or reframe it to refer to a messianic age of perfection, but without the arrival of a human messianic ruler.

Doxology: Technical term for a congregational response to an invitation to praise God; generally a single line of prayer affirming praise of God forever and ever. Examples in The *Sh'ma* and Its Blessings are the responses to the Call to Prayer and to the *Sh'ma* itself. From the Greek word *doxa*, meaning "glory."

El Adon (pronounced ayl ah-DOHN): An early medieval (or, perhaps, ancient) poem celebrating God as a king enthroned on high; it is arranged as an acrostic, that is, each line begins with a different letter of the alphabet. Nowadays *El Adon* is a popular Sabbath morning hymn.

Eretz Yisrael (pronounced EH-retz yis-rah-AYL): Hebrew for "the Land of Israel."

Gaon (pronounced gah-OHN; plural: *G'onim,* pronounced g'-oh-NEEM): Title for the leading rabbis in Babylon (present-day Iraq) from about 750 to 1038. From a biblical word meaning "glory," which is equivalent in the title to saying "Your Excellence."

Genizah (pronounced g'-NEE-zah): A cache of documents, in particular the one discovered at the turn of the twentieth century in an old synagogue in Cairo; the source of our knowledge about how Jews prayed in the Land of Israel and vicinity prior to the twelfth century. From a word meaning "to store or hide away," "to archive."

G'ulah (pronounced g'-oo-LAH): Literally, "redemption" or "deliverance," and the title of the seventh blessing of the daily *Amidah,* as well as the third blessing in The *Sh'ma* and Its Blessings; its theme affirms God's redemptive act of delivering the Israelites from Egypt, and promises ultimate deliverance from suffering and want at the end of time.

G'vurot (pronounced g'voo-ROTE): Literally, "strength" or "power," and the title of the second blessing in the *Amidah*. It affirms the power of God to bring annual rain and new growth in nature and, by extension, to resurrect the dead. Some liberal liturgies omit the belief in resurrection or replace it with wording that suggests other concepts of eternal life.

Haftarah (pronounced hahf-tah-RAH, or, commonly, hahf-TOE-rah): The section of Scripture taken from the prophets and read publicly as part of Shabbat and holiday worship services. From a word meaning "to conclude," since it is the "concluding reading," that is, it follows a reading from the Torah (the five books of Moses).

Haggadah (pronounced hah-gah-DAH, or, commonly, hah-GAH-dah): The liturgical service for the Passover eve Seder meal. From a Hebrew word meaning "to tell," since the *Haggadah* is a telling of the Passover narrative.

Halakhah (pronounced hah-lah-KHAH, or, commonly, hah-LAH-khah): The Hebrew word for "Jewish law." Used as an anglicized adjective, *halakhic* (pronounced hah-LAH-khic), meaning "legal." From the Hebrew word meaning "to walk, to go," so denoting the way on which a person should walk through life.

Hallel (pronounced hah-LAYL, or, commonly, HAH-layl): A Hebrew word meaning "praise," and by extension, the name given to sets of psalms that are recited liturgically in praise of God: Psalms 145–150, the Daily *Hallel*, is recited each morning; Psalm 136, the Great *Hallel*, is recited on Shabbat and holidays and is part of the Passover *Seder*. Psalms 113–118, the best-known *Hallel*, known more fully as the Egyptian Hallel, is recited on holidays and gets its name from Psalm 114:1, which celebrates the moment "when Israel left Egypt."

Hallel Sheb'khol Yom (pronounced hah-LAYL [or, commonly, HAH-layl] sheh-b'-khol YOHM): The Hebrew term for "The Daily *Hallel*." See **Hallel**.

Halleluyah (pronounced hah-l'-loo-YAH, but sometimes anglicized as hah-l'-LOO-yah): A common word in psalms, meaning "praise God," and the final word of a congregational response within the third blessing of the *Amidah* (from Psalm 146:10).

Hat'fillah (pronounced hah-t'-fee-LAH): Literally, "the *T'fillah*," another name for the *Amidah*. See *T'fillah*.

Hoda'ah (pronounced hoe-dah-AH): Literally, a combination of the English words "gratitude" and "acknowledgment," so translated here as "grateful acknowledgment." The title of the second to last blessing in the *Amidah*, an expression of our grateful acknowledgment to God for the daily wonders that constitute human existence.

Hoeche K'dushah (pronounced HAY-kh' k'DOO-shah): A Yiddish term combining German and Hebrew and meaning, literally, "the High *Kedushah*." Refers to a way to shorten the time it takes to say the *Amidah* by avoiding the necessity of having the prayer leader repeat it all after it is said silently by the congregation.

Inclusio (pronounced in-CLOO-zee-oh): A rhetorical style common to biblical prayer, whereby the end of a composition reiterates the theme or words with which the composition began.

Kabbalah (pronounced kah-bah-LAH, or, commonly, kah-BAH-lah): A general term for Jewish mysticism, but used properly for a specific mystical doctrine that began in western Europe in the eleventh or twelfth centuries; recorded in the *Zohar* (see *Zohar*) in the thirteenth century, and then was further elaborated, especially in the Land of Israel (in Safed), in the sixteenth century. From a Hebrew word meaning "to receive" or "to welcome," and secondarily, "tradition," implying the receiving of tradition from one's past.

Kabbalat Shabbat (pronounced kah-bah-LAHT shah-BAHT): Literally, "welcoming Sabbath," and therefore a term for the introductory synagogue prayers that lead up to the arrival of the Sabbath at sundown Friday night.

Kaddish (pronounced kah-DEESH, or, more commonly, KAH-dish): One of several prayers from a Hebrew word meaning "holy," and therefore the name given to a prayer affirming God's holiness. This prayer was composed in the first century but later found its way into the service in several forms, including one known as the Mourners' *Kaddish* and used as a mourning prayer.

Kavvanah (pronounced kah-vah-NAH): From a word meaning "to direct," and therefore used technically to denote the state of directing one's words and thoughts sincerely to God, as opposed to the rote recitation of prayer.

K'dushah (pronounced k'-doo-SHAH, or, commonly, k'-DOO-shah): From the Hebrew word meaning "holy," and therefore one of several prayers from the first or second century occurring in several places and versions, all of which have in common the citing of Isaiah 6:3: *kadosh, kadosh kadosh...*, "Holy, holy, holy is the Lord of hosts. The whole earth is full of his glory."

K'dushat Hashem (pronounced gah-doo-SHAHT hah-SHEM): Literally, "sanctification of the name [of God]," and the full name for the prayer that is generally called *K'dushah* (see *K'dushah*). Best known as the third blessing in the *Amidah*, but found also prior to The *Sh'ma* and Its Blessings. Used also as a term to describe dying for the sanctification of God's name, that is, martyrdom.

Keva (pronounced KEH-vah): A Hebrew word meaning "fixity, stability," and therefore the aspect of a service that is fixed and immutable: the words on the page, perhaps, or the time at which the prayer must be said. In the early years, when prayers were delivered orally and improvised on the spot, *keva* meant the fixed order in which the liturgical themes had to be expressed.

Kibbutz Galuyot (pronounced kee-BOOTS gah-loo-YOTE): Literally, "gathering the exiles," and the title of the tenth blessing of the daily *Amidah,* a petition for Jews outside the Land of Israel to return home to their land as a sign that messianic times are imminent. Some liberal liturgies omit the blessing or interpret it more broadly to imply universal messianic liberation, but without the literal belief that Jews outside the Land of Israel are in "exile," or that they need to or want to "return home."

Kiddush (pronounced kee-DOOSH, or, commonly, KIH-d'sh): Literally, "sanctification," the name given to the prayer recited over wine at the outset of Sabbaths and holy days, declaring the day in question sanctified. A shorter version is recited the next morning after services, at which time worshipers commonly share a meal or light refreshments together. By extension, *Kiddush* is sometimes used to designate that meal as well.

Kohanim (pronounced koe-hah-NEEM): Literally, "priests," plural of *kohen* (pronounced koe-HAYN), "priest," a reference to the priests who offered sacrifices in the ancient temple until its destruction by Rome in the year 70 C.E. Also the name of modern-day Jews who claim priestly descent, and who are customarily given symbolic recognition in various ritual ways — as, for instance, being called first to stand beside the Torah reader and to recite a blessing over the reading. It is also the title of the last blessing in the *Amidah,* which contains the priestly benediction from Numbers 6:24–25. Another more popular name for that blessing is *Shalom* (pronounced shah-LOME), "peace," because the priestly benediction requests peace. See also ***Birkat Kohanim.***

Kriyat Sh'ma (pronounced k'-ree-YAHT sh'-MAH): Literally, "reciting the *Sh'ma,"* and therefore a technical term for the liturgical act of reading the prayer known as the *Sh'ma* (See *Sh'ma*).

Liturgy Public worship, from the Greek word *leitourgia,* meaning "public works." Liturgy in ancient Greece was considered a public work, the act of sacrificing or praising the gods, from which benefit would flow to the body politic.

Ma'ariv (pronounced mah-ah-REEV, or, commonly, MAH-ah-reev): From the Hebrew word *erev* (pronounced EH-rev), meaning "evening": one of two titles used for the evening worship service (also called *Arvit*).

Massekhet Sofrim (pronounced mah-SEH-khet sohf-REEM): Literally, "Tractate [dealing with issues relevant to] scribes," an eighth-century compilation (with some later interpolations) dealing with such matters as the writing of Torah scrolls, but also including much detail on the early medieval (and possibly ancient) prayer practice of Jews in the Land of Israel.

Midrash (pronounced meed-RAHSH, or, commonly, MID-rahsh): From a Hebrew word meaning "to ferret out the meaning of a text," and therefore a rabbinic interpretation of a biblical word or verse. By extension, a body of rabbinic literature that offers classical interpretations of the Bible.

Minchah (pronounced meen-CHAH, or, more commonly, MIN-chah): Originally the name of a type of sacrifice, then the word for a sacrifice offered during the afternoon, and now the name for the afternoon synagogue service usually scheduled just before nightfall. *Minchah* means "afternoon."

Minhag (pronounced meen-HAHG, or, commonly, MIN-hahg): The Hebrew word for custom and, therefore, used liturgically to describe the customary way that different groups of Jews pray. By extension, *minhag* means a "rite," as in *Minhag Ashkenaz*, meaning "the rite of prayer, or the customary way of prayer for Jews in *Ashkenaz*" — that is, northern and eastern Europe.

Minim (pronounced mee-NEEM): Literally, "heretics" or "sectarians," and the title of the twelfth blessing of the daily *Amidah*, a petition that heresy be eradicated, and heretics punished. Liberal liturgies frequently omit the blessing, considering it an inappropriate malediction, not a benediction at all, or reframe it as a petition against evil in general.

Minyan (pronounced meen-YAHN, or, commonly, MIN-y'n): A quorum, the minimum number of people required for certain prayers. *Minyan* comes from the word meaning "to count."

Mishnah (pronounced meesh-NAH, or, commonly, MISH-nah): The first written summary of Jewish law, compiled in the Land of Israel about the year 200 C.E., and therefore our first overall written evidence for the state of Jewish prayer in the early centuries.

Mishpat (pronounced mish-PAHT): Literally, "justice," and the title of the eleventh blessing of the daily *Amidah;* a petition for just rulership, a condition associated with the messianic age.

Mitzvah (pronounced meetz-VAH, or, commonly, MITZ-vah; plural, *mitzvot,* pronounced meetz-VOTE): A Hebrew word used commonly to mean "good deed," but in the more technical sense, denoting any commandment from God, and therefore, by extension, what God wants us to do. Reciting the *Sh'ma* morning and evening, for instance, is a *mitzvah.*

Modim D'rabbanan (pronounced moe-DEEM d'-rah-bah-NAHN): *Modim* is the first word of the second to last blessing of the *Amidah,* and therefore a shorthand way of referring to that prayer. *Modim D'rabbanan* is the name given to the form of the prayer that is reserved for congregational recitation during the repetition of the *Amidah* by the prayer leader. Literally, it means "the *Modim* of our Rabbis," and refers to the fact that the prayer is composed of what were once several alternative responses, each of which was the custom of one of the Rabbis of the Talmud.

Musaf (pronounced moo-SAHF, or, commonly, MOO-sahf): The Hebrew word meaning "extra" or "added," and therefore the title of the additional sacrifice that was offered in the Temple on Shabbat and holy days. It is now the name given to an added service of worship appended to the morning service on those days.

M'zuzah (pronounced m'-zoo-ZAH, or, commonly, m'-ZOO-zah): The Hebrew word in the Bible meaning "doorpost," and by extension, the term now used for a small casement that contains the first two sections of the *Sh'ma* (Deut. 6:4–9, 11:13–21) and is affixed to the doorposts of Jewish homes.

Nishmat kol cha'i (pronounced nish-MAHT kohl KHA'i): A blessing mentioned in the Talmud as one of two benedictions in use as the *Birkat Hashir* (pronounced beer-KAHT hah-SHEER), the blessing that ends a psalm collection known as a *Hallel.* (See *Hallel.*) Nowadays, we use it 1) as part of a longer *Birkat Hashir* after the Daily *Hallel,* that constitutes the central section of the *P'sukei D'zimrah* for Sabbaths and festivals; and 2) to conclude a similar *Hallel* in the Passover Haggadah.

N'kadesh (pronounced n'kah-DAYSH): The *Amidah* is first recited silently by each worshiper individually and then repeated aloud by the prayer leader, at which time its third blessing appears in extended form. *N'kadesh* (literally, "Let us sanctify…") is the first Hebrew word of that extended blessing and is thus, by extension, a common way to refer to it.

Orach Chayim (pronounced OH-rakh CHA-yim): Abbreviated as O. Ch. Literally, "The Way of Life," one of four sections in the *Tur* and the *Shulchan Arukh,* two of Judaism's major law codes; the section containing the rules of prayer.

Payy'tan (pronounced pah-y'-TAHN; plural *Payy'tanim,* pronounced pah-y'-tah-NEEM): A poet; the name given particularly to classical and medieval poets whose work is inserted into the standard prayers for special occasions.

Perek (pronounced PEH-rek; plural, *p'rakim,* pronounced p'-rah-KEEM): Literally, a "section" or "chapter" of a written work, and used liturgically to mean the sections of the *Sh'ma.* Each of its three biblical sections is a different *perek.*

Piyyut (pronounced pee-YOOT; plural: pee-yoo-TEEM): Literally, "a poem," but used technically to mean liturgical poems composed in classical and medieval times, and inserted into the standard prayers on special occasions.

P'sukei D'zimrah (pronounced p'-soo-KAY d'-zeem-RAH, or, commonly, p'-SOO-kay d'-ZIM-rah): Literally, "verses of song," and therefore the title of a lengthy set of opening morning prayers that contain psalms and songs, and serve as spiritual preparation prior to the official call to prayer.

Purim (pronounced POO-rim, or, poo-REEM): A festival falling on the fourteenth day of the Hebrew month of Adar, generally corresponding to late February or early March. It celebrates the miraculous deliverance referred to in the biblical Book of Esther. Literally, *purim* means "lots," as in the phrase "drawing of lots," because the date on which the Jews were to have been killed was chosen by lot.

R'fuah (pronounced r'-foo-AH, or, commonly, r'-FOO-ah): Literally, "healing," and the title of the eighth blessing of the daily *Amidah,* a petition for healing.

Rosh Chodesh (pronounced rohsh CHOH-desh): Literally, "the head of the month," and therefore the Hebrew name for the one- or two-day new moon period with which lunar months begin. It is marked as a holiday in Jewish tradition, a period of new beginnings.

Rubric (pronounced ROO-brick): A technical term for any discrete section of liturgy, whether a prayer or a set of prayers. The *Sh'ma* and Its Blessings is one of several large rubrics in the service; within that large rubric, the *Sh'ma* or any one of its accompanying blessings may be called a rubric as well.

Seder (pronounced seh-der, or, commonly, SAY-der): The Hebrew word meaning "order," and therefore 1) the name given to the ritualized meal eaten on Passover eve, and 2) an early alternative term for the order of prayers in a prayer book. The word *Siddur* (see *Siddur*) is now preferred for the latter.

Seder Rav Amram (pronounced SAY-dehr rahv AHM-rahm): First known comprehensive Jewish prayer book, emanating from Rav Amram Gaon, a leading Jewish scholar and head of Sura, a famed academy in Babylonia (modern-day Iraq), c. 860 C.E.

Sefardi (pronounced s'-fahr-DEE, or, commonly s'-FAHR-dee): From the Hebrew word *Sefarad* (pronounced s'-fah-RAHD), meaning the geographic area of modern-day Spain and Portugal. *Sefardi* is the adjective, describing the liturgical rituals and customs that are derived from *Sefarad* prior to the expulsion of Jews from there at the end of the fifteenth century, as opposed to *Ashkenazi* (see *Ashkenazi*), meaning the liturgical rituals and customs common to northern and eastern Europe. Nowadays, *Sefardi* refers also to the customs of Jews from North Africa and Arab lands, whose ancestors came from Spain.

S'firot (pronounced s'-fee-ROTE; singular: *s'firah,* pronounced s'-fee-RAH): According to the Kabbalah (Jewish mysticism, see ***Kabbalah***), the universe came into being by a process of divine emanation, whereby the divine light, as it were, expanded into empty space, eventually becoming physical matter. At various intervals, this light was frozen in time, as if captured by containers, each of which is called a *s'firah.* Literally, *s'firah* means "number," because early theory conceptualized the stages of creation as primordial numbers.

Shabbat (pronounced shah-BAHT): The Hebrew word for "Sabbath," from a word meaning "to rest."

Shacharit (pronounced shah-khah-REET, or, commonly, SHAH-khah-reet): From the Hebrew word *shachar* (SHAH-khar), meaning "morning," the name given to the morning worship service.

Shalom (pronounced shah-LOME): Literally, "peace," and a popular title for the final benediction of the *Amidah,* more properly entitled *Kohanim* (pronounced koe-hah-NEEM), "priests," or, more fully, *Birkat Kohanim* (pronounced beer-KAHT koe-hah-NEEM), "blessing of the priests," "priestly benediction." See also ***Birkat Kohanim, Kohanim.***

Shanim (pronounced shah-NEEM): Literally, "years," and the title of the ninth blessing of the daily *Amidah;* a petition for a year of agricultural abundance, such as is associated with messianic days.

Shirat Hayam (pronounced shee-RAHT hah-YAHM): Literally, "Song of the sea," the song of praise and gratitude sung by Israel after the splitting of the Red Sea, and, since the Middle Ages, a prominent constituent of the *P'sukei D'zimrah,* the "warm-up" section to the morning service composed mainly of biblical material (chiefly psalms) that were intended to be sung as praise of God.

Sh'liakh Tsibbur (pronounced sh'-LEE-ahkh tsee-BOOR): Literally, the "agent of the congregation," and therefore the name given to the person who leads the prayer service.

Sh'ma (pronounced sh'-MAH): The central prayer in the first of the two main units in the worship service, the second being the *Amidah* (see ***Amidah***). The *Sh'ma* comprises three citations from the Bible, and the larger unit in which it is embedded (called The *Sh'ma* and Its Blessings) is composed of a formal call to prayer (see ***Bar'khu***) and a series of blessings on the theological themes that, together with the *Sh'ma,* constitute a liturgical creed of faith. *Sh'ma,* meaning "hear," is the first word of the first line of the first biblical citation, "Hear O Israel: Adonai is our God; Adonai is One," which is the paradigmatic statement of Jewish faith, the Jews' absolute commitment to the presence of a single and unique God in time and space.

Sh'mini Atseret (pronounced sh'-MEE-nee ah-TSEH-ret): Literally, "the eighth day of solemn assembly," and the name given to the eighth and final day of the Autumn festival of Sukkot.

Sh'moneh Esreh (pronounced sh'-MOE-neh ES-ray): A Hebrew word meaning "eighteen," and therefore a name given to the second of the two main units in the worship service that once had eighteen benedictions in it (it now has nineteen), known also as the *Amidah* (see *Amidah*).

Shulchan Arukh (pronounced shool-KHAN ah-ROOKH, or, commonly, SHOOL-khan AH-rookh): The name given to the best-known code of Jewish law, compiled by Joseph Caro in the Land of Israel and published in 1565. *Shulchan Arukh* means "The Set Table," and refers to the ease with which the various laws are set forth — like a table prepared with food ready for consumption.

Siddur (pronounced see-DOOR, or, commonly, SIH-d'r): From the Hebrew word *seder* (see *Seder*) meaning "order," and therefore, by extension, the name given to the "order of prayers," or prayer book.

S'lichah (pronounced s'lee-KHAH, or, commonly S'LEE-khah): Literally, "pardon" or "forgiveness," and the title of the sixth blessing of the daily *Amidah,* a petition for divine forgiveness of our sins.

Tachanun (pronounced TAH-khah-noon): A Hebrew word meaning "supplications," and therefore, by extension, the title of the large unit of prayer that follows The *Sh'ma* and Its Blessings, and which is largely supplicatory in character.

Tallit (pronounced tah-LEET; plural: *talitot,* pronounced tah-lee-TOTE): The prayer shawl equipped with tassels (see *Tsitsit*) on each corner, and generally worn during the morning *(Shacharit)* and additional *(Musaf)* synagogue service.

Talmud (pronounced tahl-MOOD, or, more commonly, TAHL-m'd): The name given to each of two great compendia of Jewish law and lore compiled over several centuries, and ever since, the literary core of the rabbinic heritage. The *Talmud Yerushalmi* (pronounced y'-roo-SHAHL-mee), the "Jerusalem Talmud," is earlier, a product of the Land of Israel generally dated about 400 C.E. The better-known *Talmud Bavli* (pronounced BAHV-lee), or "Babylonian Talmud," took shape in Babylonia (present-day Iraq), and is traditionally dated about 550 C.E. When people say "the" Talmud without specifying which one they mean, they are referring to the Babylonian version. *Talmud* means "teaching."

Tetragrammaton: The technical term for the four-letter name of God that appears in the Bible. Treating it as sacred, Jews stopped pronouncing it centuries ago, so that the actual pronunciation has been lost; instead of reading it according to its letters, it is replaced in speech by the alternative name of God, Adonai.

T'fillah (pronounced t'-fee-LAH, or, commonly, t'-FEE-lah): A Hebrew word meaning "prayer," but used technically to mean a specific prayer, namely, the second of the two main units in the worship service. It is known also as the *Amidah* or the *Sh'moneh Esreh* (see *Amidah*). Also the title of the sixteenth blessing of the *Amidah*, a petition for God to accept our prayer.

T'fillin (pronounced t'-FIH-lin, or, sometimes, t'-fee-LEEN): Two cube-shaped black boxes containing biblical quotations (Exod. 13:1–10; 13:11–16; Deut. 6:4–9; 11:13–21) and affixed by means of attached leather straps to the forehead and left arm (right arm for left-handed people) during morning prayer.

T'hillah l'david (pronounced t'-hee-LAH l'-dah-VEED): Literally, "A psalm of David," and the first two words of Psalm 145; hence, the rabbinic name for Psalm 145, which eventually became known, more popularly, as *Ashre* (pronounced ahsh-RAY, or, commonly, AHSH-ray). See *Ashre*.

Tsadikim (pronounced tsah-dee-KEEM): Literally, "the righteous," and the title of the thirteenth blessing of the daily *Amidah*, a petition that the righteous be rewarded.

Tsitsit (pronounced tsee-TSEET): A Hebrew word meaning "tassels" or "fringes" and used to refer to the tassels affixed to the four corners of the *tallit* (the prayer shawl, see *tallit*) as Numbers 15:38 instructs.

T'shuvah (pronounced t'shoo-VAH, or, commonly t'SHOO-vah): Literally, "repentance," and the title of the fifth blessing in the daily *Amidah*, a petition by worshipers that they successfully turn to God in heartfelt repentance.

Tur (pronounced TOOR): The shorthand title applied to a fourteenth-century code of Jewish law, compiled by Jacob ben Asher in Spain, and the source for much of our knowledge about medieval liturgical practice. *Tur* means "row" or "column." The full name of the code is *Arba'ah Turim* (pronounced ahr-bah-AH too-REEM), "The Four Rows," with each row (or *Tur*) being a separate section of law on a given broad topic.

V'hu rachum (pronounced v'HOO rah-KHOOM): Literally, "He [God] is merciful," and, because of its sentiment, a common introductory line to prayers lauding God's gracious beneficence. The best example is a seven-paragraph penitential prayer that makes up the bulk of the version of *Tachanun* (pronounced TAH-khah-noon) that is said Mondays and Thursdays.

Yigdal (pronounced yig-DAHL): A popular morning hymn that encapsulates the thirteen principles of faith composed by prominent medieval philosopher Moses Maimonides (1135-1204). These thirteen principles were arranged poetically as *Yigdal* in the fourteenth century by Daniel ben Judah Dayan (pronounced dah-YAHN) of Rome.

Yishtabach (pronounced yish-tah-BAKH): The first word, and, therefore, the title of the blessing used as the *Birkat Hashir* for weekdays (see **Birkat Hashir**). On Sabbaths and festivals, it is expanded by the addition of *Nishmat kol cha'i* (pronounced nish-MAHT kohl KHA'i), a blessing mentioned in the Talmud (see **Nishmat kol cha'i**).

Yotser (pronounced yoe-TSAYR, or, commonly, YOE-tsayr): The Hebrew word meaning "creator," and by extension, the title of the first blessing in The *Sh'ma* and Its Blessings, which is on the theme of God's creation of the universe.

Y'rushalayim (pronounced y'roo-shah-LAH-yeem): Literally, "Jerusalem," and the title of the fourteenth blessing of the daily *Amidah;* a petition for the divine building up of Jerusalem, a condition associated with the imminence of the messianic age. Some liberal liturgies interpret it more broadly to include the restoration of modern-day Jerusalem, currently under way.

Zohar (pronounced ZOE-hahr): A shorthand title for *Sefer Hazohar* (pronounced SAY-fer hah-ZOE-hahr), literally, "The Book of Splendor," which is the primary compendium of mystical thought in Judaism; written mostly by Moses de Leon in Spain near the end of the thirteenth century, and ever since, the chief source for the study of Kabbalah (see **Kabbalah**).

A Note on the Border

The border decoration used in this book is from the
Sarajevo Haggadah, one of the best-known Hebrew
illuminated manuscripts; Barcelona (?), Spain, 14th century.

NOTES

NOTES

NOTES

NOTES

NOTES

NOTES

Printed in the USA
CPSIA information can be obtained
at www.ICGtesting.com
JSHW052016140824
68134JS00027B/2508

9 781683 362104